Kidnap for Ransom

Resolving the Unthinkable

Kidnap for Ransom

Resolving the Unthinkable

Richard P. Wright

CRC Press
Taylor & Francis Group
Boca Raton   London   New York

CRC Press is an imprint of the
Taylor & Francis Group, an **informa** business

Auerbach Publications
Taylor & Francis Group
6000 Broken Sound Parkway NW, Suite 300
Boca Raton, FL 33487-2742

© 2009 by Taylor & Francis Group, LLC
Auerbach is an imprint of Taylor & Francis Group, an Informa business

No claim to original U.S. Government works
Printed in the United States of America on acid-free paper
10 9 8 7 6 5 4 3 2 1

International Standard Book Number-13: 978-1-4200-8007-0 (Hardcover)

This book contains information obtained from authentic and highly regarded sources. Reasonable efforts have been made to publish reliable data and information, but the author and publisher cannot assume responsibility for the validity of all materials or the consequences of their use. The authors and publishers have attempted to trace the copyright holders of all material reproduced in this publication and apologize to copyright holders if permission to publish in this form has not been obtained. If any copyright material has not been acknowledged please write and let us know so we may rectify in any future reprint.

Library of Congress Cataloging-in-Publication Data

Wright, Richard P.
    Kidnap for ransom : resolving the unthinkable / Richard P. Wright.
      p. cm.
    Includes bibliographical references and index.
    ISBN 978-1-4200-8007-0 (hardcover : alk. paper) 1. Kidnapping--History. I.
    Title.

HV6595.W75 2009
363.25'954--dc22   2008051284

Visit the Taylor & Francis Web site at
http://www.taylorandfrancis.com

and the Auerbach Web site at
http://www.auerbach-publications.com

Contents

ACKNOWLEDGMENTS vii

ABOUT THE AUTHOR ix

INTRODUCTION xi

CHAPTER 1   ORIGINS OF THE PROBLEM 1
Kidnapping in Antiquity (Prior to 1000 A.D.) 1
The Middle Ages (1000–1800 A.D.) 6
The Industrial Age (1800–1970 A.D.) 10

CHAPTER 2   A MODERN SCOURGE (1968 TO THE PRESENT) 19

CHAPTER 3   KIDNAPPING AND KIDNAPPERS 31
The Crime 31
Kidnappers 35

CHAPTER 4   VICTIMS, FAMILIES AND ORGANIZATIONS 47
Victims 47
Families and Organizations 56

CHAPTER 5   THE INCIDENT 63
The Nightmare Begins 63
Verification 67
External Factors 72
  Kidnap-Ransom (KR) Insurance 72
  Consultants 74
  Authorities 77
  Corruption 82
  Media 83
  Legal Considerations 85

CHAPTER 6   RESPONSE   89
             Initial Steps   89
             Establishing Responsibility   92
             Negotiator   94
             Crisis Control Center   98
             Logistics   101
             Life Support   103

CHAPTER 7   NEGOTIATION   107
             Strategy   107
             Outcomes   111
             Contact   114
             Negotiation Techniques   116
             Offer Development   118
             Pressure   121
             Communication Process   125
             Managing Money   128
             Proof of Life   130
             Offer Acceptance   134

CHAPTER 8   RESOLUTION   137
             Ransom Delivery   137
             Release   146
             Aftermath   148

CHAPTER 9   THE CRIMINAL OR TERRORIST METHODOLOGY   151
             Phase 1—Planning   152
             Phase 2—Logistics   154
             Phase 3—Surveillance   158
             Phase 4—Action   161
             Phase 5—Escape   162
             Synopsis   163

CHAPTER 10   AVOIDANCE AND SURVIVAL   165
             Personal Security   165
             Survival   178
                  As a Crime Victim   179
                  As a Hostage   182

CHAPTER 11   CONCLUSION   185

APPENDIX: PERSONAL SECURITY AND AVOIDANCE TIPS   199

BIBLIOGRAPHY   217

INDEX   221

Acknowledgments

No book is ever possible without the dedicated support of many people. At times, the writer has the easiest role to play. He simply puts thoughts on paper and turns them over to researchers, editors, colleagues and friends to look over. When the feedback is in, the actual work starts to take shape. I have been blessed with a great support team that made this work enjoyable, in spite of the somber theme.

The writing of this book would not have been possible without the first-rate research and editing of Felipe Zuluaga, who gave selflessly of his own time and energy to ensure that the work was as complete as possible. My editor, Mark Listewnik of Auerbach Publications, has been a constant source of enthusiasm, support and assistance throughout the process. Andres Edbrooke took the time to clean up some of my more egregious grammatical errors and John Hauge was kind enough to provide an author's perspective while editing every word and punctuation mark. Jorge Septien reviewed the work before publication from the perspective of one with extensive experience in the field. Any mistakes in this work are solely my own.

I also must thank a number of persons, whose full names cannot appear here for obvious reasons, for teaching me my craft. These persons taught me lessons that were then applied in helping others; without them I could not have been part of the successful resolution of so many cases. Nick showed me how kidnappers work and kept me on track throughout my first experience. Jorge, Pablo, and Don Manuel taught me the intricacies of effectively managing a response. Rodolfo and Jesus gave me a window into law enforcement's worldview and methodology and captured more than their fair share of kidnappers along the way.

I would like to thank my wonderful wife, Claudia, who has been a rock in the tempest each time I have had to attend to a case. She has been there to inspire me every time I came home scared, disconsolate and worried; she has also been strong in the face of death threats, virtual kidnapping attempts and enforced separations. Without her love and support, and that of my two children Amanda and Damian, I would have run screaming to an asylum about three days into the very first event. They have given me the strength to go on and to trust my judgment, even when times seemed darkest. Their ability to put things in perspective and offer sound contributions to my efforts has been invaluable in every case.

Most of all, I owe thanks to those families who trusted someone they had never met before their worlds were shattered, to help them through a nightmarish experience. You know who you are and I will never forget you; you are the true heroes in all of this.

About the Author

Richard P. Wright, CPP, has lived and worked extensively overseas and has more than twenty years' experience in security and crisis management. He is a veteran of the U.S. Army and holds a bachelor's degree in management studies from the University of Maryland, University College. He is a certified protection professional and serves as a member of the ASIS International Crisis Management and Business Continuity Council. He has been the principal consultant and manager in the successful resolution of numerous kidnapping and extortion incidents. He has provided crisis management program development and training to many clients and has spoken extensively on the subject in multiple international forums. He resides with his family in Virginia and may be reached at wrightsecurity@gmail.com.

Introduction

The price one pays for pursuing any profession or calling is an intimate knowledge of its ugly side.

James Baldwin

Only the unknown frightens men. But once a man has faced the unknown; that terror becomes the known.

Antoine de Saint-Exupery

This book came about as the result of a conversation with my superb editor, Mark Listewnik, at the ASIS International annual convention in Las Vegas, Nevada in September 2007. Mark noted that I was to speak on this subject, attended my presentation, and proposed that we collaborate on a book.

The true genesis of this work came in the endless hours spent with family members, friends and coworkers of kidnap victims: planning, practicing, strategizing and, above all, waiting. No one who has not participated in the resolution of a kidnapping can truly imagine the stress of keeping morale high while waiting for the phone to ring, the newspaper or postman to arrive or the delivery of a video or audio tape with news, threats, demands and, eventually, a conclusion.

Many times during those long days and nights I was asked if anything had been written on how to resolve kidnapping cases; my answer was, and as far as I am aware still is, a resounding negative. This was frequently followed by some variation of "Richard, you should write a book." One thing I discovered early in my experience as a consultant on kidnapping cases was that everyone knew someone who had been kidnapped, but no one really knew what to do when their turn came.

I hope this effort will remove some of the mystery from these cases and enable the families and organizations subjected to this scourge to at least have a better understanding of what to do and what to expect. Scattered throughout this book are italicized sections of comments and anecdotes from those who have actually suffered through a kidnapping. All have been sanitized so as not to identify actual cases. I believe these oral histories enrich the text and provide perspective that can only be gained otherwise by experience, something I wish on no one.

I am sure there are a number of other professionals who will disparage this effort as providing too much in the way of sensitive information to those who might make ill use of the data. I agonized for some time over this issue and finally decided to go forward, feeling that professional kidnappers know the majority of this information and that this knowledge should not be limited to a select few practitioners and to criminals involved in kidnapping. To my fellow professionals I can only say that I had this book reviewed before publication by one of the professionals whom I most respect, and his judgments were considered in the final manuscript.

I have also tried to present, in terms understandable both to security professionals and laypersons, an overview of the series of activities that represent the best opportunity for a successful resolution of a kidnap for ransom. I have also provided a section on defensive measures, beginning with what I believe to be the most important factor: understanding how kidnappers actually select and abduct their victims.

The first time I worked on a kidnapping case, I had no idea how true were James Baldwin's words, included on the previous page. I had worked on extortions, bomb threats and bombings, product contaminations and many other crisis situations and had been teaching crisis management to corporate clients for a number of years. Nothing prepared me for the shock and devastation of my first kidnapping case.

I received an early morning telephone call from a very important client, asking me to assist his best friend whose nephew had been kidnapped. I went to visit the family and we discussed what needed to be done to resolve the situation. I also called an old friend that I knew had some experience in these situations and hired him temporarily to help me get through the situation and be a filter, mirror and support for our efforts. Through twenty-six days of emotional highs and lows, ventures into unknown territory to recover messages, meetings with authorities, lawyers, psychologists, friends and neighbors, a constant stream of well-meaning relatives and associates, and an hours-long ordeal during the ransom delivery, we were able to manage the safe return of a young man to the waiting arms of his family. Five minutes after he arrived, we departed. I have never again spoken with any member of that family, although they have recommended me to others in similar situations over the years.

Kidnapping is among the foulest of criminal acts. There may be no impact more devastating to a family or organization than the kidnapping of an executive or family member. Taking someone by force, depriving that person of liberty and abusing him or her at will causes lasting physical and mental repercussions. Those forced by relation or position to participate as team members in the negotiation process seeking the victim's safe return also feel these effects. No one who has ever been involved in a kidnapping case will ever forget the fear, uncertainty and stress.

Kidnapping in various forms has been practiced since the dawn of time. Throughout history, slaves have been taken, armies recruited, shipmates obtained, spouses abducted, funds secured and victims for exploitation procured by this activity. Those who kidnap and those who suffer kidnappings are a group that has become larger over time and continues to grow. When I first became involved in managing the resolution of kidnapping situations, I discovered my perceptions were faulty in that I thought of kidnappers as cold-hearted monsters and victims as oppressed and tortured souls. While these generic perceptions do apply to a great degree, I learned that there are a multitude of different stories, backgrounds and scenarios. In this work I have made an effort to describe some of the concepts, measures, attitudes and individuals with whom I have dealt over the years, in the hope that this perspective brings a more human understanding to the theme. That said, I remain firmly convinced that there is no acceptable justification for committing a kidnapping for ransom under any circumstances.

No mention of those responsible for this work would be complete without including the victims and their friends and families. I rarely got close at all to a victim; I did, however, become part of a number of families for short periods of time and came to know the deepest fears and highest aspirations of many fine people placed in seemingly impossible situations. I continue to be amazed by the strength of character shown by so many in circumstances that can only be imagined by those who have not suffered such an indignity.

To claim that my level of stress ever approximated that of those who truly suffer, that is, the kidnap victim and his or her family members, would be presumptuous. They are the ones to whom this work is dedicated, the many who have suffered and wept over incidents beyond comprehension and totally out of their control.

ORIGINS OF THE PROBLEM

Whoever steals a man and sells him, and anyone found in the possession of him, shall be put to death.

Exodus 21:16

When you meet the unbelievers in jihad [holy war], chop off their heads. And when you have brought them low, bind your prisoners rigorously. Then set them free or take ransom from them until the war is ended.

Koran 47:4

Kidnapping in Antiquity (Prior to 1000 A.D.)

The practice of kidnapping is as old as recorded history. Some of the earliest written records available speak of individuals and whole segments of society being taken by force and sold, traded, or enslaved. Even entire populations have been kidnapped and removed or sold off into slavery. The removal of the Hebrews to Babylon is one of the most well-known examples of the kidnapping of an entire race of people. Not all incidents throughout history have been so significant; however, scratch the surface of any history large or small and one will encounter kidnapping in one form or another. Mention is made in a number of ancient texts that directly supports a conclusion that kidnapping for ransom was not only practiced but was much more common than one might expect. This book does not pretend to provide an exhaustive history of the practice of kidnapping and hostage taking; however, a number of examples are necessary to provide an historical context for development of the current reality.

Many of us grew up with the image graven in our minds of a caveman bonking his future mate on the head and dragging her off to his cave. Whether one views this as a kidnapping, an abduction, the taking of a hostage, the capturing of a slave, or as an old-fashioned marriage proposal, the result is the same. One individual is depriving another of her liberty and (by implication) forcing her to submit to his will. Kidnapping, slavery, and hostage taking have always been inextricably linked. Victims are taken by force, by guile, or by treaty and the only way for an individual to regain his or her freedom is in exchange for some form of compensation to the holder. The freedom of a slave can be purchased, a hostage liberated upon full compliance with agreed-upon conditions or a kidnap victim released upon payment of a ransom. At the risk of straying too far into the philosophical, I submit that human beings seem to be predisposed to the forcible deprivation of liberty. Slavery exists in the 21st century, kidnappings are commonplace worldwide, and hostages are frequently taken.

The practice of slavery has always gone forward in lockstep with that of kidnapping for ransom. Particularly in ancient times, one may infer that the victim's perceived wealth, position in a hierarchy, or social status determined whether he or she ended up being ransomed or enslaved. Wealthy or important victims were often held back from the slave markets, their captors preferring to seek direct ransom payments from families or governments, while soldiers, tradesmen, women and children were sold as slaves. Prisoners of war were frequently assigned a value and their fate determined by their family's or country's ability to pay a ransom for an individual's freedom. Captives of any sort, usually women, children and noncombatants, were considered spoils of war and judged and treated in the same manner. Ill, unfit, or injured captives were swiftly executed; the captors then made a selection of those they wished to keep for personal use or exploitation, and the remainder were sold into slavery or held for ransom.

Targeted kidnapping for ransom is mentioned occasionally in ancient texts and the ransoming of captives is frequently mentioned. What comes through very clearly is that prisoners of war or other captives who came into the hands of governments, armies, brigands, tribes, or opposing camps were carefully inspected and evaluated to determine their utility as bargaining chips and rapid decisions were taken as to their disposition. Decisions were made quickly because no self-respecting businessperson (kidnapper, slaver, tribal chieftain, governor, etc.) wants to hold onto useless inventory. The end result for those victims who were to be ransomed was the same as that of kidnap victims today. They were forced to endure a period of captivity under often dire circumstances during which an amount to be paid for their freedom was negotiated. Once payment had been delivered, if all other conditions were met and the victim still lived, he or she would be liberated.

From a legal perspective, kidnapping has been considered a serious crime since time immemorial. The Code of Hammurabi, the oldest codification of criminal laws and penalties ever discovered, prescribes death as the punishment for kidnappers. The citation from the book of Exodus in the Christian and Jewish Scriptures at the beginning of this chapter clearly states the ancient Jewish perspective on kidnapping. The Buddhist and Taoist concept of hell, dated to the Tang Dynasty in China (c. 600 A.D.), describes kidnappers as being consigned to the Chamber of Dismemberment by Sawing. Needless to say, ancient societies did not look fondly on the practice, nor were they apparently activist supporters of the concept of rehabilitation and reintegration into society.

The taking of hostages as surety for negotiated deals, debts, or ransom has been practiced for thousands of years. Hostages were exchanged as a guarantee of fealty, security for treaties, and, often, as tools for blackmail. If one party to an agreement did not live up to the negotiated or stipulated bargain, hostages could be put to death or sold into slavery. In many cases, hostages were permitted to return home after payment of a ransom. In the Sumerian poem *Descent of Ishtar*, Dumuzi is sent to the underworld as a ransom for Inanna's return. Sargon of Kish, first emperor of the Akkadian empire (c. 2300 B.C.), was reported to have used hostage taking as a punitive or control measure. Ancient Chinese texts mention the ransoming of hostages as early as the Xia Dynasty (2200-1700 B.C.) and refer to the taking of princes and family members as hostages throughout multiple ancient dynastic periods as a guarantor of negotiated treaties. The biblical story of Joseph, son of Jacob, dates from 1683 B.C. Joseph was kidnapped and sold into slavery in Egypt by his own brothers. Later, in his role as vizier, Joseph ordered his youngest brother arrested and held as a hostage to force his father to personally come and visit him in Egypt.

The mythological (or not?) kidnapping of Helen of Troy may be the most renowned ever; causing a war that lasted ten years or more and resulting in the destruction of a great city. While no ransom was apparently sought for Helen's release, her abduction spawned a great conflict and resulted in thousands of untimely deaths. Although archeological investigations conducted over the last few decades would tend to support the existence of Troy, we have only Homer's word for the story of Helen.

The ancient Greeks recorded histories to a much greater degree than most civilizations and their accounts provide ample evidence of the practice of kidnapping and hostage taking for ransom. Xenophon of Athens (c. 400 B.C.) recounts that he departed from the Ten Thousand on the march back to Greece in order to try and secure a personal fortune by kidnapping a Persian nobleman. This certainly supports the idea that kidnapping for ransom was a common practice. Curiously, Xenophon also reports that death is the prescribed punishment for kidnappers. Apparently, for a fortune-hunting Greek to kidnap a Persian nobleman was permissible; however, kidnapping among one's own was severely sanctioned. Epaminondas of Thebes (c. 400 B.C.) was renowned as a man who would call together a council of friends and decide how much each should contribute for the ransom of countrymen taken by an enemy.

Life as a hostage in the ancient world was not always deadly, dull, or difficult. Hostages often were treated almost as well as members of royal families, receiving the best care, education, and training available. In 359 B.C., Philip of Macedonia, father of Alexander the Great, took the throne from his infant nephew by regicide and established himself as king. He had been comfortably held hostage in Thebes during his early twenties and there gained much of the knowledge of military tactics that he, and later his son Alexander the Great, put to use in their wars of conquest. In 334 B.C., Darius of Persia is reported to have offered 10,000 talents to Alexander as a ransom payment for his family, captured by the Macedonians at the battle of Issus. Alexander is said to have disdainfully refused the offer on the grounds that he had become the new ruler of Persia and would henceforth maintain the royal wives and daughters.

In the Roman world, even the most famous of all persons was reportedly kidnapped for ransom. According to Plutarch, Julius Caesar was kidnapped as a young man and a ransom of twenty talents of silver asked for his release. Caesar is said to have insisted that the ransom be raised because he, as an exalted personage, was worth far more than such a paltry amount. He also is reputed to have hunted down and had his kidnappers tortured to death after he became ruler of Rome. Whether or not this story is apocryphal is irrelevant; the mere fact that a major figure in ancient times would be reported as having been kidnapped for ransom speaks to the existence and common knowledge of the practice. Many of the peoples in the Roman world also practiced the taking of hostages for ransom.

The Romans themselves practiced the taking of hostages as surety from conquered peoples on a grand scale. The historian Polybius was one of hundreds of Macedonian nobles taken hostage by the Romans in 168 B.C. after the defeat of King Perseus. The Romans held large numbers of nobles and other important individuals taken from conquered peoples as hostages to ensure compliance with their dictates. Strabo, writing in the first two decades of the first century A.D., reports that Circassian pirates often kept wealthy prisoners alive and traded them later for ransom rather than putting them to death or selling them into slavery. The Circassians, a people who specialized in maritime piracy, were the scourge of the Caucasus and surrounding areas in Strabo's lifetime. Apparently, in a manner common to good businessmen everywhere, they knew the value of their merchandise. In the early fifth century A.D., Attila the Hun was exchanged as a hostage for the Roman Aetius as surety for a treaty between Rome and the Huns. Both spent their formative years being educated in the opposite camp and they were later to lead their respective sides in the fight for domination in Gaul.

Muslims have commonly accepted the practice of kidnapping or hostage taking since the very beginning of the religion. The histories of the early Islamic leaders, including the Prophet Mohammed, describe numerous examples of prisoners being taken and ransomed. One of his wives, in fact, was a captive taken in battle who was offered the choice of being ransomed or marrying him. This practice continued for centuries, with some scholars justifying this on the basis that the civilization in which Islam was spread led to no other fair conclusion. That is, in tribal societies, once all the men are killed off, there is no one left to take care of the women and children. Therefore, marriage to a captor, becoming, in effect, chattel, is eminently preferable to slavery or death.

Throughout the latter half of the first millennium, kidnapping for ransom continued around the world. For example, Sembat I, King of Armenia, was reportedly forced to pay a huge ransom for his wife and children around 900 A.D. when rival noblemen seeking to oust him from the throne kidnapped them. The *Vita of Peter of Argos* (Theodore of Nicaea, c. 950 A.D.) states that the Cretan Muslims raided as far north as the Argolid (Eastern Peloponnese), taking hostages for ransom. During the same period, Viking raiders on the Western coast of Europe routinely practiced abduction for the purpose of obtaining ransom payments.

The Middle Ages (1000 – 1800 A.D.)

Kidnapping in the Middle Ages was also rampant; numerous European leaders and nobles used ransom kidnapping to finance their wars and conquests. War and conquest took on strong religious overtones, particularly in the West, the Crusades being the most prominent examples of primarily religious conflicts. Many of the wars in Europe and the conquest of the New World were conflicts that, if not overtly religious in nature, had religious issues as major contributing factors. The known world was also becoming smaller as news and practices from far-away locations could and did travel over longer distances. The Mongol armies were able to travel from their homeland to mid-Europe and, later, seaborne exploration opened virtually the entire world to contact.

The traditional practices of hostage taking and kidnapping for ransom continued in the Middle East during the period, gaining much notoriety during the Crusades. For example, King Baldwin II of Jerusalem was taken hostage in 1123 and held for a ransom that was later paid for his freedom. He was the chosen successor to Baldwin I, who had ransomed his prisoners back to Damascus after plundering a rich caravan in spring of 1101. Baldwin II apparently was involved in many ransoms both to and from the rulers of various Islamic states as he warred.

During the Crusades, the practice of ransoming captives was prevalent on both sides. Prisoners taken in battle or women and children captured in towns that were conquered or sacked, who were viewed as rich enough to merit a ransom, often had their freedom purchased by opposing entities or by loved ones. Prisoners not wealthy enough to be worth a ransom were imprisoned under execrable conditions, sold as slaves, or in some cases, simply executed. This practice continued throughout the duration of the crusading period, as both sides looked to profit from captives.

Many histories report that Richard the Lionhearted, King of England, was kidnapped and held for ransom in 1192. A supposed ally, Duke Leopold V of Babenberg, kidnapped Richard while he was ostensibly crossing the duke's territory in disguise on his way home from the Crusades after a shipwreck. He was reportedly ransomed just in time to return to England and retake the throne. His mother, Eleanor of Aquitaine, led the way in collecting sufficient funds to pay for Richard's freedom. In this case, a special tax was levied in all of England to raise the ransom.

In the Far East, roughly contemporaneous to Richard's experience as a hostage was that of Temujin, later known as Genghis Khan. As a young man, he was said to have been repeatedly taken hostage by various Mongol tribes. On every occasion he is reported to have escaped. The practice of kidnapping, or hostage taking, thus appears again as a common practice in the Far East. The Mongols were known to have taken many hostages during their wars of conquest and ransomed, enslaved, or executed them as they saw fit.

On occasion, guests who sought succor with neighboring princes in times of trouble became hostages to be sold for ransom when the conditions became advantageous to the host. Bela IV of Hungary fled the Mongol invasion in 1241 after the invaders decisively defeated his army. He went to the court of Prince Friedrich of Austria who willingly granted his request for asylum. In a very short time, Friedrich, looking to enrich himself, attacked Hungary, and forced the Hungarians to pay a steep ransom for Bela's freedom. Politics indeed make for strange bedfellows.

In 1356, at the battle of Poitiers during the Hundred Years War between France and England, King Jean of France was captured by the English and taken to London. He was held there and freed only after a ransom payment of three million gold *ecus*, multiple noble English hostages held by France and ample French territory. The fact that part of his ransom included freedom for English nobles amply testifies to the practice of taking hostages for ransom as widespread in fourteenth-century Western Europe. This practice apparently did not slow down; Charles V of France paid 100,000 francs to ransom Bernard du Guesclin, captured at the battle of Auray in 1364. James I of Scotland also spent eighteen years in English captivity before being ransomed in 1424.

Meanwhile in Asia, the practice of holding hostages as surety continued in China, as it had since the earliest dynasties. Of note was the attempt by Mongol leader Esen Tayisi to ransom back to the Chinese the Ming Dynasty emperor after having captured him in the battle of Tumu in 1449.

In the Americas, due principally to the virtual destruction of all written records in existence prior to the Spanish conquest, little historical information is available on the practices of hostage taking and ransoms. The Incas, however, were known to have taken the young members of royal families of subjugated tribes to their capital at Cuzco for "education", a practice that also served to maintain these individuals as hostages/guarantors against any deviation on the part of subject tribes. The Aztecs preferred to sacrifice their captives to the gods, rather than seeking any ransom. In what is now the northwestern United States, some Native American tribes permitted slaves captured in conflicts to be ransomed by their relatives.

The Spanish conquest of the Americas began with two renowned kidnappings for ransom. In 1519 in Tenochtitlan (now Mexico City), the Aztec Emperor Moctezuma was invited to lodge with the Spaniards under the command of Hernan Cortes and then held for ransom. Moctezuma offered to fill a large room once with gold and twice with silver in return for his freedom. This enormous ransom was duly paid, along with a treasure of jewels; however, the Spaniards executed or allowed him to be killed during an uprising caused by their brutal mass assassination of Aztec nobles.

In 1531, Spanish conquistadors under Francisco Pizarro seized Inca Emperor Atahualpa during a negotiating session, slaughtering many nobles and taking the emperor hostage. Pizarro agreed to release the emperor for a ransom payment of a room twenty-two by sixteen feet filled with gold. When the Incas complied and filled the room, Pizarro fabricated charges that Atahualpa was plotting a counter-revolution and publicly executed the emperor anyway.

Apparently, the Spanish conquistadores could not resist a successful methodology once discovered. In Colombia in 1537, Gonzalo Jimenez de Quesada captured the Muisca chieftain (Sun King) Quemuenchatocha and held him prisoner for a ransom in gold and emeralds. Once paid, the chieftain was tortured nearly to death in what was rapidly becoming standard practice among the conquistadores in the New World. He abdicated and died shortly thereafter.

Barbary pirates captured Miguel Cervantes de Saavedra, author of *Don Quixote*, in 1575 and imprisoned him for five years in Algiers prior to his being ransomed by the Trinitarians. The Trinitarians were a religious order founded by Saint John de Matha and dedicated to the ransoming of Christians, primarily from the Barbary States. Over the course of three centuries, the Trinitarians reportedly were able to ransom over ninety thousand captives. That amount testifies to the enormous number of kidnappings perpetrated by the Barbary pirates during their run of more than four centuries of terror in the Mediterranean.

In 1586, Sir Francis Drake extorted large ransoms for the cities of Santo Domingo, Dominican Republic and Cartagena, Colombia that he captured during raids. As a state-sanctioned privateer, he conducted his business under the English flag, holding entire cities and their inhabitants hostage. Once war was openly declared between England and Spain, the Spaniards launched the great Armada in 1588 in an attempt to conquer England. The Armada failed miserably and a number of high-ranking Spanish prisoners were held for ransom, some for nearly ten years.

Entire cities continued to be held ransom during the conflicts in Renaissance Europe. Sieges could be lifted upon payment of an agreed-upon ransom and the lives of citizens spared. Non-payment of a ransom could lead to wholesale slaughter or enslavement of the entire population. For example, the Swiss besieged the town of Eilenburg in Saxony during the Thirty Years' War in Europe (1607–1637). The Swiss commander demanded the then-enormous ransom of thirty thousand thalers in exchange for not sacking the city. Hostage taking for ransom continued all over. The Dutch made significant payments to the Ottoman Empire in the 1630s for the release of Christian hostages, while in the New World, Native American leaders were kidnapped, ransomed (and some killed anyway) as leverage to reduce attacks on trading outposts.

During the 1700s, ransom of captives from slave ships off the African coast was also commonplace; slavers would stay at anchor for a few days to see if anyone came forward to offer a ransom for one or more of the slaves on board, and thus enhance their income before even setting out for the Americas. This was, in a way, a continuation of a longstanding tradition of prisoner ransom, practiced in Africa by Muslims and non-Muslims alike.

In North Africa, the United States government paid the then-enormous sum of nearly one million dollars to the Dey of Algiers in 1797 for the release of dozens of Americans held hostage. This was soon followed by the war on the Barbary States that finally reduced the scope of their hitherto widespread activities.

The Industrial Age (1800– 1970 A.D.)

By the end of the middle ages, the practice of exchanging hostages as a guarantor of treaties and agreements between countries had pretty well ceased, except in Africa. Most countries practiced a more "enlightened" diplomacy and the need and/or the utility of hostages as surety in a bargain had decreased beyond the point of diminishing returns. The latest example of hostages as guarantors for compliance with a diplomatic agreement in Europe seems to have been the treaty of Aix-la-Chapelle in 1748 that ended the War of Austrian Succession. The treaty stipulated that English hostages were to be sent to France as a guarantee that Cape Breton Island in Nova Scotia would be returned to French control. The practice of taking hostages as guarantors of fealty continued in China until the mid-seventeenth century.

The African slave trade, however, continued apace, with millions of men, women, and children being kidnapped from their homes and either traded or sold within the continent or taken to the west for sale as slaves. An intrinsic part of this, which continued long after the slave trade with the West had ended, was the practice of kidnapping chiefs and nobles of opposing tribes and ransoming them back to their families and peoples. Caravan chiefs in the Sahara, tribal leaders in Nigeria and West Africa, and any others who were wealthy or held important positions were considered attractive kidnapping targets. Notable when discussing the African practice of ransoming kidnapped notables is the time that each case lasted. Reportedly, the time from capture to ransom probably averaged at least six months, with longer periods also commonplace.

One must consider that the opportunity for a West African captive to be ransomed in the nineteenth century, apart from the overwhelming influence of his or her socioeconomic status, was greatly influenced by geography. The immense trade network that crossed the boundaries of dozens of tribes and cultures meant slaves from a single family might be sold or taken to widely divergent locations. If a captor made no effort to contact the family or an intermediary in search of a ransom, the family or tribe of origin might seek out the captives and find only some of them. Those who were lucky enough to be identified might be ransomed if an agreed-upon price could be reached. Professional intermediaries made a living searching out enslaved or captured persons from families of a certain social or economic status and brokering a deal to arrange for ransom payment and release of the hostage.

Another practice, and a principal cause of the War of 1812 between England and the United States, was commonly called "press-ganging". In the early nineteenth century, England was at war with France (again) and in dire need of men to man her ships and serve in her armed forces. British warships began stopping American vessels on the high seas, forcibly removing sailors, and pressing them into service in the British Navy. In the case of the press-ganged sailors, few of the victims ever returned home. Ironically, United States merchant ships in the 1800s often filled their crews with men who had been "shanghaied". This practice was common in the major merchant shipping ports of the United States and involved obtaining crew members for merchant ships by virtually any ruse necessary, often including outright kidnapping. The crewman-to-be would be mugged, drugged, or both and end up as a crew member on a merchant ship at sea. The supplying of sailors in this manner by professional kidnappers, or "crimps" as they were known, continued until passage of the Merchant Seaman's Act in 1915.

The 19th century also was the period in which the practice of kidnapping that we know today really began. Stories from around the globe speak to the practice. Bandits such as Jose Maria "El Tempranillo" (the Early Bird), who committed many kidnappings, achieved near folk-hero status in Spain in the early to mid-1800s as a sort of local Robin Hood. Other bandits and gangs appear in reports from all over Spain in relation to notorious kidnapping cases. From Lady von Freygang's writings in 1811 through written reports as late as mid-19th century, the practice of kidnapping for ransom was notorious as a particularly common feature of war making in the Caucasus region.

Throughout the 19th century, kidnapping was a lucrative trade in many areas of the world. The Sulu sultanate in the present-day Philippines was basically maintained for most of the century by funds obtained through kidnapping. In Macedonia, during the struggle for independence from Bulgaria in the late 1800s, revolutionary groups often resorted to kidnapping wealthy landowners and foreigners for ransom to obtain funds necessary for continued operations. In Australia, the outlaw Ned Kelly gained fame in the latter part of the 19th century as a bank robber and kidnapper.

The practice of kidnapping free blacks in the northern United States, taking them to slave states in the South, and selling them into slavery was common in the first half of the 19th century. Slave traders would snatch up unattended children or blacks traveling alone, subdue them, and go to slave markets in Southern states where they would be sold as slaves with no questions asked by the purchasers, who were pleased to get new slaves at low prices. A particularly instructive case is that of Peter Still, kidnapped with his brother around 1806 in New Jersey, taken to Kentucky and sold into slavery, and finally able to regain his freedom in April 1850. He required a further three years to be able to raise the money to purchase his wife's and children's freedom from their owner. Hundreds of these kidnappings occurred and few victims ever returned. Freedom could be purchased, but only after diligent searching and delicate negotiations.

During the First Opium War (1839–1842) in China, the British government continued the age-old practice of seeking ransom for entire cities. The Chinese government was forced to pay ransoms of three million dollars and three hundred thousand dollars for Canton and Shanghai, respectively, to keep the British from sacking the cities. The British were able to both collect significant ransoms and continue to import vast quantities of opium into China.

The British also found themselves on the other side throughout most of the nineteenth century, as the kidnapping of British subjects for ransom was a common practice in the Balkans and many of the countries surrounding the Mediterranean.

During the American Civil War (1861–1865), hostage taking as a means of leverage to gain the release of captured soldiers was not uncommon. Multiple examples exist of the detention (kidnapping) of civilians off the streets of their towns, particularly in the South. These civilian hostages (and sometimes prisoners of war) were used as bargaining chips to ensure the arrest of men on the other side who had committed a perceived violation of the rules of war, or as trade bait for the release of captured prisoners when those prisoners were captured under dubious circumstances. President Abraham Lincoln and Generals Robert E. Lee (Confederate) and Ulysses S. Grant (Union) were not only aware of the practice, but some of their correspondence indicates active approbation.

Kidnap for ransom as the crime is typically understood today is a relatively recent phenomenon. The first kidnapping for ransom in the United States (or at least the one that is considered to be the first that drew national public attention by most historians) was that of four year-old Charley Ross who was kidnapped from near his home in Germantown, Pennsylvania on July 1, 1874. Despite national publicity and an intensive manhunt, the case was never resolved and the boy was never found.

Eastern Europe was also not immune to kidnapping during the latter half of the 19th century. In 1886, Romanian Prince Alexander was kidnapped and taken to Russia (Bessarabia) during the political intrigues surrounding the relations among the Ottoman Empire, Germany under Bismarck, and Russia. He was released at the intervention of his cousin, Tsar Alexander III of Russia, and returned to rule for a few months before abdicating and retiring to Austria.

Kidnapping also appeared in well-known 19th century works of literature as well. Sir Walter Scott included the story of a kidnapping of the scion of a wealthy family in his book, *Guy Mannering*, set in the 18th century. Robert Louis Stevenson wrote his famous work, *Kidnapped*, in 1886. A subject such as kidnapping appearing in popular works of fiction indicates that, at least among the English-reading populations, kidnapping had indeed become a commonly known practice by this time.

Toward the turn of the century, kidnappings, although sparsely reported, continued to occur all over the world. No region was safe, from the Philippines to Africa to Latin America and North

America. For example, numerous reports exist on the widespread practice of kidnapping and ransom of many French citizens in Tonkin (Vietnam) around the turn of the century. This practice (not limited to the French) was endemic to the border area in an unstable China at this time.

In the late 19th and early 20th centuries, legislation defining the crime of kidnapping and prescribing harsh punishments for wrongdoers was formally adopted for the first time in many places. Interestingly, sentences for kidnappers varied dramatically in different countries and continue to do so today. Defining the crime in its multiple manifestations has apparently been an arduous task that no two lawmaking bodies have ever been able to agree upon. One may recall the punishments prescribed for kidnappers mentioned earlier in this chapter. Perhaps modern-day legislators could take their cue from Hammurabi.

At the turn of the century in the United States, the 1900 case of Edward Cudahy, Jr., scion of a wealthy Omaha, Nebraska meatpacking family, drew significant attention again to the crime. Interestingly, press coverage of the case included recommendations and commentary on the ransom process. Some editorials advocated that the family pay nothing so as not to encourage future kidnappers; others disparaged the family's suffering by ridiculing the ease with which the family could pay the then-princely sum of twenty five thousand dollars. Still others took a more measured approach, lauding the efforts of family and law enforcement and taking a more supportive tone. The press response to the Cudahy case is very instructive to anyone wishing to consider the implications of releasing information about a kidnapping in progress. One can never be sure how the press will report on any given case and whether or not the coverage will be ultimately helpful or detrimental in resolving the case. One must think very carefully before playing with fire.

Worldwide, kidnapping for ransom slowly became more and more common, never reaching the heights of the last quarter of the twentieth century, but occurring in many places and at many times. In Mexico in 1915, the Grey Automobile Gang achieved notoriety for committing a number of high-profile ransom kidnappings. During the lengthy Mexican revolutionary period, in 1922, United States citizens Bruce Bielazki (former head of the Secret Service) and Jose Barcenas (Los Angeles businessman) were kidnapped near the caves of Cacahuamilpa in Mexico State. Barcenas was released and Bielazki later escaped, although many different versions of the tale have been told and no one ever talked formally to investigators. The kidnapping is generally believed to have been the work of supporters of Mexican revolutionary general (and former president) Victoriano Huerta, who had been apprehended by Bielazki and later died in a Texas prison hospital.

The so-called Black Hand, primarily Sicilian mobsters centered in New York, committed numerous kidnappings and extortions for ransom from 1900 to the late 1920s, only desisting when the public outcry became such that they were forced to seek other methods to obtain funds.

In the ravines of the Chambal River valley in the Uttar Pradesh region of India, bandits known as *dacoits* (criminals dedicated to robbery, kidnapping, and murder) developed into full time criminal gangs that committed kidnaps for ransom as a staple of their criminal activity since at least the 1920s. The local population viewed many early dacoits, such as Man Singh, as heroic figures who robbed the rich and fed the poor; however, most modern dacoits are perceived as common criminals interested only in money. The Indian press reports regularly on kidnappings committed by dacoits with significant ransoms being commonly paid.

Probably the most famous kidnapping in the United States was that of Charles Lindbergh, Jr. in 1932. This case, more than any other, made the crime notorious in the United States. The apparent railroading of suspected kidnapper Bruno Hauptmann has been the subject of innumerable books and articles in the intervening years. The 1935 kidnapping of George Weyerhauser, heir to the Weyerhauser paper fortune, made the news shortly after the Lindbergh event and added to the publicity surrounding ransom kidnapping as a common crime.

The first known case of kidnap for ransom since colonial times in Colombia, considered for most of the past two decades as the world leader in kidnappings, was that of Elisa Eder, three year-old daughter of industrialist Harold Eder, in 1933. She was released after the payment of the then-considerable sum of fifty thousand pesos.

Simultaneously, guerrillas in the southern states of Mexico (Chiapas, Guerrero, Oaxaca) began a campaign of kidnappings to finance their revolutionary activities. This trend has continued into modern times, with many kidnappings in the last twenty-five or so years traced to insurrectionist groups seeking to finance their activities, not only in Mexico but in many locations worldwide.

During the Second World War, the Nazis in Germany kidnapped thousands of people from their homes. Not only was this part of the Final Solution—the Nazis' program to eradicate Jews, gypsies, homosexuals and other "undesirables," the Nazis also sold the freedom of many Jews and others as a way to obtain capital for the state or for corrupt officials. This was virtually a state-sponsored tactic that resulted in numerous ransom payments being poured into Nazi coffers. Japanese kidnapping of Korean women (estimates vary between 100,000 and 400,000) who were forced to serve as "comfort women" (sex slaves) to Japanese soldiers during 1932–1945 is well documented and resulted in a formal apology from the Japanese government in 1993. The Soviet Union, at the end of the war, dedicated tremendous efforts to kidnapping and returning citizens who had previously emigrated to Eastern European countries. These were not ransom kidnappings per se; most, if not all, were either executed or imprisoned by the Stalinist regime.

During the 1950's baby boom in the United States, ransom kidnappings continued to occur. The Greenlease case in Kansas, in which a six year-old boy was kidnapped and murdered, garnered national attention. The 1958 kidnapping in Cuba of star Argentine racecar driver Juan Manuel Fangio also achieved worldwide notoriety, as did the 1963 attempt to kidnap Jean Claude "Baby Doc" Duvalier in Haiti. This first notorious kidnapping attempt in Haiti was seemingly a precursor to the actions that have led Haiti to become the worldwide leader in per capita kidnappings over the last few years.

The 1960s saw a number of attempted and successful high profile kidnappings that drew more attention to the theme and may have been an inspiration for terrorists in the campaign of aircraft hijackings and kidnappings later in the decade. American beer baron Adolph Coors III was murdered during a botched kidnapping attempt in 1960; no ransom was ever paid and the criminal was apprehended and convicted. Contemporaneously, four year-old Eric Peugeot, son of the founder of the automobile dynasty, was kidnapped in France and released in a few days after a significant ransom payment. Also in 1960, the kidnapping (not for ransom) of Adolf Eichmann from

Argentina by Israeli intelligence agents occurred with the full support of an established government in violation of the sovereignty of
another. One of the most famous kidnappings in U.S. history was
that of Frank Sinatra, Jr. in 1963. He was held for only a few days
before released after a ransom payment and the kidnappers were
later jailed.

2

A Modern Scourge

(1968 to the Present)

There can be no doubt as to the debilitating effect of kidnapping on the law-abiding majority, the fear and anxiety it creates and the extent to which it contributes to the perception that our country is not safe.

Patrick Manning

The tragedy of life is what dies inside a man while he lives.

Albert Einstein

After around five thousand years of recorded history during which pirates, statesmen and crooks used the art of kidnapping as a tool in sporadic bursts, the practice underwent a worldwide sea change in the late 1960s and early 1970s and began to take on the shape that we recognize today. A combination of terrorist and criminal actions propelled kidnapping to the forefront of consciousness of many in the world and there is no sign of a letup. Terrorists and revolutionaries use the tactic to make political statements or to raise funds, while criminals commit kidnappings for profit, straining the ability of law enforcement and terrorizing entire populations.

One aspect of the recent problem is the blurring of the distinction between criminals and terrorists. Many of the most active criminal kidnappers began as terrorists and many terrorists were formerly criminals (although most people believe that they still are). Members of both worlds are in constant contact with one another, providing support and assistance as necessary. For example, human traffickers smuggle terrorists across international borders; kidnappers purchase arms and plans from terror groups; and drug traffickers foment and actively participate in kidnappings.

By the end of the 1960s, international terrorists, revolutionary groups and common criminals had begun to commit ransom kidnappings on an historically unprecedented scale that has continued to increase almost unabated to the present. Kidnapping for ransom as a common practice began in the early 1970s, principally as an outgrowth of the many terrorist aircraft hijackings and the kidnapping of diplomatic personnel with the aim of freeing "comrades-in-arms.". Militant groups the world over began to hijack airliners and kidnap public and private figures to secure the release of imprisoned comrades, insist on publication of some sort of manifesto in the local or international press, or for ransom to finance their operations. Hostages were frequently executed or disappeared if all three conditions were not met. Criminals quickly joined in the trend.

Many self-styled "revolutionary" terrorist movements such as the M19 in Colombia, ETA (*Euzkadi ta Askatasuna*, Basque Fatherland and Liberty [or Basque Homeland and Freedom]) in Spain, Baader-Meinhof in Germany and the Red Brigades in Italy began to commit kidnappings in the late 1960s and early 1970s as a method of financing their guerrilla operations. Other criminals, such as the Rodriguez Orejuela brothers in Cali, Colombia, used kidnapping as a measure to finance their entry into the large scale trading of narcotics. The funds recouped from the kidnappings were used to arm, train and promote guerrilla movements, often with the active support of major intelligence agencies from both sides of the Cold War. "The enemy of my enemy is my friend" was a working justification for all sorts of different activities, and intelligence agencies on all sides were up to the task of providing training, intelligence, financing, weapons, equipment and contacts across international borders. This support helped in no small measure to facilitate the growth and increased sophistication of international terrorism. In a very short time, groups all over the world were in contact. Years later, as ideological partners changed sides and the world situation evolved anew, their original supporters paid (and are still paying) a heavy price. For example, the Soviets' practice of fomenting and supporting radical Muslim terror groups across the Middle East throughout the sixties, seventies and eighties led to situations the world is still confronting today in the Middle East, not to mention the severe ethnic and religious problems that the Soviet Union faced in the Central Asian republics in the 1980s. Another example is the United States' efforts to arm and train the Mujaheddin fighters in Afghanistan during the Soviet invasion. Many of these leaders became the Taliban rulers of Afghanistan and a number are now fighting in their home country and in the Northwest Frontier Provinces of Pakistan.

A significant number of incidents involving so-called revolutionary organizations were concluded violently; this seemed to be a harbinger of things to come as the movements attempted to demonstrate their levels of commitment or seriousness. In the early 1970s some international incidents perpetrated by guerrilla movements, particularly in Latin America, involved the execution of kidnapping victims, such as CIA Station Chief in Uruguay Dan Mitrione in 1970 by the Tupamaros and German Ambassador Karl Maria von Spreti in 1970 by guerillas in Guatemala. The Guatemalan government refused to aid the German government's efforts to negotiate payment or release of "political prisoners," and von Spreti was murdered soon thereafter.

Possibly the most famous terrorist kidnapping of the period was the takeover of the Israeli dormitory at the Olympic Village in Munich, Germany by commandos from the Palestinian terrorist organization Black September in 1972. Although the German government indicated a willingness to accede to their demands, a botched hostage rescue attempt led to the deaths of nine members of the Israeli Olympic team and five of the kidnappers. Another case was that of the Israeli rescue of kidnapped hostages in Entebbe, Uganda in 1976. Terrorists from the Popular Front for the Liberation of Palestine (PFLP), acting in collusion with Ugandan dictator Idi Amin Dada, hijacked an Air France flight to Uganda. Israeli commandos were able to successfully rescue all except one of the hostages. These two incidents, while not ransom kidnappings in the strictest financial sense, brought even greater worldwide attention to the practice.

Meanwhile, ransom kidnappings of diplomats and industrialists continued in many locations. The Tupamaros in Uruguay kidnapped British Ambassador Geoffrey Jackson in 1971, held him for eight months and released him after payment of a ransom. Jackson became famous as a "stoical hostage" due to his equanimity and good humor in the face of his tribulations and later wrote a book about his experience. Kidnappings by the ETA of German Consul Eugenio

Biehl (1970) and Spanish industrialists Lorenzo Zabala (1972) and Felipe Huarte (1973) were some of the first kidnapping actions by a group that has become internationally known as the experts on how to conduct a ransom kidnapping. The ETA has provided or sold kidnapping plans and expertise for years to criminals and terrorists alike. The ETA was formed in 1959 as a revolutionary group seeking an independent homeland in northern Spain and southwest France. They have committed many terror attacks in Spain, have long had an established presence in Mexico and Central America, and have been actively involved in many kidnappings in the region.

The kidnapping and ransom of Paul Getty in Italy in 1973 (variously imputed to the Mafia or to the Red Brigades) was one of the first recent famous cases in which mutilation of the victim was used as a pressure tactic. The kidnappers sliced off one of his ears and sent it to the family with a threat to remove the other unless a ransom was swiftly paid. The family did so and the young man was released a few days later. The trauma suffered by young Getty undoubtedly contributed to his lifelong drug problem and early demise. The Montoneros movement in Argentina was responsible for numerous ransom kidnappings in the early 1970s, including, in 1974, that of the Born brothers, heirs to a food and cereal fortune, for whom a ransom of some $60 million was paid. This amount still stands as the largest known ransom ever paid. In 1974 the Symbionese Liberation Army kidnapped publishing heiress Patty Hearst in the U.S.

In the early to mid-1970s, criminals, both large organizations and small groups, having observed the success of terrorist organizations in conducting kidnappings for ransom, began to commit increasing numbers of the same crime.

Italy gained international notoriety in the 1970s as the place for kidnappings. A long tradition of organized crime related extortion and kidnapping became more and more well known to the public. The case of Cristina Mazzotti, kidnapped and murdered despite payment of a $2 million ransom in 1975, was notorious and brought much scrutiny to the crime. Another important case was that of former Premier Aldo Moro, kidnapped in 1978 by the Red Brigades. After nearly two months of fruitless negotiations (no money was requested, only the liberation of other terror group members), Moro was assassinated by his captors.

The number and frequency of kidnappings in Italy maintained the country as a worldwide leader throughout the late 1970s and most of the 1980s until public outcry forced the Italian government to act. The government instituted a series of measures designed to combat the kidnapping plague, including freezing the assets of kidnap victims and making kidnap-ransom insurance policies illegal. They further empowered magistrates to freeze the assets of anyone who might be considered a potential contributor to ransom payments. This, in combination with implementation of hooded prosecutors and reforms in the law enforcement system, began to reduce the numbers of kidnappings in the early 1990s. By then, however, countries such as Colombia, Mexico and Brazil had raced past Italy into the top spots on the worldwide list.

The Colombian experience has been widely reported in fact and fiction. For many years the Revolutionary Armed Force of Colombia (FARC) in particular have been financing their projects through illicit activities, first kidnapping and now drug trafficking. During the 1970s, the M-19 and FARC committed thousands of kidnappings for ransom. Many rural mayors, businessmen and landowners were kidnapped or forced to pay an extortive "war tax" or "vaccination" fee to the guerrillas. Those who refused to pay often were kidnapped and their families forced to come up with large ransoms. Colombian criminals observed the activities and took advantage of the opportunity to commit innumerable kidnappings for profit, most of which were blamed on the insurrectionist groups. To this must be added the kidnappings committed by paramilitary groups under the guise of counter-revolutionary activity; creating a toxic mix in which no one in the country was immune to being kidnapped. By the end of the 1980s, as many as four thousand kidnappings for ransom were reportedly occurring yearly in Colombia.

The Colombian government took drastic measures to slow down the rate of kidnappings, freezing the assets of kidnap victims, making outside intercession illegal (a number of people were prosecuted under the statute), and increasing penalties for kidnappers. The measures had little or no effect, and the kidnapping rates continued to spiral out of control throughout the 1980s and 1990s. The continued activity of the FARC on one hand and of the paramilitaries on the other, combined with untold numbers of opportunistic criminals, has kept the country at or near the top of every list for most of the last three decades.

In Mexico In the late 1980s, the kidnapping problem began in earnest with a series of high-profile kidnappings of industrialists and well-known figures. These kidnappings were, for the most part, committed by national and international groups with an eye toward raising funds in support of revolutionary activities. Multimillion-dollar ransoms became commonplace and, as common criminals became aware of the ease with which kidnappings could be committed and the gains that could be achieved from these crimes, Mexico began an ascending spiral that took her to at or near the top of all lists of kidnappings.

During the early 1990s, criminals in Mexico began to commit kidnappings on a larger and larger scale. No one was immune and some kidnappers established a pattern of kidnapping, receiving payment, spending the money and returning to kidnap again with victims almost never reporting the incidents. An overwhelming lack of trust in the authorities and refusal of the citizenry to report more than a small fraction of incidents engendered a situation in which kidnappers operated with virtual impunity. The sheer numbers of kidnappings grew to the point where Mexico took over as the "kidnap capital of the world" in 2004, a dubious distinction that no country wishes to hold.

In 1993 in Managua, Nicaragua, an ETA safe house exploded, apparently due to faulty work on a bomb in preparation. In the rubble, Nicaraguan authorities discovered (among other things) a list of kidnapping targets throughout Latin America, many of whom had already been the subject of intense and detailed surveillance. I have seen copies of the data acquired by the ETA on many of the individuals on the list and the depth of information obtained on each is striking. Much of the information could only have been obtained by direct observation and tenacious investigation. Not surprisingly, many of the names on this list are individuals who were later kidnapped.

The information recovered at the house in Managua teaches important lessons. Kidnappers are typically not just a bunch of street thugs who grab the first person they see. They are professionals, dedicated to their craft and willing to invest the necessary time, effort and resources into identifying, observing and attacking a target. A friend once told me that if a band of kidnappers is willing to invest sufficient effort in kidnapping someone, there is virtually no chance that person can avoid becoming a victim. The level of effort and sophistication demonstrated by the ETA in Nicaragua supports this contention. Similarly, investigations revealed that the kidnapping of General James Dozier by the Red Brigades in Italy in 1982 was only committed after months of surveillance; this included at least one incident where the kidnappers gained access to his residence under false pretenses.

Terror groups were not idle during the 1990s either, a significant example being the takeover of the Japanese Ambassador's residence in Lima, Peru in December 1996 by Marxist guerrillas of the Movimiento Revolucionario Tupac Amaru (MRTA). After holding hundreds of hostages for more than four months, the terrorists were killed and the hostages freed in an attack by Peruvian Special Forces soldiers. Peru's Truth and Reconciliation Commission stated in their 2003 report that, in keeping with the practices of other revolutionary movements, the MRTA had systematically practiced kidnapping as a fund-raising tool during its entire existence.

Central America has slowly become a hotspot for ransom kidnappings as well. During the wars in Guatemala and El Salvador in the 1980s and 1990s, kidnapping or abduction of persons on both sides of the conflict was common. Most of these kidnappings led to execution or torture; few resulted in ransom payments. The Mara Salvatrucha gang originated during the war in El Salvador among immigrants to the United States fleeing the conflict. After the war and ever since, as gang members were deported or repatriated back to their home country, the Maras began to grow significantly in influence and scope. As they have spread to other countries in Central America, the scourge of ransom kidnapping has appeared again in Guatemala, grown dramatically in Honduras and El Salvador, and is increasing significantly in Costa Rica and Nicaragua. The operational presence of the ETA in the region, willingness on the part of gang members to commit virtually any crime for profit, and weak law enforcement have combined to make this a particularly problematic area. Characteristic of Mara tactics are short-term abductions (express kidnappings) and extortions, rather than longer-term kidnaps for ransom. The Maras use these tactics to avoid the heavy prison sentences associated with traditional ransom kidnappings.

Venezuelan criminals began to copy their Colombian neighbors in the mid-1990s and, within a few years, moved the country onto everyone's top ten list. They started by kidnapping mostly ranchers and landowners in the states bordering Colombia and the practice gradually spread to become a nationwide plague. Recent developments in the Venezuela–Colombia border area could lead conspiratorial thinkers to suspect that the first wave of kidnappings in Venezuela may have involved a certain level of FARC participation as well. In any case, by the first decade of the twenty-first century, Venezuela has become firmly entrenched as one of the countries with a very high rate of kidnaps for ransom. The problem spilled over from Venezuela into neighboring Trinidad and Tobago in the early years of this decade. Trinidad and Tobago is a very small state that was the scene of a significant number of ransom kidnappings for a few years that led the country into the top ten rankings for per capita kidnappings worldwide. Major efforts by the Trinidadian government reduced the numbers to more acceptable levels, although many incidents still occur.

Brazil, where soccer is nearly a religion, has long been plagued by extraordinary numbers of kidnappings. Since 2004, however, the families of soccer stars have become fair game for Brazilian kidnappers. Historically, famous players were treated as heroic figures and their families received a free pass from kidnappers. Starting with the kidnapping of star player Robinho's mother in 2004, a number of family members of football players have been kidnapped and significant ransoms paid for their return. Overall, Brazil continues to suffer one of the highest kidnapping rates in the world.

In the Philippines, the tradition of kidnap for ransom continued unabated. By the early 1990s, reported kidnappings in the hundreds and estimated kidnappings in the thousands flagellated the populace. The Tsinoy (Chinese–Philippine) minority, representing less than 2% of the total population but with significant economic power, was and continues to be victimized, suffering an estimated 25% of all kidnappings. Government efforts to curb the spread of kidnapping have done little more than ensure a constant rotation among gang leaders. As each is killed or captured, a replacement steps up to take the reins of the band. In addition, Communist and Muslim insurgent groups scattered throughout the archipelago commit multiple kidnappings for political or fundraising purposes. Other Southeast Asian countries with recurrent kidnapping incidents include Indonesia (mostly insurgent groups) and Malaysia.

In the Middle East, beginning in the 1980s, tribesmen in Yemen regularly kidnapped oil company workers and tourists, as the country was slowly opened after centuries of isolation. Contrary to most ransom kidnappings, the tribesmen have basically used their victims as tools to pressure the Yemeni government for concessions, and many hostages have received very good treatment from their captors. There also, however, have been a number of cases of kidnap for ransom or political kidnapping by radical groups. An enormous amount of attention has been paid (and rightfully so) to the terrorist kidnappings and beheadings in Iraq and many other related types of politically motivated abductions throughout the Middle East over the last few years. Lost in the haze and hysteria of more publicized and politicized cases have been numerous reports of kidnappings in which significant ransoms were paid for the release of hostages.

Abductions are common in Afghanistan and ransom kidnappings have been reported. In neighboring Pakistan, however, kidnap for ransom is a major problem. In the northern and western provinces, kidnapping for ransom is ongoing and large amounts have been paid for victims, both national and international. There is debate as to how many of the ransoms are for common criminals and how many are put to use for political ends; however, the number of incidents continues to rise.

India has long been one of the world's busiest kidnap-for-ransom markets. As mentioned in the previous chapter, in some regions kidnappers have been viewed almost as benefactors for the poor and downtrodden. All across the country, from the Kashmir to the Bangladeshi border, literally hundreds of kidnappings are reported each year. The government has shown little ability to control the proliferation of incidents, and payment of ransoms is common throughout the land. Sorting out the kidnappings committed by common criminals from those committed by insurgents or extremist groups is difficult; however, for the victims the result is always the same: a ransom payment for the return of a loved one or in many cases, death.

After the fall of the Berlin Wall in 1989 and the subsequent breakup of the Soviet empire, entrepreneurial criminals from Kazakhstan to Eastern Europe took advantage of their newfound freedoms and began a wave of kidnappings that still continues. In Russia and the former Soviet republics, criminal organizations have practiced kidnapping with virtual impunity, taking ransoms for businessman, family members and persons of all socioeconomic levels. Rampant corruption and less than effective law enforcement have fostered an environment in which kidnapping flourishes.

In the twenty-first century, Nigeria has become one of the world's most active locations for kidnapping. Hundreds of locals and expatriates are kidnapped every year and massive ransoms are paid. In the oil-rich state of Rivers, white western oil company executives are referred to by gang members as "white gold," for their value as pawns in the kidnap and ransom game. In recent years the practice of kidnapping westerners has become increasingly common, although the threat existed as early as the late 1960s, when my father traveled there regularly on business. Nigeria is the leading kidnapping state in Africa (although Somalia competes favorably) but is far from the only location. The practice continues in states such as the Sudan, Niger, Chad, South Africa and others. Remember that slavery and kidnapping are intertwined, nowhere more so than in Africa; the continued existence of the practice of slavery in many places and the taking of hostages for ransom continue to plague societies across the continent. South Africa also has a continuing problem with ransom kidnappings that is considered particularly pernicious in some major cities.

Western European nations and the United States have not been immune to kidnappings either. Every year, thousands are reported. Many of these crimes are abductions for sexual exploitation or parent–child kidnappings in which spouses in conflict try to resolve their differences by taking the children and running away. Kidnap for ransom, however, continues to occur and, although press reporting of these incidents is overshadowed by the more sensationalistic types of crimes or abductions, some incidents result in large ransom payments. Contrary to popular belief, not every ransom kidnapping in the United States is solved, nor are all of those in Europe.

Kidnapping is a worldwide phenomenon. For every difference that one can detect there are significant similarities. Kidnappers in Mexico use the tactic of cutting off ears or fingers to pressure families and organizations to pay. In Colombia, the bodies of dead hostages are ransomed back to their families for proper burial. In Iraq, Muslim terrorists have taped the beheading of kidnap victims and posted videos on the Internet. In the former Soviet Union where universal dental care was provided by the state, kidnappers would extract a tooth with pliers and send it to the family as a proof of life or demonstration of possession of the victim. The evil that men do may vary slightly, but, in the end, individuals are forcibly deprived of their freedom through no fault of their own and their families or organizations are forced to pay a substantial sum to (hopefully) ensure their safe return.

3

KIDNAPPING AND KIDNAPPERS

This miserable measure the wretched souls maintain of those who lived without infamy and without praise. Mingled are they with that caitiff choir of the angels, who were not rebels, nor were faithful to God, but were for themselves. The heavens chased them out in order to be not less beautiful, nor doth the depth of Hell receive them, because the damned would have some glory from them.

Dante Alighieri, The Divine Comedy

The criminal element now calculates that crime really does pay.

Ronald W. Reagan

The Crime

The question should be asked: How widespread is kidnapping throughout the world? A precise determination is impossible. Accurate statistics on kidnappings are impossible to obtain, citizens mistrustful of their own police forces are unwilling to report the crime, governments skew statistics for political purposes, and a universally accepted legal definition of the crime of kidnapping is lacking. Thus, comparisons are difficult and all data must be extrapolated from incomplete and often incompatible sources. There is, however, considerable evidence that speaks to the scope of the problem. Press reports, survivor stories, arrest records and governmental reports and declarations certainly indicate that kidnapping is a large and growing problem everywhere. For every success story, such as the reduction of incidents in Italy and Trinidad and Tobago, there are ten more countries in which the number of incidents has increased exponentially.

Kidnapping is viewed as an easy way to make money in countries where government and law enforcement are weak or where corruption is rampant, flourishing in places where the rule of law is tenuous. This, unfortunately, describes many countries across the world. Globalization has enabled kidnappers and other criminals and terrorists to transfer funds anywhere in an instant, allows them to stay up-to-date on the latest tactics and techniques and permits surreptitious, confidential, virtually instantaneous communication both locally and across vast expanses of territory or international borders. Technology has also enabled the use of throwaway cellular phones, instant digital videotape and photography for counter surveillance and numerous other benefits of which kidnappers take full advantage. A leader in Zimbabwe can manage a kidnapping band in Argentina; a kidnapping may be committed in Indonesia and the ransom paid in Kazakhstan.

There has been a definite political slant to many ransom kidnappings over the years, as insurgent groups take hostages to finance their activities. These cases are not unusual and normally involve larger amounts of money, more protracted negotiations and, once the group has gained experience by committing a number of abductions, a greater degree of sophistication than a typical criminal ransom kidnapping.

There is no precise and generally accepted legal definition for kidnapping across the world. In the United States, there are numerous state and federal laws against various forms of kidnapping. Depending on the country or region, kidnapping is called illegal privation of liberty, abduction, hostage taking, illicit detention and numerous other terms. This leads to a jumble of terminology, penalties and definitions, some of which make life simpler for the criminal. The legal tangle surrounding kidnapping would be better served by a standardized international definition accepted everywhere. This, however, is unlikely to occur. Local laws, be they more or less stringent, are those that rule and kidnapping for ransom is considered a crime everywhere.

Religious laws must also be considered. In certain predominantly Muslim countries, Sharia law takes precedence over any standard legal precedent understood by the Western mind. For example, in parts of Nigeria, the Sharia law is interpreted as permitting kidnapping and forcible conversion of non-Muslim women. The Koran is also used in many locations to justify kidnapping as acceptable, although a number of Islamic scholars have denounced the practice. Christians have no immunity from similar acts throughout history, either. The famous kidnapping and raising as a Catholic of Edgardo Mortara in Italy in the 1850s was the subject of a well-known recent book. Apparently, the practice was not unusual in that numerous children, baptized without their parents' knowledge, were taken by the church and raised as Christians. Religions change their views, positions and sanctions over time; mistakes are made and adjustments follow. Where religious law takes precedence over secular law, however, someone will be there to provide a justification for immoral acts, including kidnapping.

To seriously discuss kidnapping, one needs an acceptable definition. Webster's Dictionary defines kidnapping as "to seize and detain a person unlawfully, usually for ransom." Since over time there have been so many variations on the crime, a more focused definition is necessary.

Ernst Kahlar Alix, in his seminal 1978 work, *Ransom Kidnapping in America*, defined fifteen different types of kidnapping extracted from one hundred years of news reports:

white slavery
hostage situation
child stealing
domestic relations kidnapping
kidnapping for rape or other sexual assault
kidnapping for murder or other nonsexual assault
kidnapping for robbery
romantic kidnapping
ransom skyjacking
ransom kidnapping hoax
plot or abortive ransom kidnapping
ransom threat for extortion
developmental ransom kidnapping
classic ransom kidnapping
miscellaneous kidnappings

Alix's definitions are useful in understanding that multiple types of kidnapping occur and not all involve the payment of a ransom. The history of kidnapping includes all of these crimes. The remainder of this work will, however, focus almost exclusively on what Kahlar defines as classic ransom kidnapping, with some attention paid to other situations such as extortion and situations that begin as other crimes and subsequently develop into ransom kidnappings.

To understand some of the most commonly accepted current terms in the press, security industry and public domain, let us begin with a definition of the types of kidnapping that are the principal subjects of this work:

Ransom kidnapping—This is a situation in which one or more individuals are taken by force or guile and held against their will pending the payment of a ransom. These events are characterized by a long-term negotiation ultimately leading to the payment of a ransom for the victim's freedom. Long-term can mean anything from three days to years, depending on the location and the kidnappers. Most ransom kidnappings today last, as a general rule, from six to sixty days, during which kidnappers communicate demands to the family or organization, a process of negotiation is followed, agreement is reached and the victim is released after payment. A large percentage of victims are treated relatively well, supplied with food and medicine as needed, and return home safely after their ordeal. Accurate statistics are impossible to come by and some areas of the world have higher death rates than others in these incidents; however, the most common estimates cite a survival rate of more than 90% for victims of ransom kidnapping. Kidnappings that last more than approximately six months are primarily political acts; hostages normally are held on a long-term basis for other than exclusively financial reasons, although ransoms are negotiated and paid as well.

Express kidnapping—This term came into vogue in the 1990s and describes a kidnapping that occurs quickly and is over in a very short time, usually less than 24 hours. Kidnappers typically grab an individual from a bank kiosk, parking lot, school, nightclub, restaurant or other public place and immediately place a call to the family demanding a rapid payment. The victim will normally be taken to various bank teller machines in an effort to extract as much immediate cash as possible, while the family scrambles to put together as much money or other easily transferable goods as can be made available on a crash basis. The negotiation is conducted in a matter of hours, frequently using the victim's personal cellular phone and ransoms are relatively low, although some impressive sums have been noted. Once payment is delivered, the victim is released and able to return home. This crime is usually considered to be a variation of the "ATM abduction," in which the victim is taken in the same manner and driven around to various ATM machines in order to withdraw as much cash as possible in a short period of time.

Virtual kidnapping—This is a crime that became increasingly popular in the 1990s as well. A victim must be isolated and out of communication for only a couple of hours and the kidnappers must be able to convince a family that they have him or her in their power. The classic case is that of a young person going to a movie, sporting event or other location in which he or she will be out of touch for a few hours. The criminals extract personal data from the individual under some pretext, often taking photographs as well, and immediately call the family claiming to have committed a kidnapping. These are extremely short in duration; families must come up with whatever they can, usually in less than two hours; and criminals basically are forced to accept whatever is offered. The unknowing victim returns home after the event to a shocking story.

Psychological kidnapping (Extortion)—This is an increasingly popular method among criminals and is based on fear. Kidnappers, more correctly extortionists, communicate a threat to the family or organization that one or more members will be kidnapped or killed unless a payment is made. In a climate of fear and uncertainty in which numerous kidnappings are in fact occurring, a threat can be sufficiently believable to cause a family or organization to pay almost as a form of insurance. This tactic has been used for a number of years in Latin America in particular to extract substantial sums of money from victims without ever having to seize anyone. This is an extremely low-risk, high-reward crime if the victim makes no report. For our purposes we will focus on extortion via the threat of kidnapping, although threats to murder a family or organization member also are used as extortion tools.

These four basic types of kidnapping are the focus of this work, although some ransom kidnappings have other factors in common such as political overtones, family and child custody issues, sexual abuse and slavery.

Kidnappers

How does a man or woman leave home in the morning, make the sign of the cross and ask for blessings on the day's labors, then proceed to violently deprive another individual of his or her liberty for ransom? This question may best be answered by sociologists or psychologists with far greater qualifications and experience than my own; however, the ability to do so is common to kidnappers all over the world. Religious affiliation may vary, some kidnappers may ask for the blessing of Allah or the Virgin Mary and some may have no religious beliefs at all. Kidnappers, as a rule, perceive themselves as normal working people whose job is to make money the best way they know how.

Most kidnappers are professionals who dedicate themselves to their craft. Those who do not learn from their own mistakes and those of others have very short careers. Few, if any, start out to become kidnappers; circumstances lead them to make the decision to commit these crimes. This does not justify their actions; kidnappers are the vilest of creatures and should be severely punished. Kidnapping is so wrong on so many levels; uprooting an individual from his or her family and forcing the family to pay for a safe return is degrading, disgusting and truly amoral. The blood, sweat and tears of the victims and their families cry out for justice; no punishment can ever replace lost lives, limbs, hopes and dreams.

Kidnappers may come from anywhere. In the political kidnapping arena, from which many ransoms are paid, the perpetrators are often former university students who have turned to "revolutionary" activities as a way of seeking redress for perceived social or economic inequities in their country or in another. These are generally intelligent, well-educated people who have made a conscious decision to commit kidnappings, justifying them in the name of their "cause," whatever that may be. They may have started out with the seemingly noble aspiration of changing the world for the better; however, having turned to activities such as kidnapping, they place themselves squarely in the ranks of wrongdoers who merit only contempt. Some of these individuals turn from their political activities and become enamored of their role, dedicating themselves to kidnapping as a lucrative profession.

Religion has also been a source of many kidnappers; fanatics of every stripe seem to gravitate to the activity. I know of no religious source material in which any given deity promotes or authorizes kidnapping; however, some religious leaders can convince followers that almost any activity is sanctioned by the deity they worship. In the end, the result is the same whether based on religion or politics. Undeserving individuals are deprived of their liberty at a tremendous cost to families, organizations and/or governments.

Many common ransom kidnappers begin by committing armed robberies, bank heists, carjackings or any number of other crimes. Some are attracted to kidnapping because they perceive that it offers a better opportunity in risk–reward terms than the crimes they currently perpetrate. This is absolutely true in countries in which kidnapping has been referred to as the "best business going" or the "best business in (insert country name)." The attractiveness of a low-risk, high-reward business is undeniable for anyone, much less a criminal, and this leads to ever-greater numbers of kidnappers. On occasion, law enforcement authorities, after arresting notorious kidnappers, have held press conferences at which recovered booty was prominently displayed. Instead of the intended effect of discouraging potential kidnappers, these have served to animate other criminals to take up the activity.

Imagine yourself as a poor working youth in a third-world country. You see no real hope for success, jobs are tight and those that are available pay very little. You live with your whole family in a one- or two-room apartment and are constantly exposed to television and radio advertisements for the "good life," none of which you can ever aspire to afford. You watch the news and see that Joe Smith the kidnapper has been captured. The police parade him in front of the press, but your eye is drawn to the stacks of bills, gold coins and jewelry on the table behind him. While the police proudly display the fruits of his labor recovered during the arrest, you begin to wonder whether you might not consider taking up the profession.

The decision to become a kidnapper can be relatively easy for an individual inclined toward criminal activity who does not perceive much of an opportunity to join the mainstream in the future. In countries in which society is stratified and the lower classes have little hope of achieving a dramatic leap forward, corruption among police and politicians is rampant, and there is only a marginally functional criminal justice system, kidnapping can become a very attractive option.

Kidnapping bands are organized for the most part like any other business operation. The typical band of kidnappers is composed of a maximum of eight to ten persons, with a leader who controls the group and selects the targets. He or she also normally receives a very large percentage of the ransom and doles out the rest to followers. Each member is allotted specific tasks to perform, in line with demonstrated abilities or talents. Many arrested kidnappers report that they started their own groups after participating in a few cases to learn the business.

A significant percentage of kidnapping bands start out as groups of childhood friends, school acquaintances, or criminal associates who decide to change tracks. These groups are normally made up of people who already know and trust each other. The old saw "honor among thieves" holds true to some degree. As their level of experience progresses, others are recruited into the band as necessary, always after a careful vetting. When the authorities break up a band, those members not arrested will start new groups. This "hydra effect" contributes to the continual propagation of additional kidnapping bands.

The largest percentage of those individuals apprehended, prosecuted and incarcerated for kidnapping is composed of low-level participants; those individuals contracted as actual kidnappers, lookouts and caretakers rather than the brains behind the organization. This further contributes to the spread of kidnapping, as those in charge tend to insulate themselves from apprehension and prosecution and, with the vast amounts of money involved, are able to easily recruit new members or pay protection as necessary. Kidnappers have learned from drug traffickers and vice versa; the littlest fish in the pond are those most likely to be swallowed up, while the largest continue to swim freely.

In my neighborhood, a house was being remodeled. From my friend's bedroom window, we could see that the construction looked like a series of rooms with no windows, sort of like storerooms. This house was a place where the guys who came and went had really nice cars, Mercedes and BMWs, and everyone in the neighborhood thought they were narcos (drug dealers). I was curious, so I started hanging around with a guy my age who used to go in and out of there regularly. He always had money to pay for drinks at the local bar. After a while, he asked if I would be interested in working with him. He wouldn't tell me what the work was; only that it paid well, the work might be dangerous and that I could get killed for talking about it.

I said why not; anything was better than the miserable minimum wage job I was working and I wanted to get some nice things for my mother and me. He said he would set something up so I could meet his boss.

A few days later he took me in a taxi to a bar on the other side of town. We met with a guy wearing dark glasses and a large mustache that was obviously false. He asked me about my family and copied down all my personal information. He wanted to know if I was willing to do anything he told me and let me know that, if I wanted to work for him, my family would suffer if I betrayed him. I told him I was up for anything as long as the money was good. He said they would be in touch and ended the interview after about fifteen minutes.

About a week later my buddy picked me up one evening and we took a taxi ride into the city. We started hanging around an overpass as night was falling and he told me that we were there to look for a certain vehicle. We were supposed to make a note of the first five cars that followed the vehicle and call them in. After a while the vehicle came by and we did this. Then we went to another place and did the same thing. This went on for a few hours and then we went home. The next day he came up and gave me a hundred dollars, reminding me to keep my mouth shut. This was easy money and I wasn't sure what to think, I had thought we were working for the narcos, but now I began to think it might be something else.

A few days later he picked me up and we went outside the city. He handed me a pistol and taught me how to shoot; after a while, I got the hang of it. Then he asked if I was willing to work all night for a while, guarding some merchandise. I said sure and he told me to come over to the house in the neighborhood at around ten that night. When I showed up, there was a real scary guy I had not met before who made me swear that I would obey orders without question and again threatened my family if I ever betrayed them. He gave me a gun and took me to the new part of the house and told me to stand guard outside one of the doors. He told me that if the person inside called out or I was told to go in; that the person had better be wearing a blindfold when I opened the door or that I should tell him in the morning. He further told me that if the person inside tried to come out without permission, I was

to shoot him on the spot. That's when I realized that our business was
kidnapping, not drugs.

In most countries, the judicial system is such that kidnappers are very rarely apprehended. Those who are captured go through the legal process just as any other criminal. In many countries, the sheer volume of cases makes the process of investigation, apprehension, trial and incarceration very slow; in others, corruption is so common that many can buy their way out of trouble. Those convicted are frequently sentenced to long prison terms that are routinely cut short due to overcrowded conditions in local penal systems. The time that kidnappers spend in prison is similar to the experience of other criminals. Prison is considered to be the equivalent of a university education in criminal activity. Inexperienced kidnappers become much more sophisticated and those sentenced for lesser crimes can learn how to move up to kidnapping. When a kidnapper is released from prison, he or she is much better prepared to operate a band and avoid capture in the future.

Once any individual becomes an active participant in kidnapping, the situation is akin to that of a drug addict. As the easy money flows, the possibility that a kidnapper will pull away from the activity and "go straight" becomes increasingly remote. He or she is pulled into a cycle of kidnap, negotiate, receive payment, spend the ill-gotten gains, and return to kidnap again. Very few kidnappers have the preparation, education or mindset to look at kidnapping as a short, lucrative career that will enable them to rapidly become financially secure and then retire or do something else. Most kidnappers are given to spending freely between each incident and, when money runs out, performing another job. The most sophisticated gang leaders may make investments or seek to shelter their money in tax havens, but this is unusual.

Kidnapping bands also make extensive use of subcontractors for many separate individual tasks. The most professional groups have adopted cellular structures drawn from Cold War-era espionage tactics, in which separate cells are used for each individual task, and none of the members knows anyone outside the cell. For example, there might be different cells for the actual kidnapping, transportation, holding the hostage(s), and communications and the baseline team may only really be involved in negotiating, recovering the ransom and delivering the money to the leader for counting and distribution. Subcontractors are paid fixed fees for their work and go on to other business.

The use of cellular structures makes law enforcement's task much more difficult. A cell can be rolled up and the members arrested; however, their inability to identify the others involved leads to multiple dead ends. This makes the task facing law enforcement much more difficult and has been an important factor in the dramatic expansion of kidnapping worldwide. A little context for this contention is necessary. After the fall of the Berlin Wall in 1989, thousands of professional intelligence and security officers from the Eastern Bloc were suddenly out of work or forced to seek new careers. Many sought opportunities as consultants throughout the world, a number of them training criminal and terrorist organizations in tradecraft and other useful skills. The cellular organizational structure grew out of the development of terrorist tactics in earlier years, many of whose members had been trained by Soviet-bloc intelligence operatives, enabling criminals to become significantly more sophisticated in terms of their organization, communications, tradecraft and ability to avoid detection and capture.

This activity can be seen in multiple cases worldwide. In one case the group of five individuals involved in the actual taking of the victim was arrested within 24 hours of the kidnapping. The highway patrol found a member of this group using the victim's car to transport stolen electronic equipment from one town to another. The family was contacted and immediately notified the specialized anti-kidnapping unit of the state police. The individual was interrogated and the other members of the group swiftly taken into custody. A raid was then conducted on the building (a residence in a slum area) to which the victim had been delivered. When the police entered (30 or so hours after the kidnapping occurred), all they found were the clothes the victim had been wearing when taken and no trace of any information that might lead them to his whereabouts.

Despite intensive interrogation of all five members of the group, no useful leads were developed that contributed to identifying either a location at which the victim might be found or the identity of any members of the band of kidnappers. The arrestees turned out to be a group of carjackers hired for their evasive driving ability and willingness to commit violence if necessary. In this case, in which the initial ransom demand was around $300,000, the actual strike team was to have received $2,000 for a few hours work.

While some courage is needed to actually snatch the victim off the street, from his or her car or from any public or private location, captured kidnappers often prove to be weak and easily intimidated. For some reason, many of those who kidnap seem to demonstrate the same character traits as school bullies; they fold immediately when pressured. Torturing and abusing a helpless victim does not require any moral or physical courage, only a sadistic streak. Many victims report that their caretakers were almost apologetic, only to turn violent and threatening the moment any potential threat materialized or when someone higher up in the organization appeared on the scene.

In addition to the unimaginable psychological strain placed on any kidnapping victim, mistreatment and physical or sexual abuse of kidnapping victims is rampant. Many victims report that immediately after reaching a safe house, they were forced to hand over their clothes and change into a sweat suit or similar togs and subjected to an invasive and degrading physical search. Therapists, speaking unofficially, report that a significant percentage of victims, particularly (but not restricted to) females, report varying levels of sexual abuse at the hands of their captors.

The inclination toward abuse when in a position of authority is well documented, whether that abuse is psychological, physical, sexual or a combination of the three. The Stanford Prison Experiment conducted in 1971 used a group of randomly selected college students to participate as guards and prisoners in a two-week simulation of prison conditions. The actions and pathologies observed clearly demonstrated that apparently normal college students, when placed in a position of complete authority over their peers, very quickly began to administer harsh and abusive treatments to those under their control. The effects were so dramatic that the experiment was called off after only a few days. Military prison guards at Abu Ghraib in Iraq demonstrated a similar willingness to abuse prisoners as they saw fit. Kidnappers, who have absolute power of life and death over their hostages, and generally do not come from university or military environments, routinely tend to do the same.

If members of the kidnapping group have any tendencies toward violence or sexual abuse, they will likely emerge during the situation. The most prone to this type of activity are those who function as caretakers, that is, the individuals assigned to provide 24-hour security on the victim at the location where the hostage is detained. Depending on the leeway given by the leader of the group or the autonomy that the caretakers have (they are frequently subcontractors or provide a service holding multiple hostages for different groups), the guards can basically have their way with hostages, as long as the victim's survival is guaranteed.

The leader of a kidnapping group sets the tone for the behavior exhibited by all members of the group. Kidnapping bands are usually dictatorships in which the leader's word is law. Deviance from his or her instructions can be, and frequently is, punishable by death. If the leader is a sociopath, the members will normally have the freedom to be much more abusive than in cases where the leader wishes to run the operation more like a business.

A young woman reported that she had been selected by the leader to be his object of affection and band members were warned that only he could touch her. He sexually assaulted her regularly during her captivity, leaving emotional scars that may never heal completely. She was held in a safe house in which a number of other rooms held other victims of the same group and, when recounting her story, repeatedly asserted that she had been fortunate compared to others. She reported that two other young women had been kidnapped together and were repeatedly gang-raped by any members of the group who so desired. Her designated guardian told her that this was because they were "stuck up," deserved the treatment and that "the guys" needed to have some fun.

Although sexual exploitation of kidnapping victims is common, physical violence is even more so. One victim mentioned that every time the negotiator returned from speaking with his family and reported that they would not pay the requested ransom, he received a beating. Since he wore a pacemaker for a heart condition, his captors confined their beatings to kicking him from the waist down to avoid precipitating a heart attack. Many victims report that beatings are commonplace when the kidnappers have spoken to the family or organization and received a reply that does not satisfy their demands.

In extreme cases, serious physical violence is perpetrated on the victims as a method of pressuring the family or organization to pay a higher amount and do so quickly. In Mexico, the famous *mochaorejas* (ear-cutter), Daniel Arizmendi, delighted in cutting off a victim's ear and sending it to the family or posting the ear in a public place for the family to recover. He was a sociopath who gleefully committed the worst atrocities to "see what I could get away with." His tactics enabled him to gain multimillion-dollar ransoms from frightened families; however, the tactic also contributed to his downfall as intense public pressure to apprehend and prosecute him finally overcame the massive protection payoff system he had arranged. He is serving a long prison sentence in a maximum security prison.

Other kidnappers specialize in cutting off fingers, pulling teeth and other forms of torture designed to pressure families and organizations into prompt payment. Forms of pressure commonly used are the threat or actual commission of acts of nonlethal or nondisfiguring violence against the victim; menacing or performing acts of sexual depravity; threatened or real withholding of food, water or medication, and simply the threat of holding the hostage as long as necessary to achieve the desired result. These, in combination with the ever-present possibility that the hostage could be executed at any time, combine to apply intense pressure on the family or organization.

Fortunately, sociopaths like Arizmendi represent only a small percentage of kidnappers worldwide. Various sources estimate that around ten percent of all victims of ransom kidnapping are killed and that a further ten to twenty percent suffer serious physical injury. Ransom kidnapping is a business and, like any good businessperson, the kidnapper must sell mostly undamaged merchandise for anyone to wish to participate in the transaction. If the merchandise (victim) were always damaged (seriously injured or killed), the market would soon dry up.

The typical kidnapping band conducts a detailed study of the victim prior to striking. They observe the potential victim's habits and routines to determine whether he or she is a viable candidate for kidnapping and how best to undertake the actual operation. They also investigate the potential victim's financial situation to estimate the ability to pay, including properties, other assets and apparent liquidity. If the victim meets their criteria, a kidnapping is performed. The more information they can obtain, the easier they find pricing the victim and negotiating a higher ransom. Neither they nor families nor organizations are served by a continued insistence on payment of an unattainable sum. This is not to say that this does not happen, but kidnappers normally have a pretty good idea of the family's or organization's capacity to pay and target accordingly, although initial ransom demands are frequently astronomical, with kidnappers hoping to occasionally "hit the lottery." After all, who knows when a family might fold and immediately pay what is demanded?

Most kidnappers take care in selecting their victims. There are those who circle, simply looking for individuals in late model cars. They attack, take the victim and negotiate for whatever they can get. Many of these are incidents in a gray area between express and ransom kidnappings. Quite a few do, however, last a few days as ransom kidnappings and require a more detailed response. In some cases, small bands of kidnappers take victims with the express purpose of selling them to larger, more experienced groups that have the wherewithal to conduct a lengthy process of negotiation in search of a significantly greater ransom.

4

Victims, Families and Organizations

The peculiarity of punishment of this kind, in which what is pitiless, that is to say, what is brutalizing, predominates, is to transform little by little, by slow stupefaction, a man into an animal, sometimes into a wild beast.

Victor Hugo, Les Miserables

Hostage is a crucifying aloneness. It is a silent, screaming slide into the bowels of ultimate despair. Hostage is a man hanging by his fingernails over the edge of chaos, feeling his fingers slowly straightening. Hostage is the humiliating stripping away of every sense and fiber of body and mind and spirit that make us what we are. Hostage is a mutant creation filled with fear, self-loathing, guilt and death-wishing.

Brian Keenan, Hostage in Lebanon

Victims

Kidnapping victims come from all walks of life. There is no magical formula that can be used to predict whether any given individual will be more or less prone to kidnapping, although selection of targets in certain countries or locations follows a more or less predictable trajectory. For example, in Nigeria, white westerners are colloquially referred to as "ATMs" (automated teller machines) because they represent quick cash to the various kidnapping bands that operate there. In Mexico, ethnic or religious communities (e.g., Spanish, Jewish, Lebanese, etc.) have been repeatedly victimized by separate waves of kidnappings. In those and other countries, some kidnappers seize upon apparently attractive targets of opportunity (new cars, flashy jewelry, ostentatious behavior), while most others make a more detailed study of potential victims.

One thing all victims have in common is suffering. The trauma of being kidnapped and forced to survive at the whim of a band of criminals is truly astonishing. Every victim with whom I have ever spoken mentions an overwhelming sense of utter terror and helplessness at his or her plight. The total lack of control was to many victims a significant factor in their experience. Victims report varying types of treatment, ranging from an almost friendly style (food to order, low-threat, and baths) to savage abuse at the hands of their captors.

I was held in a small room, about eight feet square. There was a little window high up on one wall through which I could see the side of a mountain or hill. I had a small bed and a bucket for my necessities that was taken out once a day. In four weeks, I never got a chance to shower, wash, shave or brush my teeth.

Victims range in age from the very young to the very old. The youngest victim of a ransom kidnapping that I personally know of was five and the oldest eighty-four; other reports indicate that even younger children have been taken (e.g., the Lindbergh baby). Gender is also not necessarily a factor; both men and women are taken. The main issue in gender selection seems to be accessibility; that is, when a family or organization is targeted, kidnappers seek the target that can be most easily taken. In some places there is a tendency to go after male heads of households as the most tempting targets; however, some kidnappers tend to attack other family members, feeling that they can more quickly negotiate a settlement when the primary decision maker remains free and is available to make a deal. This is more typical in family kidnappings than in corporate situations, because an organization will have other executives with whom a negotiation can be conducted, although in most countries the preponderance of male executives in senior positions implies that they will comprise a correspondingly high percentage of kidnap victims.

In some cases when the head of household has been taken, obtaining the release of funds for ransom payments can be difficult. If he or she is the only one with authority to release certain funds, that money is not available for the ransom. This has led in some instances to a hostage being released at a much lower level of payment than expected. In other cases, the hostage is released with the promise that the ransom will be paid. Some follow up and pay and some do not, depending primarily on how far the family or organization believes the kidnappers will go to recover "their" money. A number of highly publicized escapes reported in various countries were actually cover stories promulgated to permit the family or organization to privately make agreed-upon payments without intense public scrutiny. As well, a few "escaped" kidnap victims have fallen prey to "accidents" within a year or two of having returned home.

Once an individual becomes a hostage, he or she loses control over the most basic of life's functions. Hostages are told when to eat, sleep, use the bathroom, wash and clean; even the amount of natural or artificial light to which they are exposed is controlled. This permits kidnappers, under certain circumstances, to be seen as magnanimous by simply providing a crust of dry bread (see Stockholm syndrome below). As insane as this may appear to be under normal circumstances, if you have received no water for two days, the man who smiles when he hands you a full glass can quickly become your best friend. The lack of control over the simplest of things can seriously affect victims of any age and is frequently cited as one of the most difficult aspects of captivity. Victims often report a terrible sense of impotence at not being able to take care of the smallest details in their daily lives.

When I was taken, they handcuffed me to a bed in a dark room and kept the radio blaring on a popular music station twenty-four hours a day. When I wanted to go to the bathroom, I had to wait until they brought me a bucket. Sometimes, they would leave the bucket in the room for twelve hours or more, just to harass me. The sense of humiliation I felt at not even being able to decide when to use the bathroom was tremendous. Even worse was having to do my private business while blindfolded, with someone standing there watching me, and having to beg them for toilet paper. This was absolutely the worst aspect of the whole experience for me.

No one ever thinks that he or she will become a kidnap victim and few persons ever make any real preparation for the eventuality. In many countries, security companies and major organizations offer courses that include some instruction on hostage survival techniques. These courses range from very good to very poor, depending on the skill level and knowledge of the instructors. Few potential kidnap victims attend such courses and a very small percentage of those attending truly pay attention. Most people seem to feel either that a guardian angel will protect them or that "it can't happen to me." When tragedy strikes they are woefully unprepared and suffer the consequences.

I was one of those people who, although a number of individuals I knew had been kidnapped, figured that this would never happen to me. My family had taken a course on personal security, defensive driving and stuff like that. I was kidnapped at 0630 in the morning on my way to the university. My day started off like any other; I got my coffee, got in the car, turned on the radio and headed for campus. At a stop sign about three blocks from my house, a car bumped into me from behind and I heard glass crunching. I jumped out to yell at the other driver and suddenly, these two guys pulled guns and made me get into the back seat of their car face down on the floor. I remember thinking that I wished I had paid more attention when we went to that weekend seminar on security and that my parents would be very worried.

Victims report all sorts of psychological pressures and attempts by their kidnappers to enlist their aid in pushing the family or organization to raise more money. Many report that they are interrogated about every conceivable facet of the family's finances. Families also find that the kidnappers will suddenly come up with information on money they were unaware of or a piece of heirloom jewelry that could be sold for more. Often, the victim, in exchange for information, is "rewarded" by a lessening of the mistreatment or provision of some sort of favored foodstuff, a book or another small item to make the captivity a little more bearable. This is, unfortunately, only part of the psychological gamesmanship brought to bear. Kidnappers completely control the environment and can grant or remove the smallest of privileges as a whim. Everyone has a breaking point, and kidnappers become quite proficient at detecting and exploiting even miniscule weaknesses.

Brian proved very resistant to physical abuse; he was able to withstand savage beatings without breaking down. After a while the beatings ceased and his treatment improved; he was even given a few books to read. After a short period of time, the books were taken away and he became disconsolate. In a vain attempt to have the books returned, he told the kidnappers everything he could think of and answered all their questions. Not only did the kidnappers not return the books, they regularly mocked him for his weakness and teased him about how the information he had provided was being used to squeeze every last cent out of his family. He returned home suffering from an extreme case of depression that required years of treatment.

Kidnappers have also been known to use their hostages to develop information on other potential victims. Many victims report that they were pressured into providing the kidnappers with a list of detailed information on fifty to one hundred acquaintances who might become future victims. This led in a number of cases to ruptured friendships and long-term enmity between formerly tight-knit groups of friends and associates. Each time the kidnappers took a new victim, they made sure to reveal who had identified him or her as a potential target. Each victim was forced to provide in turn his or her own list of other potentially attractive targets, thus furnishing the kidnappers with a continually updated and easily verifiable target list. Some victims contacted everyone whose name they could remember immediately upon release to warn them; however, the majority were embarrassed and made no mention of the situation to their friends and neighbors until the practice became an open secret.

My kidnappers asked me on the very first day to make a list of one hundred people I knew that might be of interest to them. Naturally, I refused and they beat me so badly that I couldn't stand up. The next day they came in and beat me again. The pain was incredible and I did not know what to do; when I begged them to stop they just laughed and kept kicking and punching me. On the third day they took all my clothes, beat me and threatened to rape me. That night the leader and three others came into my room; they held me down while he sodomized me. They all laughed and told me how much I liked the treatment. The next day they asked me again for the list of all my friends and contacts and promised they would not hurt me anymore if I cooperated. I had no choice, I wrote down as much information as I could on everyone I knew, anything to keep him from doing that again. After I made the list for them, they pretty much left me alone, except when the leader was angry with my parents over the pace of the negotiations.

The trauma to which victims are subjected is tremendous. Kidnappers play on their fears and emotions to get what they want or just to cruelly tease the victim and make the experience even more degrading. The young man in the previous anecdote underwent a course of therapy after his release but he still has nightmares about the incidents. He feels guilt over having informed on all his acquaintances, some of whom were later kidnapped, as well as his own problems resulting from the abuse suffered at the hands of his kidnappers. The psychological effects of a kidnapping on the victim are far-reaching. They often suffer severe bouts of depression and some have been known to become completely reclusive. During a kidnapping, victims' emotions tend to run the gamut from intense hatred of the kidnappers to a surprisingly supportive viewpoint or even active cooperation and support. The development of positive feelings on the part of the victim toward the kidnappers is called the Stockholm syndrome.

The phenomenon is very real and affects all kidnap victims to some degree. Families and organizations need to understand this and realize that the victim will surely have been affected. This reaction is an almost subconscious survival strategy or technique that is more a result of the intense duress to which a kidnapping victim is subjected rather than a conscious decision made by the hostage. This mandates care and discretion in comments made by family and organization members and begs discretion when speaking of the kidnappers in front of the former hostage. The hostage may be surprisingly supportive of those who have held him or her for a period of time and this can be exhibited in unusual ways.

The Stockholm syndrome is named for a phenomenon that was first noticed during a six-day bank hostage-taking in Sweden in 1973. After their release, interviewers noted that the hostages had begun to identify with their captors. In this case, some of the hostages resisted being liberated and many actually verbally defended the captors after their release. In psychological terms, the Stockholm syndrome is a defense mechanism. A hostage cannot really exercise sound judgment in an unendurably stressful situation such as a kidnapping. He or she therefore begins to identify with the kidnappers; the smallest of kindnesses is magnified as perspective wanes and the person's normal coping mechanisms are perverted. Many sources report that the syndrome begins to take effect within three to four days and that the length of captivity thereafter is irrelevant.

Pedro was a young man who had been held captive for many days. Upon his release, his parents asked him to go with them to see the police so that they could make a statement. He absolutely refused, stating, "They were nice people, they gave me pizza whenever I wanted." The parents were confused, and the father's vehement denunciations of the "low-lifes" who had kidnapped his son only contributed to a hardening of Pedro's position. At the time, without a declaration from the victim, police in that country could not act. He never did make a statement and the gang continued to kidnap other victims for some time afterward.

Among the many documented cases of Stockholm syndrome that have achieved international notoriety, a few in particular come to mind. The nascent urban guerrilla group, the Symbionese Liberation Army (SLA), kidnapped Patricia Hearst, heiress to the Hearst family publishing fortune, in February 1974. After two months of captivity, in which she was reportedly kept in a closet and repeatedly raped, she participated with the group in a series of bank robberies for which she was later convicted. When arrested, she listed her occupation as "urban guerrilla." To the audience in the United States, she is the poster child for Stockholm syndrome. A more recent example in the United States is that of Elizabeth Smart, a Utah child kidnapped and reportedly kept as a sex partner for nine months in 2002–2003, who passed up numerous possible escape opportunities.

To a Latin American audience, no better example exists than Clara Rojas of Colombia. She was a legislator and former vice presidential candidate, kidnapped by the Revolutionary Armed Forces of Colombia (FARC) in 2002. During her captivity, she gave birth in April 2004 to a son fathered by one of her captors. The child was taken from her after eight months and eventually ended up in the care of the state. Rojas was released in January 2008 as part of a deal brokered by FARC ally and Venezuelan President Hugo Chavez and she was reunited with her son shortly thereafter. The news of her pregnancy and the fact that a guerrilla fathered her baby has been the subject of intense discussion in Colombia and around the world. What is clear is that any relationship she may have had with the baby's father could not have developed under normal circumstances.

In Europe, the case of Natascha Kampusch, kidnapped as a ten-year old and kept locked in a basement for eight years by her captor before escaping, gained notoriety in 2006. She was widely reported to have been traumatized and suffering from Stockholm syndrome, and public statements by her psychiatrist made reference to this assertion. Her attachment to her captor was dramatically demonstrated by reports that she wept after hearing of his suicide.

Kidnap victims also report extreme feelings of frustration; many express a feeling of utter helplessness at not being able to positively resolve the situation. The need to depend on the kidnappers for communication, news and movement fosters feelings of impotence, particularly among those accustomed to making decisions and acting immediately.

One of the most frustrating aspects of my captivity was the lack of an opportunity to do anything to influence the outcome. I could not tell the kidnappers what to say, that would have been stupid. They asked me a lot of questions but I only told them about our bank accounts here and nothing about our money overseas or any investments. I wanted to get involved in the negotiations, but I remembered that when we attended a security training class they said to never try and negotiate as a hostage. I had to wait helplessly while my wife did everything to gain my freedom. The kidnappers kept telling me that the police were involved, but I knew better and told them so all the time. My wife would never willingly go to the police. We used to say that if our house was robbed, not to call the police because they would come back the next day and take the rest. When I told that to the kidnappers, they laughed and agreed. I did not find out until after I was released that she had contacted a consultant who helped her through the whole process.

Kidnappers also like to play with a victim's expectations and hopes of returning home. Some are very professional and keep the hostage informed as to the progress of the negotiations. Many gratuitously create false expectations, only to dash the hostage's hopes repeatedly. This also is a method of enhancing control over the victim and may be one of the cruelest measures of all.

I had been held for over two months. My captors liked to tell me at least once a week that, "tomorrow, you are going home". The first few times, I really got my hopes up and was crushed when nothing happened. I finally stopped believing that I would ever get out of there. The day before I was released they told me the same thing, but this time they made me scrub the entire room where I had been held. They told me that I had to do this to make things ready for the "next guest." Since they had never done that I was pretty sure they were either going to kill me like they had threatened to do so many times, or let me go. Fortunately it was the latter.

The impact that this type of treatment has on victims is always significant and the severity of resulting traumas will vary; however, families and organizations need to understand that the ordeal of being a hostage in a kidnapping is most stressful on the victim and that some symptom of the Stockholm syndrome will occur. The only real treatment is time and therapy, as the victim comes to grips with his or her ordeal.

Some victims report extremely brutal treatment at the hands of their captors. The practice of cutting off ears or fingers to pressure families or organizations to pay more and pay faster has gained much notoriety in many areas. I used to frequent an upscale ethnic restaurant for breakfast in a major Latin American city. Every time, there were a number of men there at different tables with at least one finger missing. When I questioned a close friend and member of the ethnic community about this, he told me that the same group or groups that had been specifically targeting their community had kidnapped most of them. Other brutalities include pulling teeth or committing sadistic acts on film to foment a sense of panic and try and force a rapid conclusion. Much has been made of this type of activity that represents, fortunately, only a small percentage of kidnappings worldwide. The filmed beheadings of hostages in Iraq belong primarily in the political arena, as the "ransom" requested in such cases is frequently more political in nature than financial.

Families and Organizations

There are also those left behind during a kidnapping, the family and other members of an organization to which the victim belongs. Attempting to compare the anguish of family members to that of the victim directly is pointless; both suffer a great deal. The fellow members of any organization also suffer from the victim's absence, depending on their level of empathy and closeness to the situation. Well-meaning friends and acquaintances often can unintentionally exacerbate the situation, rather than helping.

I tried to see the situation as some sort of illness that would end after a period of time. I was sure everything would work out and I tried to just continue going to school and acting normally. My biggest difficulty in dealing with my brother's kidnapping was that everyone started treating me differently, like I was going to explode if they touched me or said anything. All anyone would say is, "How's it going?" or "Are you doing okay?" All I wanted was to do normal things, like playing ball or

Nintendo, but everyone treated me like I had some sort of disease. Then there were the people I didn't even know very well who would come up to me and offer me their shoulder to cry on, as though I was suddenly going to pour out all my feelings to someone I didn't even like very much. Nobody knew what to do or how to treat me; I'm not sure that I would have known either but what they did was not very helpful.

Friends and family members undergo intense anguish for the kidnapped person. They suffer the uncertainty of wondering how the victim is doing, if he or she is being well treated, receiving medical treatment and, above all, the uncertainty of not knowing how long the situation will last. Family members also commonly rage against the injustice of the situation. They question why their brother, sister, son, daughter or parent was taken in an apparently arbitrary act that makes no sense and completely disorders their world. This disorder is extreme; suddenly, all activity is focused on the hostage situation. Work, school, vacations and other normal routines are abruptly truncated or radically reorganized as the family tries to come to grips with the new reality. Sleep patterns are disrupted; insomnia and nightmares are commonplace events.

When my sister was kidnapped I couldn't sleep at all. Every night I tossed and turned until the early morning and then would fall into a state that I can only describe as a waking nightmare. Every time I closed my eyes I thought of her and what those bastards might be doing to her and I got very angry. I could not do anything to help myself and, finally, I started taking sleeping pills just to get some rest. This went on for the entire six weeks that she was kidnapped.

The kidnapping is a period of terrible uncertainty. No one knows how long the situation will last nor what the final result will be. This can go on for months or even years, and the pressure is unending. Every evening before bed family members must wonder where the missing one is and how he or she is doing. Every morning brings a frantic search for news of the victim. This is particularly pernicious; any information that comes from the press is unlikely to be good.

Someone, however, must review the news and see if a body has turned up or if pertinent information is forthcoming.

When my cousins were kidnapped, I stopped by the local newsstand every morning and looked at all the scandal sheets to see if there was any news. After we paid the ransom and they still didn't appear, things were even tenser. One morning, I saw a picture of some dead bodies in a trash dump and just knew that it was they. Nothing could have prepared me for this; I had to break the news to my aunt and uncle. That was without a doubt the very worst day of my life.

Every day, every hour, every minute is filled with dread and anticipation. Will the kidnappers call? Will we receive videotape or an audiotape? Will there be news from an outside source? What is next? The family or organization passes endless hours just waiting for the next contact from the kidnappers. Every single time the phone rings a jolt surges through everyone present, and the letdown that follows a wrong number or unrelated call is intense.

Every time the phone rang, I got a tremendous surge of adrenaline. I would wait while my father and our consultant went into the office to take the call and try to listen at the door to see if I could hear anything. All I could hear would be muffled voices and the calls seemed to go on for hours, when they really only lasted a few minutes. After a little while, my father would come out and tell my mother and me what was happening. Then we would wait for the next time the phone rang and the whole dreadful cycle would start again. The worst part was when the phone would ring, everyone would get ready, and it would be a wrong number or a friend who did not know not to call on that line. Sometimes my dad would shout at people or get really angry with them for calling a wrong number; he even yelled at a couple of my friends from school. For months after my sister came home, I would jump every time that particular telephone rang, even after we changed the number.

In spite of all this, life must go on. Other family or organization members need to eat, sleep, work, study and play. If children too young to fully understand the events are involved, the effort to maintain some semblance of normalcy is even more difficult. The pervasive fear that everyone feels must somehow be subjugated to enable some semblance of a normal life to go forward.

Organizations also must consider the impact of a kidnapping on their operations. The abduction of a senior executive or family member, particularly an expatriate, can leave the organization in a state similar to a ship without a rudder. Staff and even families are quick to sense a lack of resolve when a crisis situation strikes, and the organization must receive clear and unequivocal messages of support and leadership. Quick and decisive action is necessary to ensure that staff and families are reassured that business will go on as usual and that the company is supporting the victim's family. This can often be a delicate balancing act; no organization likes to openly take responsibility for resolving a kidnapping; however, all members of the organization must be confident that support is being provided.

A majority of larger organizations have prepared contingency plans to deal with the kidnapping of an employee or family member. These plans are often no more detailed than those of the average family; however, many organizations fully prepare. This is normally reflective of the location(s) in which the organization operates; a higher threat level spawns a greater interest in contingency planning. No matter the status and sophistication of established plans, most organizations will respond in a similar manner when a staff or family member is kidnapped.

The organization will typically provide logistical support to the victim's family; this may include transportation, communication, housing and food if necessary, and other items to aid in maintaining as normal a situation as possible. If financial support is provided, this is usually done very discreetly. Legal aid and facilitation of contacts with local authorities can also be provided in most cases. If the kidnappers' focus is on the family, an organization may well consider allowing that to continue as the best course of action, while providing covert support.

Security measures throughout the organization will normally be enhanced while decision makers attempt to determine whether others are threatened as well. If so, family members or other members of the organization will be extended the necessary level of protection. Most organizations make every effort to ensure that the incident is not publicized, not wanting to deal with the resulting attention from other members, stakeholders, police and government, press and the public.

Managers in any organization must be prepared to deal with the effects of trauma resulting from the kidnapping. Members with no direct involvement are likely to suffer adverse reactions when they become aware of the situation, and management must be prepared to deal with these reactions both individually and as a group.

When our director was kidnapped, nobody told us anything. The rumor went around the company like wildfire that he had been taken on the street in front of the plant and that he would be killed if the company didn't pay millions of dollars in ransom. Everybody was very nervous and started calling home and checking on their spouses and children. A whole bunch of people got sick and had to leave work right away. I was scared and asked my boss what was going on. She had no idea either but gathered our team together and asked everyone to be calm, told us she would try and find out what was going on and get back to us. By that afternoon she told us that he was kidnapped and that work should go on as normal.

The director was gone for four weeks and was replaced right after he was released. The whole time he was gone and for a while afterward, production was really low and people would act really strange and paranoid. I wish the company had done more to help the rest of us. I mean; you know they paid for him and to get his family out of the country and probably for their group therapy, but the rest of us suffered, too.

In the preceding case, management did not properly inform the organization's members nor was any provision made to address the effects of a traumatic situation on all members of the organization other than the director and his family. Production suffered, as did many of the staff, when a program of support might have alleviated many of the problems. This is, unfortunately, all too common in organizations; attention is paid to the needs of the victim and his or her family, while other affected members receive short shrift.

Whether in a family or in an organization, everyone involved, directly or indirectly, needs understanding, compassion and support to get through the situation and the aftermath. The effects of a kidnapping have been likened to post-traumatic stress disorder (PTSD) shown by soldiers returning from combat and can be manifested in physical, mental, behavioral or emotional symptoms. Anyone involved in a kidnapping would do well to pay attention to the needs of all those affected.

5

THE INCIDENT

Today the ringing of the telephone takes precedence over everything. It reaches a point of terrorism, particularly at dinnertime.

Nils Diffrient

The most terrible of motives and the most unanswerable of responses: Because.

Victor Hugo, Les Miserables

The Nightmare Begins

The insistent sound of the telephone roused Carlos from a sound sleep. He checked the clock on the nightstand, 0545 hours. As he groped for the telephone, he wondered why anyone would call at such an hour. He immediately thought of his daughter, Serena, who routinely left for school at around 0520 hours in the morning. Did she have an accident, a flat tire? he wondered as he grabbed the receiver. "Baby, is everything alright?"

"Is this Carlos?" sounded a menacing voice on the line. "Yes, who's calling?" he replied. "Shut up and listen to me. We have your daughter. If you want to see her alive again, we require four million dollars by tomorrow. No police and no press or else she dies; we will call you back in two hours with instructions."

Fully awake in an instant, Carlos asked to speak to his daughter. Roundly rebuffed in the most obscene terms, he could think of nothing else to say as the apparent kidnappers hung up. He turned to his wife, who had also awakened and said, "Honey, they've taken our baby", and collapsed in tears.

Thus began a tortuous 23-day martyrdom for the family, one that would tax resources and relationships to the breaking point.

Carlos' experience was similar to many I have witnessed. A family member is out of the home, en route to school, work or shopping, and suddenly a telephone call is received reporting that he or she has been kidnapped. The typical initial reaction is disbelief; followed immediately by shock and horror. No one wants to believe this could happen to him or her, although in many countries every person of means knows a friend or neighbor who has suffered through the same difficult situation.

The immediate reaction is almost always to place a call to the victim's cellular telephone. Carlos did, and when he received no answer, utter panic ensued. The feeling of complete helplessness that the initial call generates is indescribable; most family members report that they come together for a short period of weeping and despair. They then immediately start calling trusted friends or relatives to find someone, anyone, who might be able to help. Almost never is the first response to call the police.

Kidnappers frequently make outrageous statements, such as demanding an enormous sum of money and promising to call back within a very short time. This only augments the pressure on the family or organization and can preclude rational thought. Had Carlos thought clearly about the situation, he would have known that no one could reasonably expect him to get together four million dollars between 0600 and 0800 on a weekday; after all, banks do not even open until 0900 hours.

Kidnappers often make such statements in order to confuse and apply pressure on the victim's family. This is a classic control mechanism. Keeping the family off guard and uncertain aids in maintaining control over the situation; calls to the family can be used as rewards or punishment, depending on how the kidnappers choose to move forward. The kidnappers seek to create a family or personal crisis and prevent the victim's family or organization from preparing an ordered response with the assistance of outside consultants and/or police. This is one reason why they constantly insist that no outsiders become involved; they feel that by dealing solely with the victim's family they can better achieve their monetary goals.

Carlos carefully watched the early news shows to see whether any incidents had been reported that might involve his daughter or that might produce a witness to whom he could speak. None were forthcoming and, meanwhile, he began to call friends and relatives in a frantic search for assistance. I received a call at around 0830 hours from a friend of a friend (the normal way in which these issues are approached). I called Carlos, we spoke for the first time and I assured him that I could be there by 1200 hours. He was in a state of panic and wanted to see me five minutes ago. Convincing him that the kidnappers would not call back before evening, if then, was no easy task.

The pressure caused by the initial telephone call from the kidnappers is always intense. Any family, particularly in the first few hours after receiving word that a loved one has been kidnapped, is in danger of coming apart at the seams. I am constantly amazed by the strength of character shown by individuals under such enormous stress. A majority of families hold together through the incident no matter what pressure is applied. In Carlos' case, he and his family were able to withstand enormous stress and constant threats and maintain a startling equanimity throughout the entire ordeal until his kidnapped daughter was safely home.

A number of concepts, best presented as "Do's and Don'ts", should be considered in the initial contact with kidnappers. While professional consultants and negotiators understand and routinely apply these concepts, laymen do not and they are normally the ones who have to confront the initial contact without support. Properly implementing these concepts can go a long way toward setting the stage for the successful resolution of the situation.

Do:

Attempt to verify that the kidnapping has actually occurred.
Start a case record or establish a journal of all events.
Tape all conversations, if possible.
Demonstrate a willingness to cooperate in reaching a solution.
Let the kidnapper know that you are taking the conversation seriously and making notes.
Make sure they understand that you are not the final arbiter and that you will facilitate communication with those who can actually make decisions.

Obtain and write down specific detailed instructions, demands, comments and requirements.

Try to obtain a code by which to identify the kidnapper in future communications.

Establish a time frame for subsequent communications if possible.

Don't:

Make any promises that later cannot be kept; specifically avoid offering a specific sum or agreeing to ransom demands.

Provide any additional information to the kidnapper.

Threaten the kidnapper or engage in verbal abuse or confrontational rhetoric.

Beg or show nervousness, fear or suspicion.

Become sidetracked by outside disruptions or allow yourself to become distracted.

Accept conditions; later calls will establish parameters and conditions.

Even seasoned professionals can have difficulty maintaining their composure and following through on these recommendations. Family members who have never experienced such a situation normally do not do well, particularly those who have never received any training. The initial conversation more often is most similar to that of Carlos than to a reasonable professional exchange. That said, families, and organizations in particular, should strive to prepare possible recipients of kidnapping calls so that they have had at least a modicum of exposure to a typical scenario.

To expect that any family or organization will successfully resolve all of the aforementioned actions before and during the initial contact is unrealistic. The point of preparation is to be as ready as possible and set the table for future contacts. There is no reason for regret if one or more of the items is not properly handled; every step taken is a step forward and will doubtless help in working toward a satisfactory resolution. The important issue is to be as prepared as possible to optimize the efficiency of any response.

This is where prior training can play a significant role. If an organization has an established crisis management program and trains for such scenarios, part of the program should deal with preparation for any eventuality. Those individuals expected to play key roles in resolving a kidnapping situation should know the basic steps necessary in preparing for a contact with kidnappers.

In family situations, preparation is more difficult, but potential targets for kidnappers would be well served to consider making at least rudimentary preparations. Not every family should prepare a kit for a kidnapping; that would be an exaggerated response and would signify certain surrender to the inevitable. Far more important for any family is a sound security plan directed toward preventing such situations.

Verification

In the absence of any immediate eyewitness reports, the family has no choice but to believe that the victim has been kidnapped. Normally, they try to call the victim's cellular phone repeatedly and usually will check with best friends or significant others. Since most victims have little or no direct experience with kidnapping, the effort to verify a reported incident is slipshod and disorganized.

This is also not unusual in the professional sector. Very few organizations have taken the time to define a concrete set of measures to verify that a kidnapping has actually occurred. This lack of preparation is surprising, especially given the number of feigned or "virtual" kidnappings that have occurred in recent years.

Virtual kidnappings include many reported incidents in which families or organizations have been victimized by purported kidnappings, only to later learn that the victim was alive and well and was just out of touch for a while. A classic case is that of an adolescent who goes to the movies. Before entering the theater, he or she is approached by an apparent talent scout for a modeling agency, who asks to take a few photographs, records personal data, and promises to call in a few days to schedule a formal audition. Once the youth enters the movie theater, the scam artist knows that his or her cellular phone will be turned off for the next few hours. They immediately drop a picture in the home's mailbox and call the family to insist on an immediate ransom payment. The family, unable to contact the missing member, scrambles to put together as much money, valuables and acceptable property as immediately possible and deliver the ransom in order to save the life of a loved one. Payments of over fifty thousand dollars have been recorded in cases such as this. The reaction when the supposed victim returns from the movies is never a pretty picture.

False kidnapping scams are limited only by the criminal's imagination. In one case, a criminal retrieved the wallet from a dead fellow passenger in a bus crash and used the information to negotiate a substantial ransom from the victim's family while the body was buried in a potter's field. In another case, an executive on a golf outing left his cellular phone in a clubhouse locker. When he returned after 18 holes to shower and change, he found that the round of golf had actually cost more than twenty-five thousand dollars. There was nothing to be done; the supposed kidnappers called and convinced his wife that they had abducted him; she gathered together all available resources and delivered a payment; and he called from the clubhouse shortly afterward.

Once a kidnapping is reported, the most important requirement is to immediately do everything possible to verify that the incident has in fact occurred. In addition to ensuring that the report is not false or just a joke in very poor taste, the flurry of activities involved enables those affected to burn off some of the nervous energy that begins to accumulate immediately upon receipt of the first phone call.

The verification effort must be as discreet as possible. There is nothing to be gained by announcing to the world that someone has been reported kidnapped and that one is trying to determine whether or not this is actually the case. In many countries, this can be foolish or even dangerous, particularly in places where the authorities cannot necessarily be trusted. Information should be sought quietly and without attracting unwanted attention. Remember, one of the first demands from virtually all kidnappers is that authorities and press be kept out of the picture.

There are a number of actions that can be taken to verify a kidnapping, depending upon the circumstances:

Transportation schedules—If the victim is traveling by air, train, bus or ship, call the carrier to verify schedules and passenger manifests. Most common carriers will provide (albeit grudgingly in this day and age) information on whether specific passengers reported for the trip if the user code and other data are available to the enquiring party. At the very least, information on delays and rerouting of transportation can be obtained.

Secretary or assistant—The victim's schedule can be verified through a secretary or administrative assistant in many cases. Discreetly enquire as to the victim's schedule and whereabouts. Depending on the relationship, direct questions may be feasible.

Medical facilities—Any hospital or clinic that the victim may have passed can be queried to determine whether any unidentified patients or bodies have been processed. A level of detail sufficient to determine whether personal investigation is merited can usually be obtained via telephone. If any doubt exists, a trusted friend or family member can be dispatched to the facility to view the injured person or identify the deceased.

Traffic conditions—Many staged or false kidnappings have resulted from traffic problems. Care should be taken to ensure that the area through which the reported victim has passed is not the site of major congestion, accident or disruption. Demonstrations and marches can often disrupt traffic patterns and force delays, and these should be thoroughly investigated.

Routes—Any routes that the victim may have taken on foot or in a vehicle should be traversed from beginning and end to look for any indications of unusual activity, including accidents, disruptions, and signs of violence or delays. Dispatching separate parties from each end of the route saves time and provides increased opportunities to observe any anomalies.

Cellular phone—Calling the victim's cell phone, Blackberry, beeper, radio or whatever personal communications device is routinely carried is an obvious action. If the victim answers, he or she should be able to confirm that all is well or, conversely, that a kidnapping has, in fact, occurred. In the first hours of a kidnapping, many kidnappers will allow the victim either to answer or take calls directly to show that they mean business. This depends on their level of sophistication and perception of local authorities' ability to track such devices remotely.

Inquiries at residence—If the report has come in to an organization, there may be a need in the early stages to inquire at the purported victim's residence without alerting family members to an incident. This is an issue that requires deft handling and a very discreet approach. "Hello, Mrs. Jones, was your husband really kidnapped this morning?" is not the type of question likely to help the situation. If the family has already been called by the kidnappers, communication from the organization will almost assuredly lead to a sharing of information.

Witnesses—If any witnesses have been identified, they should be interviewed as soon after the actual event as is feasible and sworn to silence, if possible. While there may be no hope of keeping news of the kidnapping out of public channels if witnesses come forward, try to avoid any release of information until absolutely necessary.

Police blotters—False kidnappings have also been staged when a purported victim was arrested or detained. The police stations nearest the route traveled by the victim should be checked to ensure that this is not the case. Cover stories used with the authorities, particularly in countries in which they are not completely trustworthy, must be simple and believable. Remember, the object is only to learn whether a family member or coworker has been arrested or detained, not to alert the authorities that a kidnapping has occurred.

Business contacts or appointments—When the victim's schedule is known, his or her presence at scheduled events should be relatively easy to verify. Calling a company to ask to speak to an individual from another organization who is in a meeting will normally be sufficient to verify the presence or absence of the potential victim. More creative solutions abound if progress is difficult.

Girlfriend or boyfriend—History is replete with examples of kidnappings that have occurred while the victim was with his or her "second front". Aside from the obvious complications that this causes, contact must be established with anyone with whom the victim is romantically involved to verify his or her whereabouts.

Social engagements—Any social gatherings or events the victim might have attended or planned on attending must be checked. Where the victim is attending a large convention, sporting event, or similar size gathering, under no circumstances should any funds be released until the incident can be verified.

Mortuaries/coroners—Each country or region has different ways of treating unidentified bodies found on the streets. Depending on where the kidnapping occurs, these offices should also be contacted to check for recent arrivals.

Companions—If the victim was accompanied by anyone else, those persons should be located and immediately questioned. If they are not to be found, contact with their organizations or families should be established and discreet inquiries initiated.

Schools—If a child who is supposedly in school is reported kidnapped, calls should be made to confirm his or her absence or attendance. As my wife can testify from personal experience, school administrators often tend to overreact, so discretion is most important.

A thorough verification effort is necessary to avoid falling victim to any type of false or simulated kidnapping. These occur frequently and can be nearly as painful as the real thing. A student who returns after going to a movie and finds his family in tears over his kidnapping, a double blow to the family of an accident victim, or the payment of a ransom for someone who is simply stuck in traffic near a construction zone are events that have occurred and should never have been allowed to come to fruition.

Discretion is a key factor in any verification process. A famous quote attributed to Benjamin Franklin states that "Three may keep a secret, if two of them are dead." This is the level of discretion that must surround any effort to verify a kidnapping. As the number of individuals cognizant of the situation increases, so does the likelihood that outsiders or persons without a need to know will become aware. This opens the door to unwanted and dangerous potential intrusions by reporters and/or members of law enforcement not specifically selected by the family or organization, as well as expanding the possibility that a third party with knowledge of the case will try and interject himself or herself into the negotiation and profit thereby.

In any case, mistakenly making a payment for a false kidnapping is decidedly preferable to the actual kidnapping of a loved one. Unfortunately, no matter how extensive or complete the verification effort, kidnappings do occur and the release of hostages must be secured. During the effort to verify a kidnapping and immediately thereafter, an enormous amount of preparation is required to afford the family or organization an opportunity to obtain the safe return of a loved one.

External Factors

Many external factors influence how a kidnapping situation is managed. Each must be carefully considered prior to beginning a negotiation; failure to address each factor could lead to disaster. Some issues can have a major impact on the outcome, particularly if one or more have been ignored and later come into play. Specific factors particularly affect cases in which the victim is an expatriate or a foreign national visiting another country. The actual negotiation will likely proceed much more smoothly if the terrain has been adequately prepared.

Kidnap–Ransom (KR) Insurance

Kidnap-ransom (KR) insurance is a specialized branch of the insurance industry. These policies have traditionally been offered primarily through a number of insurance brokers, mostly based in London. However, in recent years demand for KR policies has led to a significant expansion of the market, to the point where virtually all major insurance companies now offer some type of KR coverage. Many organizations purchase KR insurance for senior executives and family members, particularly those operating in foreign countries or in known trouble spots.

Like other types of insurance, KR insurance cannot be purchased after the fact; once an executive or family member has been kidnapped, no policy is available to cover the incident. Virtually all insurers offer similar terms: a substantial annual premium guarantees that a multimillion-dollar ransom may be paid if a covered individual is kidnapped. These policies also normally cover extortions and include a series of additional benefits that can include some or all of the following:

Coverage for kidnapping ransoms
Coverage for extortion demands, including:
      Intentional or accidental product contamination

Loss or theft of trade secrets, copyright-protected material
or proprietary information
Malicious software attacks of any type
Cost of salaries and wages to affected members of the
organization
Coverage for psychotherapy or specialized medical treatments
Costs associated with product recall
Costs of additional security requirements related to the incident
Development of crisis management and business continuity plans
Specialized consulting and risk management services
Benefits related to accident or death of an affected employee or
community member
Personal financial losses suffered by covered individuals
Expenses related to travel, job retraining and relocation of
affected individuals and family members

In KR policies, the policyholder must accept the assistance of specific specialized consultants in support of the negotiation. These consultants are generally highly experienced professionals who provide guidance to the negotiator and lead the family or organization through the situation. Refusal to allow the designated consultant to participate in the negotiation process automatically voids most policies. In some cases, these professionals will actually conduct the negotiation, although this varies among companies and scenarios.

In spite of their demonstrated professionalism, victim's families and organizations need to understand that KR consultants work for insurance companies. One of the consultant's primary responsibilities is to protect the insurer's interest as well as those of the family or organization. In a number of cases, this has led to the payment of ransom demands at levels that skew the local market upward and consequently raise demands across the board. For example, if a victim is insured for $5 million and, in the interest of a rapid solution, the insurer agrees to pay a three million dollar ransom, this can and has led to other kidnappers in the same venue insisting on higher ransoms. Kidnappers have their own networks of information and are as ego-driven as other businesspersons.

The impact of this activity could be considered significant in some places. Payment of high ransoms leads to a vicious cycle in which kidnapping is seen as more remunerative by more criminals; larger numbers of victims are taken; higher ransoms are sought and paid; and the frequency of kidnappings in a particular country or region begins to spiral out of control. This is not to imply that the dramatic increase in worldwide kidnapping over the last couple decades can be attributed to the actions of KR consultants; only that, in some cases, payment of exaggerated ransom demands by insurers has raised the bar for everyone.

A significant percentage of large companies and international organizations carry this insurance; however, knowledge of the policy's existence is restricted only to covered individuals and those in the organization with a specific need to know. No matter the circumstances, no family or organization should ever allow any outsider to be aware that a KR policy exists. This must be a closely held secret; common knowledge of the existence of KR insurance is equivalent to declaring open season on the family or executives of any given organization.

Any organization or family that has a KR insurance policy should be prepared to obtain the assistance of a qualified external consultant, responsible only to them, in case of a kidnapping. This will help insure that the family or organization has a knowledgeable representative who serves only one master involved in the process.

Consultants

Many consultants specialize, or claim to specialize, in managing kidnapping situations. As in all business transactions, *caveat emptor* (let the buyer beware) should be the guiding principle in selecting and hiring a consultant. An experienced professional consultant can be a tremendous asset during the management of a kidnapping, while a less than professional consultant can lead to disastrous results.

A professional consultant is normally not a negotiator. A consultant will organize and direct the response to a kidnapping, relying on experience and training to ensure that the myriad details associated with the situation all receive the requisite amount of attention. He or she does not decide on what will be offered or when; rather guidance is provided to enable the family or organizational decision maker(s) to select the most appropriate course of action.

This is not a haphazard distinction. Consultants provide advice; they are not the ones who make fundamental decisions and this can be critical in places in which any other forms of activity or participation would be illegal. Furthermore, only the individual(s) directly responsible for the negotiation can make concrete decisions on how the negotiation will be approached. A quality consultant knows when to push and when to back off and will provide advice that helps develop a strategy, implement that strategy and prevent the family or organization from deviating in a manner that would negate the effects of an effective negotiating technique.

Most professional consultants have sufficient professional experience, training and preparation to function as a negotiator and, if necessary, can take over the direct communication with the kidnappers and conduct negotiations. This is an issue that must be considered in each case; however, circumstances and the kidnappers will dictate whether a professional can participate. In most cases, the direct intervention of a professional indicates a certain level of resources to the kidnappers that leads to a higher ransom as a result.

A consultant provides an experienced, minimally biased view of the crisis based on his or her experience. He or she will normally be able to evaluate the situation and present options to the family or organization considering the pros and cons of each option. Resolving a kidnapping is a team effort and decision makers must be provided with a view of all sides of the problem.

Consultants are normally referred by word of mouth. A victim's family or organization makes calls to find out who is available to assist and then calls in one or more consultants for an interview. This is a very rapid process, since time is of the essence, and victim's families normally are under the impression that another call or communication from the kidnappers will come at any time.

The family requires an explanation of the process that is occurring. They need to know what to expect, how long the process will last (within reasonable parameters) and what are the expected or possible outcomes. We normally discuss the situation in their area (other cases, statistics, etc.) to provide the family with some perspective on the situation. They must be shown that there is a solution to the problem and that a structured methodology exists via which the victim can most likely be safely returned. This helps develop confidence and empathy between consultant and family as well as aiding them in confronting a totally foreign situation. Emphasis should be placed on the fact that if any violence is to be inflicted on the victim, that decision has probably already been taken. Since kidnapping involves the use of force and, frequently, violence, any consultant who guarantees a safe return of the hostage should immediately be shown the door.

I prefer to meet with those who will be making decisions in the negotiation process to determine whether we are a good fit as a team. These situations are intensely stressful and require that strangers quickly establish a rapport and an ability to work together. A strong bond of trust must be immediately established that will stand up to the stresses placed on all those involved. If the client cannot put his or her faith and the fate of their loved one in my hands, they would do better to look elsewhere.

This normally takes a discussion that lasts anywhere from thirty minutes to two hours, depending on the time available. Once we have finished our discussion, during which I describe the process, explore capabilities and possibilities, and establish parameters, I normally step outside and await a decision. If the decision is made to work together, we begin immediately to address outstanding issues and prepare for the struggle. If the client decides not to use my services, I may recommend another professional he or she might talk to, and take my leave.

Any professional consultant should be bound by the obligation to be honest with the client. He or she must provide dispassionate advice without veering into scare tactics or self-promotion. Cases have occurred in which consultants, in the interest of furthering reputations or as a tool for future business development; exaggerate the threat faced by the family or organization in order to make his or her actions appear heroic. For example, a case I became aware of when contacted by the victim's family after the fact amply illustrates this point.

The consultant's conversations with the family had been taped without his knowledge. They came to me after their daughter had been released and asked me to help them establish a family security plan. As part of the executive protection program, I was asked to listen to the tapes and reinforce or comment on the recommendations made during the negotiation process. What came through loud and clear were the consultant's attempts to take advantage of an extremely difficult situation to promote his services and exalt his contributions. When asked whether the family should report the case to the authorities, he suggested they wait until the victim had returned, since the authorities "could not be trusted". He further stated there were three hundred members in the band of kidnappers and that, while the police might arrest eight or ten of them, the rest would pursue the family looking for vengeance. I had to diplomatically inform the family that there were no bands of kidnappers operating in the country that had more than about fifteen members. Once they realized what had been done they were justifiably angry, since the father particularly wanted to see justice done but had been scared off by the consultant's statements.

Authorities

There are valid reasons for reporting a kidnapping to the authorities. Every case that is reported enables the authorities to form a clearer picture of the scope of the problem. Obviously, cases that are not reported go unsolved, fomenting further kidnappings by the same group. This has been referred to as "inventory rotation," that is, kidnappers convince victims not to report the crime, leaving them free to pursue other victims and, frequently, return to the same proven source of revenue at a later date. The fact that a majority of victims worldwide do not report kidnappings is the single most important factor in enabling kidnappers to operate with virtual impunity.

Dealing with the authorities varies dramatically from country to country. In some countries, local, state and federal police are all considered to be honest and trustworthy and can be approached directly to report a kidnapping. In others, police or their agents are responsible for a significant percentage of kidnappings committed and should only be approached with the utmost circumspection and, preferably, through an intermediary. An approach to the wrong authority can lead to disaster if that individual or unit is part of the kidnappers' circle.

The single most important factor to understand in dealing with authorities in any country is to know the law. In many countries, failure to report a kidnapping carries the same weight as committing a kidnapping. While this may sound absurd, the practice has grown out of the absolute refusal of the populace to trust the authorities, thus engendering legislation to try and force the issue.

In most countries in which such laws exist, they are routinely ignored; however, that is of little solace to the consultant who finds himself in jail in a far-away place for having become involved in illicit activities, no matter how well intentioned. Most of these types of laws do not allow release on bail, so anyone who is jailed on such charges can expect to spend considerable time behind bars until a solution can be arranged.

The level of competence of the authorities is another vitally important issue. The roles and functions of the units or individuals involved in pursuing a kidnapping investigation vary, but almost all countries have specialized police units, some are called anti-kidnapping units, that attend to such crimes. There is a wide disparity among state and federal units in terms of equipment and experience in most countries; federal units normally enjoy a dramatic technological advantage.

This, however, is not always an indication of competence. I have worked with state-level anti-kidnapping units that were far better investigators than their federal counterparts. In most countries, this is experientially driven. If the state team has been working together and the federal unit is in a state of flux, the state unit will be superior in spite of having less equipment and funding. Particularly in the developing world, international aid programs go first to the federal authorities and this contributes to a constant reshuffling of organizations with a concomitant decrease in both professionalism and experience.

Competence can also be affected by the political situation in any given country. Governments in countries in which there is an active insurrection, a severe narcotics trafficking problem or a particularly lawless society tend to place less emphasis on solving ransom kidnappings; law enforcement and security funds are directed toward other, higher threat or higher profile criminal or terrorist activities. The reduced emphasis on kidnapping fosters a more propitious environment for potential kidnappers and they tend to move quickly to take advantage of the opportunity.

In a number of countries, and with good reason, many of the specialized anti-kidnapping units have abysmal reputations due to a history of involvement as kidnappers themselves. This is an issue that has resulted from a long tradition of police corruption and graft in many locations. The problem for any consultant, family or organization is to know and understand with whom they are dealing. Selecting which police organization with which to establish contact is a difficult decision and wrong choices can have a significant impact on the outcome.

Police need to be informed when a kidnapping occurs. They can provide useful intelligence on the band of kidnappers, since most have a database of events that can be evaluated to identify trends, tendencies and similarities to prior cases. This is very useful in determining a negotiating strategy; most kidnappers have a defined comfort level at which they will release victims. If offers fall too far below this predetermined level the danger increases; when offers too far above the level are made the danger becomes extreme.

Also, police must be provided with copies of all communications between kidnappers and negotiation teams. Whether they have already tapped the telephone lines is inconsequential; providing tapes of each conversation is a professional courtesy that goes a long way toward establishing a rapport among families or organizations, consultants and law enforcement authorities. When communication is written, conducted through want ads or by any other form, authorities should be kept informed and provided with any hard copy material that may have been handled by the kidnappers.

The police will be able to implement a tactical operation if the opportunity or necessity arises. In some cases, intelligence is obtained that identifies the location where a hostage is being held or where members of a band of kidnappers are located and identified. If an acceptable professional level of coordination has been established, the police will normally consult with the family or organization before mounting a tactical operation against the kidnappers. If no prior coordination has been established, they may move against the kidnappers, risking the lives of hostages, without understanding the parameters of the negotiation or considering the family or organization's wishes.

In cases where violence (e.g., mutilation, possible murder) is suspected or confirmed, the attractiveness of a tactical operation rises dramatically, since such actions exhibit a callous disregard for the victim's well-being and call into doubt his or her eventual survival. A tactical operation therefore becomes much more feasible and prior coordination will have been essential.

The issue of a hostage rescue operation is a complex and dangerous subject. Hostage rescues are famous, particularly in the arena of political kidnappings. The retaking of the Japanese Embassy in Lima, Peru (1997); the rescue at the Iranian Embassy in London (1980); the recapture of the hostages in Entebbe, Uganda (1976) and other incidents have made worldwide headlines. Unfortunately, so have failed rescue attempts such as the attempt to rescue the Olympic athletes in Munich, Germany (1972) or the attempted retaking of the Supreme Court in Bogotá, Colombia (1985).

Law enforcement operations to rescue hostages are usually much less notorious. In most cases, the operation might receive a mention in the local or even national press; however, worldwide attention is virtually unknown. This does not imply that these operations are any less risky for the participants or that the impact of a rescue is any less significant for the affected family or organization members. Worldwide, quite a number of kidnap victims have been rescued and numerous members of law enforcement have given their lives in attempts to rescue them.

Remember that the authorities may or may not consult with the family or organization before mounting any operation; they are under no legal obligation to do so in most countries. If they do request input or approval prior to undertaking a rescue mission, the risks and rewards of any operation must be carefully examined before consent is given. Families and organizations should consider factors such as the level of training and equipment of the strike team, the particular circumstances surrounding the case (violence, gang history, etc.), and the assessed potential for a successful rescue. Once a decision to move forward is taken and an operation mounted, later recriminations are pointless if things do not work out as hoped.

When dealing with the authorities, never afford individual members of the law enforcement team direct access to the money. As ransom offers rise throughout the course of a kidnapping, no police official should ever be allowed to know for certain where the ransom funds are being kept or how much is available. This is a simple but important protective measure; in most countries police are grossly underpaid and there is no reason to openly display a tempting source of immediate wealth to an underpaid and underfunded law enforcement officer. Additionally, police in many countries have been found to be in collusion with kidnapping gangs, and letting the authorities know how much money is available can disrupt a negotiation or lead to real difficulty in reaching an acceptable solution. In cases in which a tracking device is to be placed with the ransom (not recommended in most cases), the officer who places the actual device is the only one who should have physical access to the money, and this only for a moment immediately prior to dispatch of the ransom.

The authorities should also never be allowed to take full control of the situation. For all their experience and best intentions, law enforcement's mission is to detain and prosecute criminals. The family or organization has the absolute priority of obtaining the victim's safe return, and these two goals can sometimes be in conflict. Most police agencies practice great respect for families' interests and will not intervene in a situation until the hostage is freed. Situations have occurred, however, in which apprehension of the criminals became the highest priority, at the victim's expense. Families or organizations must maintain control and always strive to be the final arbiter of any decisions taken with respect to the incident.

In sum, dealing with the authorities is a complex and delicate ballet. The issues of trust, control, access and honesty must be carefully considered prior to contacting any police agency and safeguards must be implemented to ensure that the family or organization maintains control and makes decisions with respect to the negotiation. There are, however, fundamental and important reasons for reporting these events and all should be formally denounced. One must always remember that kidnappers are criminals! While a family or organization may feel that its efforts provide the best opportunity to safely retrieve a victim, parallel efforts by law enforcement provide a valuable resource if the negotiation begins to go poorly, the victim is not returned, or, if tragedy strikes. Involving law enforcement in the process from the earliest stages permits the authorities to develop information and to be prepared to intervene in short order should this become necessary. If this is not accomplished and things go awry, chances that the victim will return safely are diminished.

The significance of reporting every single kidnapping incident to the authorities cannot be overstated. Kidnappers rely on secrecy and intimidation; each case that goes unreported foments further kidnappings. The only way to diminish the frequency of these incidents is to place the kidnappers under a microscope and to allow law enforcement to do its job. In places where law enforcement is unreliable, constant reporting will help augment public pressure on the police to reform and take measures to stop the epidemic.

Corruption

This can mean life or death to the victim. In the developing world, corruption is extensive and deciding whom to trust is like navigating a minefield. In many countries, numerous specialized anti-kidnapping units have been repeatedly disbanded and reorganized due to involvement of their members as active participants in kidnappings, both at state and federal levels. Many officials have been incarcerated in a number of countries; however, given the reality that police in most locations are underpaid and under-appreciated, corruption remains a problem.

The amount of money involved in kidnapping transactions is second only to that in narcotics trafficking. Poorly paid police officials can be susceptible to bribery by kidnapping bands when, at a single stroke, they can receive amounts of money equivalent to months or years of salary. This then leads to a situation in which the very authorities who are charged with investigating and resolving a kidnapping are suspect.

On two separate occasions, senior anti-kidnapping commanders have told me that a ransom offer should be raised to a certain level to guarantee a rapid solution to a kidnapping. How did they know? The question I had to answer was whether the advice was given based on long experience and knowledge of the gang's activities and modus operandi, or if the fix was in and a deal had already been cut.

In one case, after extensive discussions with the family, a decision was made not to quintuple the offer and follow the recommendation. Six weeks later, a badly beaten man was released after payment of a ransom that was almost half the recommended amount. One can never know whether there was collusion behind the scenes between police and kidnappers, or if the scenario played out naturally. In another situation, the family immediately doubled the offer (to an amount approximating the suggested number) and the victim was released within ten days, after a few more telephone calls.

Another common practice is for the family or organization to provide "operating expenses" for the specialized anti-kidnapping units. This basically means that the victim's family has to pay the police to investigate. The operative cover story is that the police have no money for gas, food or incidental expenses related to the investigation. This is undoubtedly true in some cases; I have seen commanders take money from a freshly delivered envelope and distribute the cash to team members so they could go to the gas station and/or get something to eat.

Individual agents have told me that the contents of envelopes provided to their bosses did not often trickle down and asked that they be included in future disbursements. The level of corruption always amazes; paying the police to do their job and hoping that payment guarantees that they are on your side is not a practice that inspires confidence.

Corruption is such an inherent part of doing business in the developing world that one should not be surprised that the effects are noticeable even in kidnapping cases. Make very sure of your territory before moving forward. The possibility of a misstep that could lead to tragic consequences both for the victim and personally cannot be overestimated.

In societies in which corruption and graft are *de facto* accepted practices, expecting police to operate on a higher moral plane is ridiculous. Police department budgets are tight, pay is abysmal, and many officers are routinely faced with a stark choice: steal or starve. Under these circumstances, it should not be a surprise when corrupt actions become an integral part of any scenario.

Media

Dealing with the media during a kidnapping is always difficult. In today's market, what sells worldwide is scandal. The bloodiest reports receive the most coverage and reporters are under extreme pressure to develop and report on stories that can attract and keep the public's limited attention span. Yellow journalism has become a standard in most countries and the practice impacts kidnapping situations as well.

Media awareness of a kidnapping situation changes the panorama to a great extent. Kidnappers and victims' families and organizations are normally not interested in having any media involvement; this only increases pressure on all sides to achieve a resolution, forces posturing and brings unwanted attention from the authorities. Police involvement is guaranteed following media involvement and this generally is not to the kidnappers' liking. Kidnappers have, however, been known to publicly release embarrassing or humiliating information, pictures or videos to try and pressure the family or organization into complying with their demands. They also have used the rumor mill to help augment pressure and try and force compliance.

If the media is aware of a kidnapping, homes and offices will be staked out, press conferences are needed on an almost daily basis and much additional futile effort is required of those involved in managing the situation. In a number of well-known cases, negotiations have practically been carried out through the media; this does not facilitate a clean and rapid solution, as both kidnappers and victims are forced to be more intransigent in their demands and counteroffers.

Once media representatives are involved, a number of measures must be taken. Communication with media outlets should be conducted only through a single designated spokesperson and the extensive, preferably exclusive, use of press releases is encouraged. Written statements can be crafted to provide sufficient information and leave the management team free to attend to their primary responsibilities. If necessary, press conferences can be held to answer questions from reporters.

When engaging in dialogue with members of the media, a designated spokesperson should be truthful and forthright. Lying to reporters is dangerous, particularly if the facts can be independently verified. Telling the truth does not, however, equate to telling all! Some facts and issues are not to be discussed with the press under any circumstances. These normally include ransom demands and offers, presence or absence of violence, timelines and any information on involvement of the authorities. Stating that a particular subject is confidential or is under development is safe to do; "no comment" often leads to speculation and complications, as reporters will often invent their own reality.

Many organizations have developed crisis communications plans that should be implemented immediately once a kidnapping is verified. If the press is not aware of the situation, there is no need to voluntarily come forward with the information; however, communications planning should be conducted in case the information leaks out. For those organizations or families that do not have preexisting plans, an abundance of usable information is available on the Internet, and any professional consultant will have access to quality information or experience in managing a situation with media involvement.

No matter what, when the media is involved in a kidnapping situation, establishing empathy and support through the media is important. The very last thing that a family or organization wants is the press portraying the kidnappers as "Robin Hoods" or as a band of poor, deprived individuals struggling against the oppressor. This only increases pressure on the victim's side to pay more and accede to kidnappers' demands. Every effort must be made to gain a sympathetic ear from the media, rather than permitting them to be a witting or unwitting ally of the kidnappers.

The media has been unknowingly used on many occasions to communicate ransom demands and offers, usually through classified advertisements. For example, a kidnapper will insist that the victim's family or organization place a want ad for a house with a selling price that is actually the quantity offered as a ransom. Kidnappers will respond via another housing advertisement or a personal ad with a counteroffer, and the process will continue until an acceptable number is reached. This is a tortuous process that delays resolution and makes proof of life difficult; however, many kidnappers insist on avoiding telephone conversations for fear of call tracing and cellular location capabilities.

Legal Considerations

There are two distinct legal areas that should be of concern to anyone involved in managing the resolution of a kidnapping. The first is the local law with respect to kidnapping. Local laws and the definition of kidnapping vary from country to country. Some countries refer to the crime as abduction, some as kidnapping. In many places the crime is broken down into multiple different styles, with varying penalties for different types of crimes. The labyrinth of crimes and punishments militates for a profound knowledge of applicable laws in every case.

Worldwide, ransom kidnapping is considered a serious crime and is viewed as a form of terrorism in most places. Kidnapping carries criminal penalties; these penalties are harsher in some places than in others. The strength of local laws and penalties can have a significant impact on how a negotiation is conducted. The stronger the penalty, the more likely kidnappers are to commit violence against a victim if they feel threatened or insist on higher ransom payments. This is a simple risk-versus-reward equation that must be considered. Kidnappers who feel they have nothing to lose will be more prone to violence in locations where the death penalty or extremely long prison terms are in play, typically less so in countries in which the punishment is light or parole is easy. I once was present at a debriefing of a kidnapping victim who told us that her kidnapper had put a gun to her head during what he thought was a police raid, saying, "Ten years for homicide or forty for kidnapping, I have no choice." Fortunately for her, the supposed raid was only a helicopter landing a couple blocks from the safe house and she survived the incident.

In many countries, the law requires an immediate criminal complaint. In most of these countries, that requirement is virtually ignored by a populace that has little or no faith in the authorities and minimal confidence in their investigative capabilities. Families and organizations will go to great lengths to avoid reporting kidnappings; in Latin America the most reliable estimates place actual versus reported kidnappings at a ratio of 8:1 or greater. Government statistics are notoriously unreliable for two primary reasons. The first is the lack of confidence in, and hence, reporting to, the authorities when someone is kidnapped. The second is that governments throughout the world are interested in portraying themselves in the most favorable light possible. Therefore, kidnapping statistics, similar to those for other crimes, tend to rise and fall as new regimes are established or power changes hands during elections.

An initial step for any organization or family that has suffered a kidnapping and wishes to make a formal complaint is the hiring of a qualified attorney to represent them to the authorities. An experienced attorney will normally know the most efficient way to approach the authorities and put together a criminal complaint in such a way as to minimize interference with the negotiation, engender the most professional investigation possible, and reduce the possibility of information leakage. Establishing contact at the highest level possible within the police organization that will receive the complaint is important as well. The higher the level of the individual receiving notification of the situation, the tighter the circle of those in the know can be.

Many countries, states and cities have specialized channels for (supposedly) discreetly reporting kidnapping incidents in order to keep them out of the public domain. These channels should be used if at all possible. Where none exist and all criminal complaints become part of the public record, incentive to report the crime is reduced to nearly nil. No matter how or with what agency a criminal complaint is registered, representatives should always obtain signatures and complete, official copies of every relevant document.

A primary consideration in hiring an external consultant is to evaluate the legality of his or her presence and work. Many countries have laws that prohibit or strictly limit what consultants can and cannot do during a kidnapping. For example, in Mexico, Article 366 of the Criminal Code makes it a felony offense for any outsider to profit from a kidnapping. This has been construed to mean that any consultant who levies a charge for his or her services is liable to arrest and prosecution; and this offense is not one for which bail can be granted.

In a famous case in Colombia from 1993, Rene Higuita, goalie on the Colombian national soccer team, was incarcerated for acting as an intermediary between kidnappers and a victim's family. The law in Colombia prohibits private citizens from acting as intermediaries in kidnapping cases; Higuita served seven months in prison before being released.

Many other countries have similar laws, so the use of consultants, although imperative, must frequently be done in a discreet manner or hidden from prying eyes for the protection of all involved. Most laws that have been enacted to limit or ban consultants have been implemented to force families to report and denounce kidnappings. These laws have had marginal success and have led to very few prosecutions. Any professional consultant operating within a target country will know the laws and be able to operate within them.

6
RESPONSE

Strategy without tactics is the slowest route to victory. Tactics without strategy is the noise before defeat. Pretend inferiority and encourage his arrogance.

Sun Tzu, The Art of War

If you are prepared, then you are able to feel confident.

Robert J. Ringer

Initial Steps

Mounting an efficient response to a kidnapping requires an extreme level of attention to detail from the very beginning throughout the entire process. The first step is to initiate and maintain a journal or log of all that transpires. If sufficient numbers of reliable persons are involved in a family situation, the responsibility can be devolved on a family member or trusted acquaintance. In a corporate situation, a specially briefed administrative worker will normally be used. Whoever performs this task can often be responsible for both maintaining a journal and transcribing all telephonic communications from the kidnappers.

If the negotiation is being conducted in a language other than that of the parent organization, translation will also be necessary. Professional translation services are normally to be avoided, because they bring outsiders into the situation. If at all possible, a trusted family member, friend or employee should perform all translation. This, of course, is only valid if an individual within the circle of those who are aware of the situation possesses sufficient capability in both languages and whose time can be made available to perform the work.

A dedicated telephone line should be set up for all future communications. Only the designated negotiator will answer this line; no one else should take any incoming calls. In family situations when the negotiation is being conducted on the primary telephone line at a residence, other parameters apply. In areas in which a caller ID system is available, other family members may answer calls from known acquaintances only. Acquaintances and friends aware of the situation should be discouraged from calling on the line used for negotiation, because each time that telephone rings there occurs a flurry of activity and a tremendous spike in adrenaline levels.

In all cases, potential recipients of calls from the kidnappers should receive a briefing on what to say and do. This does not mean they must be made aware of any more details than are absolutely necessary to be able to answer a call, to ask the caller to stand by while the call is transferred, or immediately provide a number to which future calls should be directed. Organizations and families need not preoccupy themselves with concerns that the kidnappers will call once, become angry, and never be heard from again. Kidnappers are very interested in establishing direct contact with the person with whom they will negotiate and, although they may threaten and bluster, will almost always quickly take direction and call the number indicated or accept that the call must be transferred. In some cases, they may insist that the negotiator take the call on the line they have used, in which case modifications can be made, using call forwarding, rerouting or simply by having the negotiator take the call and work out an alternative arrangement.

Family members of the kidnap victim must be isolated and protected from external threats, particularly in the early stages of a kidnapping. While actual threats to other family members are unusual (as opposed to stated or implied threats from the kidnappers), a sufficient number of instances in which other family members have been targeted exist to warrant immediate action to protect all family members, at least until the situation is more clearly understood. In any case, once a kidnapping is reported, all family members must be located and measures taken to ensure their immediate security. In the specific case of school-age children, this can be a difficult issue. Most parents want their children to continue in school in order to maintain as normal a life as possible under the circumstances. This must, however, be weighed against any potential threat and decisions taken.

The families of kidnap victims need to carefully evaluate those around them and endeavor to identify who can be considered a friend or an ally. When a head of household begins asking his or her friends for loans to build a ransom for rescuing a family member, doors immediately begin to close. In many situations, I have dealt with family members who were shocked and demoralized when the rich uncle, brother or business associate suddenly invented financial difficulties as an excuse for not being able to provide any resources to assist in resolving the case. Help may also come from unexpected places; however, more doors close than open when a ransom is required.

In organizations, family members of the victim should know very quickly to what extent the organization will go to help resolve the situation. If the victim is insured by a KR policy, the insurer will reimburse the ransom paid up to the insured amount, provided all conditions are met. If not, the organization will have to determine how much of a commitment to make and how it will be managed. The financial director or other senior financial official should sit down with the affected family at the earliest opportunity and clearly delineate the scope and limits of any financial support.

Those who know the hostage best should prepare proof of life questions immediately. These questions should be simple, require short answers that are hard to garble when passed from a stressed-out victim through an interrogator to a negotiator, and should not be about obvious things. If the questions are too easy, kidnappers may well have already gotten the answers during the initial interrogation of the hostage and be able to provide the correct response, even though the hostage has already been murdered or incapacitated.

Questions such the name of a favorite pet or a family member, the color of a car or an address should routinely be avoided. Questions that are too complicated can also result in confusion, either among the kidnappers or the hostage. Remember that the hostage is under an enormous amount of stress and may not be thinking altogether clearly. I once was present in the 1990s when a brother posited the following question for kidnappers to pass along to his sibling, "Remember when we were in Dallas in '86 and we went over to that great restaurant after the ballgame the second night we were there. There was a blond waitress that was hitting on me all night. What was her name?" The kidnapper's laughter was clearly audible on the recording. His response was unprintable, but consisted of a rather direct request for a different type of question. Needless to say, another question had to be chosen and passed along.

Multiple questions should always be submitted to ensure that at least one or two are received and answered to an acceptable degree of certainty. There are endless options; however, correct answers to a series of questions such as "What was the name of your youngest sister's first boyfriend?" "How old is your Aunt Clara?" and "Which team won last time we went to the ball game?" will normally elicit sufficient response to make a judgment on the victim's safety and reasoning ability. The victim may not remember the score or even who won the game, but he or she will often pass on information about the game that only they could know. The responses received must be analyzed considering the stress on the victim and the possibility of a garbled transmission of the question and/or answer by the kidnappers.

A number of psychologists with whom I have worked have always insisted that no questions related to death, violence, alcohol, drug abuse or sexual encounters should ever be asked, feeling that these type of questions might lead the kidnappers to start thinking in darker directions.

If the victim suffers from any medical condition that is being treated, this must be identified and information on medicine and treatment must be on hand for provision to the kidnappers. A significant percentage of kidnappers will provide limited medical treatment to their hostages to keep them in relatively good health until the ransom is paid. Withholding or threatening to withhold necessary medicine is a favored negotiating tactic; however, kidnap for ransom is a business and damaged goods command a lower price. Being in possession of accurate medical information will also be very important once negotiations have been concluded and the hostage is to be released.

Establishing Responsibility

A critical initial decision is who will lead the negotiations. In my experience, forcing or convincing the kidnappers to deal with family rather than with an organization accrues greater benefits.

In a majority of cases the family does not have similar resources and kidnappers may be forced to adjust their demands to the perceived reality of the family's economic situation, rather than going after the organization's deeper pockets. This also enables the family to make a more compelling appeal to whatever sense of decency the kidnappers may have, although not much faith should be placed in the decency of such people. The family will require covert financial and logistical support from the organization. Errands need to be run, equipment purchased, life support issues addressed and myriad other details attended to.

The extent of the organization's willingness to support the family must be clearly understood by all before any negotiation begins. If financial support is to be provided by the organization, how much will be contributed and under what conditions? Will monies contributed to the ransom need to be repaid or are they a donation in support of a kidnapped team member? If the employee is covered by an insurance policy, professional help is automatically offered to the family and upon acceptance, dispatched. The family needs to agree to accept that help in order to benefit from the insurance policy. The use of outside consultants must also be addressed. Consultants must be paid, and who will do so and at what rate needs to be determined. As well, consultants provided by insurers often do not always agree to work with outside consultants and this issue must be resolved. Legal assistance may be necessary and responsibility for liaison with local law enforcement must be assigned.

When my father was kidnapped, the general manager of his company assured us that the firm would support us in everything and contribute significant sums of money for the ransom without expecting repayment. He provided an estimate of the amount, told us that he would confirm right away how much money would be made available and we started negotiating based on that premise. I called him every day for a week and always received one excuse or another; finally he called and told me that they would be responsible for a much smaller amount, but that the company could loan us money if we needed to borrow funds. This turned the negotiation upside down; we are not rich and had been bargaining in good faith with the kidnappers, expecting to receive money from the organization to cover all that we had borrowed on a temporary basis from family and friends.

Another critical issue is clearly deciding who makes the final decisions on the overall negotiation. This can be the negotiator who will speak with the kidnappers; however, affording the negotiator the flexibility to state that he or she must check with someone else is virtually always a positive force in the negotiation. In organizational situations this is an obligatory step; no kidnapper will ever be allowed to speak with the senior decision maker in any organization. In family situations, often only the decision maker is willing and able to perform the negotiation and, hence, he or she is the final arbiter. If, however, a layer of insulation can be placed between the decision maker and the kidnappers, this can be a boon to the negotiating team and a valuable step forward.

Negotiator

This is the single most significant role in resolving any kidnapping situation. The negotiator is the only person to whom the kidnappers will speak directly and is the conduit through which all management decisions will be communicated to the kidnappers. A principal function of the negotiator is to obtain or extract the maximum amount of information possible from the adversary, while providing a minimal amount of information.

Negotiating is all about relationships. The negotiator must seek to develop a rapport with the adversary that leads to a swift and "equitable" solution (although paying a ransom for a kidnapped loved one can hardly be considered equitable in any normal sense of the word). A level of rapport should be sought that enables the negotiator to gradually convert the adversary into somewhat of an ally. Establishing a credible relationship with the kidnappers' negotiator normally leads to development of an "us against the world" mentality, in which the adversary is slowly won over to the side of the victim and actively advocates a solution. Some are more susceptible than others to this tactic; however, most will come around over time.

In family situations, the negotiator is most often a trusted friend or family member. The decision to choose a friend to conduct the negotiation is not to be taken lightly; no matter how close a friendship exists, there is a difference in the level of emotional commitment to the case. This can be advantageous; friends are often able to be much more dispassionate than family members and are normally less susceptible to threatened or implied violence. Family members however, are in the best position to know exactly what is possible and can often develop empathy or the appearance of empathy with the adversary that is difficult for friends to achieve. If the kidnapping band is a small one, family negotiators often can use the directness of contact as an advantage, appearing to be emotionally affected while playing the sympathy card with the adversary. The best practice for choosing a negotiator; however, is to always seek someone with the ability to maintain as much emotional detachment as possible.

In many instances the choice is a *fait accompli*; the kidnappers will insist on speaking to a particular individual and will not accept communication with anyone else. This often is attributable to a kidnapper's perception that the selected individual is the decision maker or that a certain person is more susceptible to pressure. They may reveal much of their strategy by insisting on direct communication with a parent or sibling. For example, insistence on speaking to the father when a daughter is kidnapped is frequently a sign that threats of rape and torture will be used to try and pressure the family into a rapid settlement at a higher figure than might be otherwise negotiated.

Each case is different, and only experience and judgment serve to determine whether the negotiator should be accepted or changed. Change can be forced in a number of ways, but is always a delicate operation. In one case I attended, the father of a teenage daughter was a member of Alcoholics Anonymous. He had made an initial offer of almost two million dollars when the kidnappers called demanding four million dollars immediately after taking the daughter. In order to establish a negotiation that would lead to both the daughter's safe return and vaccinate the family against future incidents, the negotiator had to be changed on the first day of the incident. When the kidnappers called that afternoon, they were told that the father had taken to drinking (an antecedent they could verify with the daughter) and that they would have to deal only with the mother. They insisted for ten days on speaking with the father before they capitulated and negotiated seriously with the mother. The daughter returned home safely after more than three weeks at a fraction of the cost of the original demand.

I have also seen cases in which the negotiator burned out one or more adversary negotiators. The mother of one kidnapped young man was so astute at running circles around the adversary that the band changed negotiators three times in a week. She was able to turn the negotiators into advocates for an immediate settlement almost overnight, by detecting and playing on the adversaries' emotions. Smaller kidnapping bands routinely have one member assigned to conduct the actual negotiation and are uncomfortable making changes. In general, kidnappers will change if they feel that their negotiator is making no headway or that a different negotiator might have better success.

There is also some propensity to conduct a "good cop, bad cop" type of negotiation to pressure the family. This occurs when one adversary negotiator applies tremendous pressure by making constant threats against the victim, while the second adversary negotiator plays the role of a friendly sort who only wants to achieve a settlement to spare victim and family further pain and suffering. The "good cop" negotiator tries to convince the family or organization to raise the ransom offer, taking the tactic that he or she is working with them to keep the "bad cop" from ordering violence against the victim. This not an uncommon tactic can be very effective against inexperienced or unsupported negotiators.

The designated negotiator must have absolute fluency in the local language. Kidnappers often come from the lower strata of society and speak in an argot that is only understandable to a native linguist. This can have a dramatic impact on communication and perception. Misspoken words or misunderstood statements can have tragic results, regardless of the experience level of the negotiator.

An individual I once worked with used the phrase "No tienes madre?" (Don't you have a mother?) during a conversation with a kidnapper while trying to establish empathy. In Mexican-style Spanish, this exact phrase can also be perceived as a grievous insult, meaning basically that the individual has no redeeming virtues. The kidnapper took the phrase for an insult and immediately went ballistic. There followed an extremely tense five minutes of threats and imprecations until the negotiator was able to clear up the misunderstanding and get the conversation back on track.

This is one reason why a consultant or an outsider (particularly a foreigner) normally never takes the phone and speaks directly to a kidnapper. The language barrier is not easy to overcome and the mere fact that an outside consultant has been brought on board communicates information to the kidnappers that they most definitely do not need. Whenever an outside negotiator intervenes directly in the negotiation, kidnappers can immediately assume one of two things, either of which will likely contribute to a significantly higher ransom payment. The kidnappers will automatically assume that the victim has KR insurance and that a significant amount of money is available. They normally start making statements such as, "Your insurance will pay for this" or "It's not your money anyway." Moving them off such a position can be extremely difficult. In a case in which they are insufficiently erudite or lack the necessary experience to perceive the possibility of insurance, or can be made to accept the fact or believe the fiction (as the case may be) that the family or organization has none, they will assume that if there are funds available to pay a consultant, there is plenty of money to pay the ransom demand. They will also immediately assume that any outsider is a police officer, which can cause all sorts of undesirable consequences.

Whoever is chosen to be the negotiator should be able to think quickly and react spontaneously to an ever-changing situation. Kidnappers like to inject variables or to do the unexpected in the hope of breaking down defenses and achieving their goals. The negotiator must be able to remain calm, yet show the necessary emotion when required. An emotionless negotiator has difficulty in establishing credibility with the adversary. The negotiator must also be able to respond to external guidance while in the middle of an incredibly stressful discourse with a kidnapper, as well as maintaining a dialogue that leads to meeting the goals of each communication.

At the heart of any negotiation is the issue of credibility; kidnappers need to be able to believe that what they are hearing is true. If a negotiator is not credible, no matter how well he or she implements a strategy, the negotiation will be long and painful, and the results less than expected. For this reason, families and organizations should always have a secondary negotiator prepared to step in. This person should be involved in developing the strategy, should listen to recordings of all communications, and be available to step in and take charge of the communication at a moment's notice. A back-up negotiator who is unaware of the details of a case is both inefficient and dangerous.

In order to effectively negotiate, the individual selected should, insofar as possible, adhere to the following practices:

- Be on call 24/7 in case the kidnappers initiate communication.
- Avoid other obligations as much as possible to focus on the negotiation.
- Regularly seek to speak to the victim or request proof of life.
- Understand the need for and maintain strict confidentiality.
- Always remember the absolute priority is the victim's well-being.

Crisis Control Center

Whether in a family situation or in a more structured organizational environment, a kidnapping needs to be managed from a crisis control center, equipped with all the necessary tools to facilitate an appropriate response.

In a family situation, basic requirements normally exist on a smaller scale than in an organization. Families may be prepared for a kidnapping; however, I am not suggesting that a room in every home in which a potential victim resides be prepared for use as a center for kidnap management. There are, however, basic supplies that should either be available or easily obtainable during an emergency situation. The room to be used should have the following characteristics:

- isolated from view by passersby or outsiders (not visible from street)
- ability to restrict access to the control room by unauthorized persons (service staff, friends, relatives, etc.)
- no easy access to exterior or adjoining walls or windows by unauthorized persons
- adequate telephone service and electricity and ventilation
- sufficient wall space for posting charts (normally six to ten "butcher-block" pages)
- chairs and worktables as necessary

In residences, a spare room, office or bedroom is normally used. This often requires some modification to enable installation of the necessary equipment and to create sufficient space. In a crisis, an acceptable workspace can usually be set up within a very short time by simply moving or rearranging furniture and bringing in the necessary supplies and equipment. There is, however, a need to control access to the workspace and preclude unauthorized access to adjoining spaces. When a kidnapping occurs, experience has shown that, in a significant percentage of cases, someone on the inside is involved. Access control is therefore crucial, as is limiting the number of persons with detailed knowledge of negotiating parameters.

Most organizations have designated conference or other facilities that are to be used in a crisis situation; however, few are prepared and equipped to the necessary level. Frequently, one finds a dusty manual that refers to the "Incident Management Center" or "Crisis Control Room" and sometimes contains a list of necessary equipment and supplies. One seldom encounters a fully prepared and functional center, in which operations can be immediately conducted. A kidnapping rapidly drives home the truth of the old saying, "for want of a nail, a shoe was lost." An unprepared organization starts out at a significant disadvantage.

An organizational crisis control center requires the same basic characteristics. The facilities available should correspond to the size of the organization and membership of the crisis management team; however, this is not always the case. I have been in crisis control centers of large organizations that were no more than a cement-walled room about twelve feet square, with a single electrical outlet and no telephone jacks. Attempting to determine how the organization ever came to believe that a crisis could be managed from such a location is an exercise in futility.

I have also seen fully equipped, first-class facilities in organizations that had no written plans or procedures in place to deal with a crisis. These showrooms are excellent tools for impressing the odd visitor or stockholder; however, the lack of a coherent plan, identified and trained participants and a clear strategy makes even the most palatial accommodations virtually useless. Every organization needs to determine exactly what the requirements for a control center are and then build, modify or equip a facility to suit their particular needs. Admittedly, as the hierarchical positioning of the participants rises, planning factors usually tend toward a heightened level of luxury. This is not always a bad thing; more comfortable accommodations can foster a more productive working environment. The focus, however, needs to remain on function over form.

No matter where a crisis control center is located, certain electronic and communications equipment is necessary and should be purchased or obtained. In an organizational setting, this equipment should already be on hand, tested and ready for use at any time. In a family situation, there is a likelihood that some or all of the equipment will need to be purchased immediately. In either case, minimum requirements include:

- telephone, primary or back-up, must be an apparatus that continues to function if electrical power is cut off
- working caller ID system for telephone service where available
- recording device connected to telephone that activates automatically when handset is lifted
- headphones with at least ten feet of cord connected to telephone recording device
- nearby capability to immediately duplicate tapes or CDs of caller recordings
- videocassette or DVD player to view proof of life videos
- computer with Internet connection and printer
- copier and fax machines
- backup cellular phone(s) and chargers for use during ransom delivery

During a kidnapping, the equipment for reproducing audiocassettes was set up in the control center. A family member went into the control center and listened to the latest taped conversation while the negotiating team was eating dinner. Unfortunately, he connected the telephone-recording device to the player instead of simply changing the tape. When the kidnappers called later that night, at the moment the handset was lifted, a high-volume electronic screeching filled the room, audible not only to the adversaries but also probably to every neighbor within a six-block radius. I immediately unplugged the recording device and was forced to stand by as the negotiator was verbally abused for recording the conversations, had his son's life threatened and was forced to go it alone during a lengthy and contentious discussion. Since then, I have strictly prohibited recording and duplicating equipment in the same room.

I have designed a number of modular units for client companies in which the necessary equipment is stored in portable cabinets that can be rolled out and used in the crisis control center or redeployed to another location if necessary. These cabinets can be made to fit in any type of room and provide a portable capability with all the necessary items on hand. Most organizations will include in the design space for a laptop, extra cellular phones or whatever else management deems necessary for use in a crisis. Obviously, no family is likely to prepare a specific piece of furniture and store specialized equipment "just in case" a family member is kidnapped; however, most of the items are routinely available in a majority of upper-middle class and above households.

Any location that meets the security criteria noted earlier can be used as a crisis control center in a kidnapping situation. Most locations have call forwarding services available that permit calls to an office or residence to be forwarded to another number, thus affording the negotiation team a good deal of flexibility. I know of one case in which the victim's family had calls forwarded to a residence in a neighboring jurisdiction so that the police there (who were known and trustworthy) could handle the situation rather than having to turn the case over to the local anti-kidnapping unit, a number of whose members had recently been arrested on kidnapping charges.

Logistics

The logistical support necessary for a negotiating team during a kidnapping must be the responsibility of someone other than the negotiator. In an organizational situation, this can be a relatively simple proposition; persons can be assigned to perform the necessary tasks from existing resources and this can be pre-planned as part of overall crisis management planning. In families, the issue can become much more complex; someone needs to be identified who will take charge of all the logistics-related activities in support of the negotiating team. The negotiator must be free to focus on his or her task and the individual in charge of logistics has to be responsible for all of the other necessary activities and ensure that a smooth flow of supplies is available.

The necessary supplies may vary slightly, depending on specific situational characteristics; however, the following list covers the basic necessities for almost all cases:

- briefing chart paper
- felt tip markers
- Scotch and masking tape

- cassettes and/or CDs
- batteries
- surgical gloves
- plastic bags
- writing instruments
- note pads
- cellular phone and other equipment chargers

The person in charge of logistics must also be responsible for ensuring the immediate copying of all calls or communications from the kidnappers. If a written communication is received, the document must be handled with surgical gloves, encased in plastic and immediately copied and preserved for evidentiary purposes. Newspaper advertisements or want ad placements should be copied and enlarged. Audio recordings need to be duplicated as soon as possible after each telephone call, and the required number of further copies prepared.

The individual responsible for duplicating audiotapes or CDs must be able to handle listening to their content. Particularly in the case of audiocassettes, each call is normally dubbed onto one or more master copies. Since individual calls do not normally occupy the entire side of a cassette, the duplicator (particularly when dubbing cassettes) must listen to the call multiple times while making each new copy. This can be an extremely stressful task, more so in cases in which high levels of violent threats are employed. If a junior staff or family member is tasked with copying the recordings, he or she may well be adversely affected by the contents. I normally try to employ the secondary negotiator as the person responsible; this affords him or her opportunity to become intimately familiar with all details of the negotiation while performing this important task.

In many cases, particularly those in which a multinational corporation is involved, transcription and translation into the native language corresponding to the senior headquarters or home office is also necessary. This necessitates the preparation and employment of skilled translators who should be capable of hearing the worst of humanity and remain capable of performing an accurate and timely translation. If the kidnappers are particularly voluble, a team of translators is dictated. Most corporate crisis management teams need the translated material almost immediately. Translators have only hours to perform their duties, review and make corrections, and send the translated material up the chain. Although outside translation or transcription services are generally available, security and confidentiality requirements influence the selection and employment of personnel for the task.

Very early in the negotiation process, the individual in charge of logistics needs to consider the potential requirements associated with ransom delivery and hostage recovery. These may include a particular type of vehicle, specialized supplies and equipment, airline tickets, visas, communications equipment or any of a multitude of other items, depending on the location and form of the ransom delivery. Preliminary planning should begin very early in the process and the necessary adjustments made as the negotiation winds to a climax.

Planning for the immediate medical examination of a recently released hostage can be done ahead of time by contacting a family physician or alerting a staff medical person. The services of a good psychologist should also be contracted during the initial stages of any kidnapping; often the necessity for therapy surfaces among affected family members during the negotiation process. An effective therapist can make the negotiation process go much more smoothly by providing needed psychological support to family members. I do not recommend the inclusion of psychics, voodoo priestesses, ghosts or beings from the future in developing a response.

Life Support

The negotiating team must receive full support in the most mundane tasks. In an organization, sufficient support elements usually exist to carry out the necessary tasks without a major disruption; however, selecting and clearing those persons who will participate is time-sensitive and crucial. The fewer the number of individuals aware of what is occurring, the better the possibility of controlling or preventing leaks of key information. Every single individual selected to participate in any way during the management of a kidnapping must be totally trustworthy and briefed beforehand. Each individual briefing should emphasize the need for discretion and provide the person only with sufficient information to perform his or her assigned task.

In a family situation, even meal preparation can be a source of problems. Suppose the victim's mother is doing the negotiating and she normally prepares all the meals. During a kidnapping, she cannot possibly follow her normal routine and, therefore, other arrangements must be made. If a relative volunteers to prepare and serve all meals to the family, that individual will have to clear his or her schedule in order to provide the service. If an outsider is to perform this task, he or she must be adequately vetted before access to the home is granted to ensure security. Frequently, friends and family members organize a rotating schedule to provide meals to the family; however, this must be administered so that the family is not overburdened with visitors.

If any relatives or outsiders will be staying at a residence or in a local hotel for the duration of the kidnapping, this must be arranged to place the minimum stress possible on the family. I once worked a case in which a family friend suggested I move into the victim's room for the duration of the case. The shocked stares and ensuing uproar quickly convinced him of the error of his ways. To the family, this would have been tantamount to resigning themselves to the fact that their son was never coming back. (He did, after about two weeks of negotiation.)

Visitors can be a bone of contention. Any family that has suffered a kidnap needs the support of relatives and friends; however, this support can easily become an additional trial if proper control is not established from the outset. Friends and family members should be encouraged to call or visit regularly. They should also, however, be made to clearly understand that the victim's family needs support, not smothering. I have been in situations in which upward of a dozen friends and/or family members were present in the home for up to twenty hours per day. This places an unsupportable additional burden on the family and can exacerbate an already stressful situation. Visits are welcome, but beneficial in moderation only, and all those who might wish to accompany the family need to be sure that their actions are not adding to the problem. I normally brief a number of key friends and family members to get the word out with respect to this issue.

In the initial stages of a kidnapping the enormous levels of shock and pressure frequently contribute to a lack of rest. This is normal; any parent or family member undergoing such a trauma is likely to experience sleepless nights. Countless family members have told me, "I won't sleep until my son comes home," or something similar. This is a non-starter, and actually redounds to the kidnapper's advantage if the negotiator and support team get so little rest that mental acuity and alertness are affected. Family members need to be convinced that as normal a sleep cycle as possible should be maintained in order to maximize the quality of their response to the kidnapping. As in any other situation, tired, dull-witted persons are much less effective than those who are rested and alert. Most medical professionals recommend that the average individual get seven or more hours of sleep nightly to maintain top mental condition, particularly during times of increased stress. The key is to understand that continued sleeplessness will degrade performance and diminish response to the situation. Although sleeping normally under such circumstances may seem impossible to the casual observer, experience shows that a majority of family members are able to achieve a relatively routine rest cycle after a few days.

The most mundane tasks of daily life can become sources of irritation and frustration. For example, if the family only has one telephone line, every time the phone rings the adrenaline level reaches impossible heights, the team rushes into place and the call is taken. Friends or relatives, particularly those unaware of the situation, are frequently left confused and hurt by brusque replies and curt brush-offs. In short order, answering the telephone becomes a trial felt by all. Ensuring that children continue to attend school and participate in their normal activities is also often very difficult. They also feel the stress of the situation and are affected to varying degrees. They need to be supported and lifestyles maintained as normally as possible.

Grocery shopping, paying regular bills, domestic employee management, car repairs and a multitude of daily tasks can easily be pushed aside and permitted to lie fallow while focus is on the kidnapping. If these tasks however, do not receive adequate attention, strange things can happen. Telephone service or electricity may be cut off at a critical juncture; food supplies can run out unexpectedly; or, at the moment of ransom delivery, someone may notice that none of the available vehicles has more than one-eighth of a tank of gasoline.

In an organizational situation, some of these mishaps are much less likely to occur; however, the impact of a kidnapping can cause other important issues to be neglected. Placing responsibility for life support functions in capable hands saves time and helps lead to a successful conclusion. Ignore these aspects of the situation at your own risk.

7

NEGOTIATION

Be what you would seem to be—or, if you'd like it put more simply—never imagine yourself not to be otherwise than what it might appear to others that what you were or might have been was not otherwise than what you had been would have appeared to them to be otherwise.

Lewis Carroll, Alice in Wonderland

Judgment is more than skill. It sets forth on intellectual seas beyond the shores of hard indisputable factual information.

Kingman Brewster

Strategy

The strategy to be used in negotiating the resolution of a kidnapping is absolutely the most critical decision taken during the entire process. No matter what else is done in terms of preparation and execution, a kidnapping can only be successfully resolved if a coherent and workable strategy is in place.

The most important consideration in developing a strategy is establishing priorities. The most important goal is the safe return of the hostage. This is the overriding concern that guides all actions and is far more important than any other consideration. No other result is acceptable; the hostage must be safely returned. While any number of jokes can be (and are) made about telling the kidnappers to keep the wife or offering to pay them not to return a philandering husband, no family I have ever encountered has been less than one hundred percent dedicated to the rapid return of the loved one.

An additional focus is to seek the return of the victim in the shortest possible time and at the lowest possible cost. The rationale behind a quick resolution is obvious: the family or organization wants the victim back as quickly as possible. The duration of a kidnapping is directly related to the level of risk the victim faces. As time goes on, many things can go wrong, frustration begins to rise on both sides, and chances of a mistake that could lead to tragic results increase.

The lowest possible cost issue is less obvious, but the financial impact of a kidnapping can be enormous, and the ransom cost is only part (although normally the most significant part) of the total disbursement. Other costs may apply including hiring a consultant; paying lawyers and in many cases, the authorities; sale of vehicles and other possessions that must be replaced at some future date; lost wages, sales and income; increased operating expenses; purchase, installation and operation of specialized equipment; and other miscellaneous outlays.

Aside from the need to control outlays during a critical time, experience has shown that lower ransom payments normally lead to less dire consequences. When a family or organization pays a large ransom quickly, the rapid payment may be an incentive to the kidnappers to murder the hostage and leave no trace for later investigation. As well, the process of negotiation must be developed in such a way as to convince the kidnappers that the target was selected in error and that there is no sense in returning at a later date to kidnap another executive or family member.

The family of one individual I know suffered multiple kidnapping events. In the first instance, the oldest son was kidnapped on the street and the father paid the $2 million ransom asked by the kidnappers within seven days. One year later, the same group kidnapped his other son on the way home from school and he paid another $2 million, again within a week of the incident. Two years later, the father was kidnapped and his children quickly paid a similar amount for his freedom. After the third event, he became completely disillusioned with the security situation in his adopted homeland, sold his businesses and returned to his native land. Had he negotiated properly the first time, he may well have been able to reduce the possibility that the kidnappers would return to kidnap another family member. The method whereby he obtained the release of both sons led the kidnappers to believe that he was an "easy money" target, and they continued to return for more money at regular intervals.

A well-developed strategy in part considers the concept of "vaccination." If the process is carried out in a professional manner, kidnappers can be convinced in most cases that the reward is only marginally acceptable and that they should seek other, more lucrative, targets for future operations. They need to be led to believe that this particular family or organization does not have the resources that would enable them to obtain hefty paydays on a recurring basis, and the safest way to ensure this is to make the process of negotiation an arduous one for the kidnappers. This does not mean that the process must be overly protracted. On the contrary, kidnappings can often be resolved in mere days at a cost equivalent to a mere fraction of the originally requested amount. This requires a well-considered and carefully implemented strategy that leads to a swift and successful conclusion.

A fundamental part of any negotiation strategy is that all actions visible to or verifiable by the kidnappers must be completely congruent with the words of the negotiator. For example, if the negotiator states that a vehicle was just sold to obtain funds for the ransom, that vehicle must disappear from sight immediately. The kidnappers may have surveillance on the home or office and simply garaging or not using the vehicle is insufficient. The vehicle must be removed to a remote location not apparently connected with the family or organization.

Gregorio owned a small printing business with about thirty employees. His daughter was kidnapped and, during the negotiation, he told the kidnappers that he was canceling payroll for his workers and putting that money into the ransom. They naturally approved and the negotiation proceeded to reach a point at which settlement became imminent. Two days later was the scheduled payday for Gregorio's employees. Much to my surprise and consternation, an armored truck pulled up at the plant and payroll disbursement was performed (employees were still paid in cash) as usual. Not surprisingly, the kidnappers called that night and accused Gregorio of lying and the discussions became much more threatening. Gregorio, thinking quickly, was able to convince the kidnappers that a fellow businessman had stepped forward and loaned him the money to make payroll so that he could keep the business open and continue to get more ransom money.

Congruence is not the same as total honesty. Kidnappers have no need or right to know everything about what is going on. The only "truth" they must be told is relative to matters that they can either observe or verify, including detailed information that may be extracted from the victim. The philosophy of TMI (too much information) certainly applies in kidnapping cases; there is no requirement to provide them any more information than necessary. Frequently, families put for sale signs on homes and cars, suspend memberships in gymnasiums and golf clubs, cease ostentatious activities such as fine dining and lay off or suspend domestic staff in support of the ongoing search for resources with which to pay the ransom. Whether or not these activities are permanent or real, they must appear genuine in all observable aspects.

The best and most congruent negotiation strategy can be completely eviscerated if the victim wittingly or unwittingly provides information to the kidnappers that belies what they are hearing. Victims are absolutely the worst possible negotiators!

Frank, an elderly gentleman, was abducted and the kidnappers asked for a multi-million dollar ransom. The family was distraught, knowing there was no way they could ever reach such an amount. After a couple weeks during which amounts of around twenty-five thousand dollars were offered and rejected, the family received a videocassette. On the tape, Frank provided specific details about a retirement account that held nearly one million dollars in a bank other than the family's normal one. The family knew nothing of the account and upon investigation discovered that the money actually was present and available for withdrawal upon the wife's signature.

This type of information causes an immediate agonizing reassessment of the negotiation strategy and can lead to disastrous results. In this case, the family analyzed its financial situation and determined that payment of such a ransom would bankrupt the family and make the parents' retirement years virtually impossible to finance. They took a calculated risk and decided not to offer the kidnappers the entire retirement amount, choosing instead to tell them that the old man was confused and may have been losing his mind due to the stress of the situation. They admitted the presence of the account; however, they eliminated a couple of zeroes and continued to negotiate. The kidnappers were incensed, but they had no means of proving the lie and, after an additional six weeks of delays, threats, additional pleading videos and severe beatings of the victim, finally settled for a significantly lower amount.

While this may sound like a cold and dangerous calculation that could represent a threat to the victim's life, the band of kidnappers had been identified and the family was made aware that they had never murdered any previous victims. In the end, they were able to retrieve the victim at a fraction of the original demand, ensure that he and his wife retained the funds necessary to live on in retirement, and send a message to the kidnappers that he was not a viable target for future kidnapping.

This strategy is not necessarily viable in every case. Kidnappers often thoroughly investigate the resources available to the victim and frequently have detailed information on the victim's assets and liquidity before they strike. In this case, their lack of preparation enabled the family to make a potentially risky decision not to pay the full amount sought. In cases in which the kidnappers have better intelligence on their victims, ransom payments are often much higher.

Outcomes

In any negotiation, there are multiple potential outcomes; most are not acceptable to either the family or the organization. Although every situation is different and each outcome may vary slightly, these outcomes may be classified in a few specific categories.

Victim death or murder—Victims are killed infrequently in most areas; however, no part of the world is immune to death during a kidnapping. The reasons for which a hostage may be murdered vary, but experts agree that the most common cause of death in ransom kidnappings is futile escape attempts by the victim. Victims also have been known to die due to untreated medical conditions, heart attacks, strokes, or, in some extreme cases, malnourishment or starvation. Most kidnappers will provide access to necessary medicines or even treatment for wounds sustained during the actual kidnapping; however, some do not and this can lead to life-threatening complications. Stress-related heart attacks or strokes may occur at any time if the victim is not in good physical condition. Imagine if you will, a sedentary 55-year old ripped from an office environment and subjected to the intense stress of a kidnapping in which he or she is chained to a radiator on a cold concrete floor for weeks on end. Victims also are executed when families or organizations refuse to pay or make no effort to negotiate in good faith. Hostages have also been murdered as examples to other potential targets or to inspire future victims to pay greater amounts and more rapidly.

Take the money, kill the hostage—This is obviously the worst possible outcome for any family or organization. A ransom is negotiated in good faith over a period of time; an agreement is finally reached; instructions for ransom delivery are obtained and precisely followed; and the victim is put to death anyway. This can happen for a number of reasons aside from those noted above. The family or organization should be told early in the process that execution almost always results from a conscious decision by the kidnappers at the outset of the process. Despite the best efforts of the negotiating team, the victim may be put to death because he or she knows or is able to identify one of the kidnappers; the criminals desire to leave as little trace as possible for investigation; or simply because the kidnappers are sociopaths who have no regard for human life. A number of victims have been killed when corrupt police authorities or other criminals intercepted the ransom and the kidnappers gained nothing but a hostage for their trouble. This devastating situation is beyond the control of the negotiating team. Knowing the mind of the criminal is impossible, and so many variables impact any given case that being able to predict with absolute certainty whether any hostage will be executed is impossible.

Take the money, claim it as a down payment, and reopen negotiations—This tactic can be ruinous to a family or organization. A negotiation is conducted, the ransom agreed upon and paid, but the victim is not released. Thereafter, communication from the kidnappers states that the ransom payment was insufficient and more money must be obtained for the victim to be freed. This tactic occurs most frequently when multiple victims are taken; the kidnappers will free one hostage but insist on an equal or greater ransom payment for the other(s). They also have been known to finalize a deal, collect the money and then escalate the original amount demanded. There is no real way to protect against this type of action. In the case of multiple hostages, staged releases of one or more hostage can be coordinated with progressive payments of portions of the ransom; however, the kidnappers retain all the money and at least one hostage pending release.

Take the money, free the hostage(s), kidnap again at a later date—This result is most common when large ransom amounts are paid immediately. Kidnappers are like any other criminals in that they seek the easiest target with the greatest reward. If a family or organization pays a significant percentage of the initial demand without delay or serious negotiation, they are marked as easy money targets. Kidnappers will frequently go back to the well at a later date. This potential outcome militates very strongly for developing and implementing a sound negotiating strategy that will dissuade kidnappers from making future attempts against the family or organization. If the process is arduous from the kidnappers' point of view, and if they feel that they have gotten all they can from the family or organization even though they are not satisfied with the results of the kidnapping from a business perspective, the likelihood they will target the same family or organization at a later date is much reduced.

Take the money, release the hostage(s), and never return—This is the optimal outcome and the only truly acceptable one (other than rescue) in any kidnapping situation. None of the others are outcomes that any family or organization wishes to achieve. If the conclusion of a kidnapping can be considered successful, the victim's safe return with no repeated attempts against the organization or family is the only such outcome that can be so characterized. Obviously, the previous two outcomes are acceptable in the sense that the victim returns safely; however, a repeat of the kidnapping at a later date is something no one wishes to undergo. Developing and implementing a sound negotiating strategy that takes into consideration all the necessary variables is the only possible way to achieve the most propitious outcome.

Rescue of the hostage—This outcome obviously depends on the participation of law enforcement authorities. When law enforcement authorities are able to identify the location where the hostage is held, they will usually (not always) come to the family or organization and propose a rescue mission if they believe one to be feasible. They may or may not wait for consent to conduct the mission; this often depends on the *a priori* relationship between the two parties. In some cases, the authorities may have received the blessing of the family or organization; however, when they enter the safe house they encounter multiple hostages. The hostages from other kidnappings are also rescued; however, they are also at risk. The viability of a rescue operation is in direct relation to the professionalism of the law enforcement agency involved and varies from city to city and country to country.

Contact

The initial contact with the kidnappers is a crucial moment in the process. If the necessary information can be elicited or provided during the kidnapper's first call at the moment in which the family or organization is apprised of the situation, so much the better. More common, however, is an opportunity to speak at greater length with the kidnappers when they call to initiate negotiations, typically within forty-eight hours of the incident.

The negotiator must immediately inquire as to the well-being of the victim, and be prepared to provide information on any medical conditions or other situations that could potentially affect the outcome. This includes information on necessary medications, treatments or other health considerations. An immediate attempt should be made to speak with the hostage and, if unsuccessful, prepared proof of life questions should be on hand and the adversary urged to receive them for an immediate response. In a majority of situations, every call from this point forward should include a request to speak to the hostage.

Unless the negotiator is permitted to speak to the hostage on a regular basis, parameters for relaying proof of life questions and responses should be established. Kidnapping is a business and the kidnappers know that their best opportunity to be paid what they demand lies in keeping the hostage in good condition and ensuring that the family or organization is satisfied that this is the case. As well, the caller (once one is sure that he or she represents the actual kidnappers) should be asked to provide a specific identification or code name so that the family or organization can be sure of his or her identity in future calls. I know of a number of cases in which an omission of this very basic step led to a ransom payment to a third party.

Fred was in the process of negotiating the release of his kidnapped daughter. The kidnappers had been exerting a great deal of psychological pressure on the family, threatening violence and making use of a great deal of sexual innuendo to force the family to quickly pay an extremely large amount of money. One evening, Fred received a call from someone styling himself as a "new" negotiator. This individual stated that the "boss" had ordered him to reach an agreement at any cost, since he was having trouble restraining members of the band from physically attacking the young lady. Fred was so concerned about the well-being of his daughter that he immediately agreed to a ransom payment slightly higher than his most recent offer without thinking through the situation. He left his home alone, followed all instructions for delivery and returned to await word from his daughter. Two nights later, in a total state of panic, he received a call from the actual kidnappers who asked how much he had been able to accumulate. When he indignantly responded that he had already paid and accused them of perfidy, they became upset and cut off communication for more than a week. After a further three weeks of charges and countercharges, reopened negotiations and difficulty in convincing the kidnappers that someone had already stolen the major portion of available funds, Fred was finally able to secure the release of his daughter.

The need to establish an identification protocol is clear; failure to do so can lead to extreme complications. An identification protocol can be established simply by having the kidnapper provide a code name by which he or she wishes to be known. This identifier enables negotiators to have increased confidence that the caller is the person with whom they should be negotiating. If the kidnapper asks the negotiator to choose a name, he or she should avoid suggesting insulting or degrading terms so as not to further complicate the situation.

Another issue of immediate importance is the need to express an absolute willingness to work with the kidnappers in resolving the situation. Properly done, this creates empathy and credibility from the outset and helps facilitate a solution. Kidnappers must be regularly reassured that the family or organization is doing everything possible to resolve the situation and will continue to do so.

During any initial contact, negotiators should never agree to any ransom demand. The kidnappers should be reassured that the family or organization is making every effort to meet their expectations; however, numbers should not be discussed until a negotiating strategy has been fully developed. I have arrived to a number of situations in which an ill-conceived offer had already been made, complicating the situation and forcing delicate, and often acrimonious, adjustments.

If the kidnapping has not been reported in the media or did not immediately become public knowledge, kidnappers will insist that no police or press become involved. They do not want the scrutiny or the investigation that this will bring. They should be assured at every opportunity that no law enforcement authorities will ever be invited to participate. This can be done in the most disparaging terms if necessary; law enforcement professionals understand and encourage the practice. Negotiators need not be concerned that any derogatory remarks they make about the police will be held against them; I have witnessed many occasions in which both parties vilified the police while an officer was present in the room attempting to keep a straight face.

Denying the involvement of police, press and consultants is very important and goes to the very heart of a negotiating strategy. If the denials are credible from the outset, the kidnappers will be inclined to believe that they have and can keep the upper hand. If, on the other hand, denials are not believable or there is obvious evidence to the contrary, establishing the necessary rapport with an adversary will be difficult and can be very dangerous.

Negotiation Techniques

Kidnappers know full well that the crime they are committing is heavily penalized and can lead to long incarceration or even the death penalty. They therefore want to be sure that they are as secure as possible when conducting business with the family or organization. Negotiators must seek to indirectly play upon these fears and establish a "we versus them" mentality, in which the adversary considers that both sides are working together toward a solution. This begins with credibility. Once the adversary believes what he or she is hearing, a solution can be achieved.

Developing a strategy that will lead to a satisfactory result is virtually useless if kidnappers cannot be convinced of the veracity of the negotiator's statements. From this flows logically the kidnappers' perception that the entire scenario created by the negotiating team is true. The best arguments and most compelling realities mean nothing if the adversary feels that he or she cannot trust the individual delivering them. The more credible the arguments presented by the negotiator, the swifter and safer the resolution of the kidnapping is likely to be. Arguments must be believable on their own merits; however, the manner in which they are delivered is even more important.

Kidnappers must never be told something that they can easily disprove. If a negotiator claims that he or she is trying to sell the home to raise money, a for sale sign must be in front of the house. Similarly, if a claim is made that a family member has broken down and been hospitalized, someone needs to be lying in bed in the sanatorium and receiving treatment for a stress-related ailment.

What the victim may know and be willing to share while under extreme duress is significant. All kidnappers interview victims to some extent seeking information they can use as leverage against the family. Interrogations of victims can range from calm and cursory to hostile and exhaustive; all will lead to disclosure of "proprietary" information. What a victim knows or may state needs to be considered when responding to demands, threats and negotiating ploys. If a negotiator makes a statement that can easily be proven wrong by consulting with the victim, the credibility that has been carefully developed over days, weeks or months of intensive effort can be destroyed.

Negotiators should seek to take charge of the negotiation by engendering a relationship with the adversary in which the kidnapper feels that a bond of trust has been established and that only by working together will a solution be achieved. By gaining control of the communication from an unwitting adversary, negotiators can steer the process to a more favorable result. This is not to say that all adversaries are unwitting or that control can easily be obtained; however, in virtually every case, a sufficient level of rapport can be established whereby a solution is more easily achieved. This process takes time; no negotiator should expect the kidnappers to beg him or her to resolve the problem after only a couple of telephone calls. The process of gaining control, however, begins with an initial dialogue carefully crafted to optimize all potential advantages a negotiator may have.

Outside influences should be considered and employed as much as possible; no subject is taboo if the result is a favorable outcome. For example, if the adversary indicates directly or indirectly that he or she is Catholic, having him or her swear by the Virgin that the victim is unharmed and will be released safely helps build empathy and reduce the potential for violence. If the kidnapper is a Moslem, praising

Allah every time he or she calls may also help to a degree. Nothing is off limits; religion, politics, race, creed, sports, economics or any other subject can be used to build rapport. Obviously, this requires careful attention and a delicate touch; simply telling an adversary that since we both like baseball my son should be released is most definitely a non-starter.

The bonding between opposing negotiators is a process that can be almost immediate or can take weeks or months. Much depends on the frequency of communication, parameters laid down by both sides, probability of violence, expectations, and levels of paranoia on both sides. During a kidnapping everyone in both parties is nervous and negotiators must seek to provide an atmosphere of steadfastness to which both sides can cleave. When this is successful, both sides will look to their negotiators to provide a mutually acceptable solution. If both sides feel that the other has given everything possible, and that the proposed solution benefits both sides, a ransom can be paid and victim(s) released unharmed.

Offer Development

How much to offer as a ransom payment is a critical decision. Offer too much and the victim may be killed or the kidnappers may decide to victimize the same family or organization again at a future time. Offer too little and the kidnappers may view the situation as untenable or not serious, with concomitant complications. There is no "textbook" offer. Each situation is different and requires careful analysis of multiple factors, leading to a decision that can have life or death implications.

The first issue to consider in formulating an offer is how much money is available. Obviously, one cannot offer what one does not have or is unable to obtain. Kidnappers typically ask for sums that are unattainable and families or organizations must determine how far they are willing or able to go in putting together a ransom payment.

Expectations are often conflicting and this can lead to some extremely tense moments. In many situations, the family of a kidnap victim is shocked by the realization that an organization will not pay millions of dollars in ransom for one of their employees and that a protracted negotiation will be necessary. The family presupposes that their loved one is as valuable in financial terms to the organization as he or she is to them. When confronted with the reality that this may not be the case, arguments and conflict frequently ensue.

This is not to state that any given organization is uncaring. The dichotomy lies in any family's desire to have a loved one returned immediately, irrespective of cost, and an organization's need to look at the overall picture and make cogently reasoned decisions that may impact on all members of the organization. These issues are not necessarily in total conflict; the victim's family must understand the negotiation process and what this portends, while the organization needs to provide necessary support. A meeting of the minds is very important; a kidnapping can be resolved in spite of disagreements or injured sensibilities. A clear understanding of the lengths to which every interested party is willing to go makes for a smoother solution.

Once everyone concerned is aware of how much participation is to be expected and, in particular, how much money is available, developing an offer can begin. An offer is not made in a vacuum. Offers must be considered in the context of a strategy designed to communicate to the kidnappers both a willingness to cooperate and to make a firm statement from the beginning as to how far the family or organization is willing or able to go. Offers must be logical, justifiable and presented as part of an overall strategy.

Once available funds have been identified, a financial strategy must be developed based on three elements: the initial offer, optimum offer (often referred to as a target settlement figure) and a maximum offer. The initial offer sets the stage for the negotiation process. Depending on how much money is available, kidnappers' demands, ability to pay, information available on similar cases (market conditions), legal considerations and any information that can be developed with respect to the gang of kidnappers, an offer can be formulated.

Frequently, the initial offer is a small fraction of the demand; in other cases, the percentage is much larger. No matter the case, the initial offer is only the first step in the process. Ideally, offers will be made along a continuum that terminates in a resolution at or below the optimum figure. The graph (See Figure 7.1) below demonstrates a typical negotiation process.

Offers are made and rejected and over time and the kidnappers, as a rule, will begin to reduce their demands. Keep in mind that no real negotiation is occurring until the kidnappers move off their initial

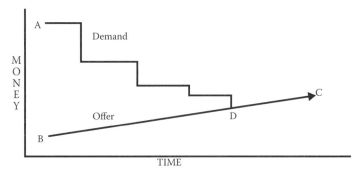

Negotiation Matrix

A - Initial demand
B - Initial offer
C- Maximum available funds
D - Settlement point

Figure 7.1

position; any offers made up until that moment are only money added to the pot. These offers are critically important; they serve to foster further communication and to establish parameters for a resolution.

Kidnapping is a business and kidnappers want to be paid as quickly and as handsomely as possible. The initial offer sends a message to them as to the family or organization's ability and willingness to pay, and this establishes a frame of reference that normally holds true for the entire case. I have seen kidnappings that were resolved in three or four days at a fraction of the initial demand because the kidnappers recognized from the beginning that the payment would end up in a certain range and that they would do well to settle and move on to the next victim. In other cases, kidnappers are patient, organized and willing to wait long periods of time to try and force families or organizations to pay more.

Once kidnappers begin to move away from their initial demand, the negotiation process has begun and progress toward a resolution, albeit very slowly in some cases, can begin. Offers typically progress slowly, in decreasing increments, from the initial offer toward the optimum figure. The two figures must be far enough apart that a few incremental offers do not take the family or organization past the optimum figure and close to the maximum available amount of money before any real movement toward closure has occurred.

Each offer must be proudly presented; this is a demonstration of how much effort has gone into attempting to obtain the funds demanded by the kidnappers. A timid offer will always be summarily rejected; kidnappers use intimidation as a favored tool and, when the offer is presented in a way that reinforces their strength, they can easily disparage and belittle the effort that went into obtaining the funds. If, however, an offer is presented in a manner that illustrates the extreme efforts being made to satisfy the kidnapper's demands, no matter what quantity is presented, the offer requires consideration. This is an essential part of the labor of convincing the kidnappers that the funds offered result from a maximum effort and should not be taken lightly. Over time, as offers are prepared and made, kidnappers will normally begin to lower their expectations and demands.

Pressure

The most difficult aspect of any kidnapping is the psychological pressure applied to the family or organization. The level of stress is truly indescribable and pressure augments steadily as time passes. Kidnappers will use any information or tactic they can devise to apply pressure and get what they want.

Kidnappers have two principal weapons with which to pressure any family or organization. The first and most important is the threat of violence. By nature, a kidnapping fosters uncertainty in the minds of the victim's family or organization. The hostage can be physically or sexually abused, tortured or murdered at the kidnappers' whim. The threat is ever present and cannot be ignored. This is the single most terrifying factor for any family or organization when dealing with a kidnapping.

Juan had been held hostage for more than six weeks. His family and the kidnappers were still speaking of widely divergent figures, although the kidnappers had significantly reduced their original demands. The kidnappers called one evening and informed Juan's son that they did not believe the family was being forthright with the offers and they were going to take action to force the family to negotiate in good faith. They instructed the son to go to a local restaurant where he would find an envelope in a stall in the men's room that contained a "demonstration of their seriousness." Two people were immediately sent to the restaurant with a discreet police shadow and searched the bathroom to no avail. Upon their return, the entire team was distraught, not having encountered anything and fearing that serious harm had been done to the victim. Shortly thereafter, the kidnappers called, insisting that the son describe for them what he had found.

He responded that there had been nothing to find and that they must have been mistaken in sending him to the restaurant. They in turn accused him of sending the police in to pick up "the finger." When he roundly denied (again and again) police involvement, the adversary insisted that he "open the envelope" and describe what he saw. By this time, the son was naturally very upset, worried that the kidnappers may have seriously injured his father and fearful that the team had not searched in the right location.

He insisted that the kidnappers repeat their instructions and sent the team back to the restaurant to look again. They again returned empty-handed. When the kidnappers called again, they replayed the entire scenario of insisting that the son describe the amputated finger. He almost agreed with them that a finger had been found; however, he was able to resist the urge to "tell them what they wanted to hear" and stick to truthful statements. The caller finally admitted that there had been no envelope left anywhere; they apparently thought that such a pressure tactic would force the family to immediately raise the offer. This also reinforced to the family the danger to which Juan was constantly exposed and the kidnappers' power over him.

The threat of violence is always present and most kidnappers do not need to emphasize the possibility at every opportunity. Many adversary negotiators use the threat of violence to apply pressure when they feel it is warranted or when negotiations seem to be stalling or breaking down. Negotiators for the family or organization, however, do not want to hear direct threats of violence and usually try to parry them with arguments as to why the use of violence against the victim is unnecessary when the capability held by the kidnappers is ever present.

I have heard kidnappers threaten to rape, mutilate or kill hostages on many occasions. Negotiators must have the strength of character necessary to listen to these threats and to respond calmly and logically to the kidnappers in a manner designed to reduce the probability of violence. Not all kidnappers can be dissuaded from committing violence against defenseless hostages; however, most recognize that their business depends on the "merchandise" being returned in good condition.

This is an important distinction, particularly when one considers how often the argument is advanced that if no one paid a ransom, kidnappings would quickly disappear. While payment of ransoms enables kidnapping to flourish, no one wants to be the first to risk his or her loved one in establishing a no-negotiation policy. This policy did not work during the Iran–Contra incident and is no more likely to do so against kidnappers than against international terrorists. In fact, terrorists seeking financing commit a significant number of high-value kidnappings each year.

Violence is a tool for professional kidnappers and is used on occasion to send messages to other potential victims as well as to a family or organization perceived as insufficiently cooperative. Violence committed by psychopathic or sociopathic individuals is a random variable that is unpredictable. While this is a cause for constant concern, negotiators can only make good faith efforts to counter threats and maintain the dialogue on an even keel. If gratuitous violence is to be inflicted on the victim, this will likely happen no matter what.

The second weapon is time; only the kidnappers have the power to decide when the situation is over. They often threaten to hold hostages for years (some actually do) and this can create immense strain. The longer a situation continues, the greater the level of stress on family and organization members. In many cases, I have heard kidnappers make statements to the effect that they have all the time in the world and that they will wait a year or two if necessary as well as other similar declarations designed to urge the family or organization to rapidly comply with their demands.

When they are not satisfied with the progress of negotiations, kidnappers will often cease communicating for a time. This can be days, weeks or months depending on factors such as the kidnapper's financial capability to wait, logistics infrastructure for maintaining the victim in captivity, belief in the family or organization's ability to pay far more than is being offered, or simply as a tactic to add pressure.

The use of time as a weapon varies between kidnapping gangs and from country to country. The longest-duration kidnappings are normally politically motivated and barely qualify as kidnapping for ransom, although a ransom may be demanded and, in many cases, paid for the victim's release. For example, many kidnap victims in Colombia have spent years in captivity before being released. Insurgent groups with the express purpose of obtaining a ransom payment may have originally kidnapped these individuals; however, their kidnappings also had a significant political aspect. In Colombia, however, the complete degeneration of the FARC from an insurrectionist movement to a caretaker organization for narcotics traffickers has exacerbated a number of long-term hostage situations. These situations have seemingly become principally an excuse or a front to maintain a "revolutionary" posture, rather than kidnappings for ransom by drug runners.

Nonetheless, the use of time as a means of applying pressure on a family or organization can never be taken for granted. When a family member has been held for a few weeks and kidnappers suddenly cut off communication for five or six days, the loss of communication can be an extremely effective weapon that places enormous additional pressure on the family to come up with a higher ransom payment offer. Frequently, families in particular, fall prey to this tactic and offer double, triple or even more money once contact is reestablished in the hope that their "good faith" efforts will be rewarded with a swift solution.

In most cases the result is exactly the opposite. The fact that a significant boost in the offer was made after cutting communication provides two things to the kidnappers. One, this proves that the initial line of negotiation was based on false pretenses and tells them that the family cannot be trusted to negotiate truthfully since they obviously had access to more funding in spite of all their previous protestations. Second, this tactic also demonstrates very clearly to the kidnappers that they can get results by cutting off communication and provides them with an incentive to repeat the tactic as many times as they wish until the desired result is achieved.

Both tactics can be countered by quick thinking and calm, reasoned responses. When violence is threatened, negotiators need to respond by calmly stating that they understand that the kidnappers are capable of performing such acts; however, these types of actions are unnecessary and counterproductive. Kidnappers must be told that violence toward the victim will not aid in a solution of the situation and that the family or organization is under sufficient pressure and negotiators must reiterate that every effort is being made to obtain the funds requested.

The manner is which this information is delivered is important and depends on the relationship established with the adversary negotiator. The adversary negotiator needs to feel that he or she is in control, but the message must be clear that violence toward the victim will likely lead to unnecessary complications and could ruin everything that has been accomplished. The focus must be returned to the businesslike nature of the situation at hand.

When kidnappers threaten to keep the hostage for an extended or indefinite period of time, a rapid response of a different type is necessary. The kidnappers should be told in no uncertain terms that time is not the issue, finances are. They need to be told that no matter how long the hostage is held, the overall financial parameters will not change, the family or organization is doing everything possible, and the amount of money available is not likely to increase significantly over time.

These arguments may not completely dissuade the criminals from committing acts of violence or extending the time during which the hostage is held captive; however, any time the kidnappers exercise these types of threats, an immediate counter is necessary. Simple, meek acceptance of threats only fosters an increased sense of dominance on the kidnapper's part and does not substantively contribute to a resolution.

Both possibilities influence the negotiation. Any time these are employed, a judgment must be made as to the probability that the kidnappers will carry out the threat. They may have made the same threat yesterday or the day before, but careful consideration is required to determine whether conditions have changed and whether the threatened activity has become more or less likely. In extreme cases, this decision can lead to a significant modification of the negotiating strategy.

Communication Process

Multiple forms of communication are available to kidnappers and negotiators. These include landline or cellular telephone, radio, e-mail, blogs, website postings, traditional letters, communication through newspaper or magazine advertisements and many other tactics. This section will focus on protocols and measures based on telephonic communication; however, the ideas discussed have a broad applicability to virtually any form of communication between kidnappers and a family or organization. In the overwhelming majority of cases, telephonic communication is the swiftest and surest way for both parties to resolve a situation.

As stated on multiple occasions, kidnapping is primarily a business, and participants must be prepared to negotiate in a manner similar to a business deal. The situation is diametrically opposed to a traditional business deal; however, it is similar to a business transaction in that a lack of preparation can lead to disastrous results. A great deal of preparation is necessary before and after each communication.

The negotiating team must establish goals for each call or communication. These goals might include lowering the kidnappers' expectations, obtaining proof of life, and establishing an improved rapport with the adversary negotiator. Two or three goals should be set for each call and every effort should be made to address these issues during the conversation. Obviously, a negotiator cannot directly state the goals nor attempt to impose his or her will directly on the adversary. Tact, discipline and subtlety are necessary to achieve substantive results. A direct approach can be useful under certain circumstances; however, this is not recommended during the course of most kidnapping negotiations.

John was negotiating for the release of his wife. He felt that rapport had been established with the kidnappers and, against advice, decided to be very direct. He told the adversary that since they were both from the same area and had so much in common, they needed to "cut to the chase" and get the situation resolved. The adversary was insulted by his presumption and told him so, informing him in choice words that they had nothing in common and that John would soon get a demonstration of what they were capable of doing. John was very surprised that the adversary had not agreed with him and nervous that he had caused a potentially problematic situation for his spouse. The negotiations basically had to be restarted and the process of establishing credibility re-initiated. This was a major factor in causing the kidnapping to last more than a month when similar incidents were resolved in ten to fifteen days.

After each call is complete, the exchange should be carefully reviewed and the potential need to refocus or reorient the negotiation evaluated.

Practicing between calls is always a good idea; this affords the negotiator an opportunity to rehearse a number of different ways to approach the issues and will highlight any particularly egregious errors prior to the next call. This should be done with a partner playing the role of the adversary and he or she should undertake to mimic insofar as possible the perceived style of the adversary.

A series of visual aids should be posted around the room in which the calls are to be taken and the negotiator should be familiar with their location and content. These may include key phrases, arguments, responses, goals, segues and any other information that might be useful during a conversation with the kidnappers. Passing a legibly written note during a call is often much more difficult than simply pointing to an already prepared talking point, argument or segue. This practice also encourages the negotiator to look up and stay focused on the task at hand rather than becoming distracted or absorbed in consideration of the victim's current state or in potential negative outcomes.

For each call, the arguments that are to be used must be evaluated and carefully considered. Each tool must be considered within the context of an approach that seeks to communicate (for example) a message that the family or organization is unable to meet kidnappers' demands and that kidnappers need to lower their expectations. This means that simply telling the kidnappers that one cannot get together the amount of money they are demanding is insufficient. Justifications, rationales and arguments must be presented at every opportunity, keeping in mind that, once a sum is mentioned, kidnappers will turn off the negotiator as quickly as adolescent children do their parents.

Arguments presented must follow a basic theme; in almost every case this is the (normally) factual line that meeting the kidnappers' demands is not possible. A series of convincing reasons should be developed and these presented each time the kidnappers call. Over time, this practice begins to build a degree of belief on the part of the adversary, no matter what he or she might believe going in. The same arguments can be presented in varied forms at each opportunity; however, a selection of reasons or statements should be developed and alternate lines of reasoning or types of arguments should be interspersed. A simple repetition of the same objections over and over rapidly becomes tiring for everyone involved and decreases, rather than increases, credibility. Remember that no argument should ever be used that can be easily disproved! This is the quickest way to destroy a credible relationship that may have taken weeks or months to develop and can wreak havoc with the negotiation process.

Negotiators must realize that this is their opportunity to communicate and begin to take control of the negotiation. The one time when an adversary is most likely to listen to what you have to say is when he or she is waiting for you to state a definitive offer. The rest of the time he or she is most likely advancing his or her agenda and usually not in a listening mode. This can lead to tense moments in which the adversary negotiator repeatedly insists on hearing how much is offered, while the negotiator patiently places his or her chips on the table only after stating the case for acceptance. While this may sound strange, remember that the adversary wants to know how much money is offered and will almost always listen, if not too carefully, to everything the negotiator has to say until a specific sum is mentioned. Once a definite amount of money is offered, there is very little likelihood that the adversary will pay much attention to anything else a negotiator says, certainly not within the next minute or so. He or she will either be communicating the offer to his hierarchy, considering the offer within the context of instructions received, or belittling the offer as insufficient, accompanied by threats of dire consequences if an increase is not immediately forthcoming.

This is the time a negotiator must be strongest. When an offer is made, one must expect calumny and threats to immediately follow. Remember, the offer just presented is based on a thorough analysis of the situation and is not just a number that can be modified at will. Raising an offer on the spot gives the lie to everything that is being constructed in terms of a relationship and the flow of a negotiation. The most adequate response is a promise to continually try to do better, accompanied by a plea for rationality and understanding in the amount being sought.

Managing Money

Kidnapping is a cash-intensive business; those who hold the hostage do not take credit cards and only the most sophisticated have been known to accept wire transfers passed through an interminable chain of relays, forwarding and dead ends. For the most part, ransoms are paid in cash and hostages are returned only after the cash has been counted and secured. This militates for careful management of all funds involved in the process, from ransom money to expenditures.

There is always a need for operational funds; food, supplies, equipment, gasoline and a multitude of other unexpected or unusual expenses always occur during the negotiation. These funds should be considered, the money set aside and never mixed with or drawn from previously offered ransom money.

Money used for a ransom payment must be securely stored, counted regularly and never commingled with operational funds. This could lead to disaster. Borrowing a banded stack of cash from a bag in which ransom money is contained in order to pay an unexpected bill leaves the ransom that much short if the kidnappers decide to accept the offer at that precise moment. If a ransom dispatched is even a little short of the agreed-upon sum, the hostage could suffer the consequences.

Ransom money should be treated in a very special manner. As funds are accumulated, they should be carefully counted, organized into bundles of specific amounts (e.g., $10,000, $20,000, etc.) and each bundle separately labeled. The serial number of each bill should be recorded. As money is put into the container in which the ransom is to be delivered, a running total should be kept of how much is on hand. Each offer to the kidnappers should be for only the exact amount contained in the ransom deposit. If the offer is accepted, that amount only will be dispatched.

When money is counted, a trusted family member should always be involved in the process. No matter who is providing the cash, a family member should always verify the count as money is placed into the ransom pool. In the words of an old Russian proverb, "Trust, but verify." This practice can avoid later misunderstandings and ensures that what is promised is what is delivered.

In some situations, I have seen excessive amounts of money on hand and a total lack of preparation for a timely delivery. One must understand that, for the kidnappers, acceptance of an amount almost always leads to delivery of the ransom within a very short period of time and the time to start counting and bundling money is not when they are anxiously awaiting departure of the delivery element. Before each offer is made, the exact amount should be prepared, counts verified by at least two different people, and the funds made ready for delivery. The money should be prepared, preferably stored in a convenient off-site location, and ready to be dispatched at a moment's notice.

The idea of offsite storage is simple; keeping large amounts of cash around a location, whether a residence or an office, from which a kidnapping is being negotiated, is both foolish and dangerous. I am familiar with situations in which criminal elements (tipped or prompted by the kidnappers?) conducted a home invasion to get the ransom money that they suspected was being kept in the home of a current kidnap victim. If this happens, the kidnappers will insist on negotiating anew and any damages suffered by the family or organization, financial or otherwise, are ancillary to the kidnapping that must still be resolved. No matter whether the funds are stored in an offsite location or kept in the same place from which negotiations are being conducted, leading the kidnappers to believe that the money is stored "at a friend's house" or some other location is always good practice.

Unless specifically instructed to do so by the kidnappers, there is no need to ensure that all bills are in any particular condition or denomination. In fact, sending only freshly minted bills of a particular denomination with their bank bands intact can be interpreted by the kidnappers as a sign that the ransom does not include all available funds. Consider that a family or organization, struggling to reach an agreed-upon sum, dispatches only fresh money. As a kidnapper, this practice would seem highly suspicious. If the negotiator has been telling the truth, funds undoubtedly would have been obtained from diverse sources and the makeup of the package should reflect that fact. Sometimes, kidnappers request at the last minute that jewelry, watches or other items be placed in the package as well. If this is necessary to close the deal, the step should be considered and carefully selected items may be included in the ransom delivery.

Proof of Life

This is obviously a critical issue in any kidnapping situation. The family or organization absolutely must know at regular intervals during the entire process that the hostage is alive and able to function. Without sufficient guarantee that the victim is alive and well, no serious negotiations can be conducted and no ransom will ever be delivered. Kidnappers are aware of this. Often, however, they will delay, deny or decline to facilitate the process. While this is normally just another attempt to put psychological pressure on a family or organization, in some cases the refusal can also indicate that the hostage has been maimed or killed. Since the family or organization has no other verifiable way of determining the victim's condition, they must insist on a proof of life at regular intervals.

This begs the question as to the nature of an acceptable proof of life. What is this proof and how can one be sure that the evidence offered is genuine? In our technologically sophisticated age, short of an actual conversation with the victim, pictures, audiotapes, video and almost everything else can be feigned. In spite of the possibility of false evidence being prepared and submitted as genuine in an attempt to deceive the family or organization, there are a number of difficult to counterfeit and almost completely verifiable measures.

The most definite proof of life and the one that should be sought at every opportunity is a chance to speak to the hostage. This is becoming increasingly difficult to achieve; kidnappers watch a lot of television programs and tend to believe that law enforcement has the capability to simply "throw a switch" and detect the exact point of origin of any given telephone transmission. They are therefore loath to permit a hostage to speak on the telephone and in those cases in which he or she is permitted to do so, the communication is kept necessarily brief. This does not obviate the need to regularly insist on speaking to the victim. The kidnappers may accede to the request and, if not, all they can do is say no.

Other less direct ways of obtaining proof of life can be, except in extremely unusual circumstances, acceptable. The most common are personal questions, the answers to which only the victim is able to provide. As discussed earlier, these questions must be carefully crafted so as not to be so simplistic that the kidnappers are able to guess the answers or have gotten the information from the victim in an interrogation. Nor should the questions be so complex that the victim, under intense stress, will have extreme difficulty answering them. I have seen cases in which the victim was unable to answer the questions asked; however, he or she provided a tale or description that was sufficiently detailed and private to convince the family or organization.

The use of dated pictures or videotapes can also be acceptable, as long as the date is shown by a daily newspaper or weekly newsmagazine held by the victim in the photograph or on the videotape. The use of videotape injects additional potential complications into the situation. The hostage may be compelled by the kidnappers, or of his or her own volition think that negotiations are stagnant and that no end is in sight. He or she therefore might make recommendations or suggestions, identify potential additional sources of funding, or even remind family or organization members where hidden sums can be located. Make no mistake: a hostage laboring under incredible stress is absolutely the worst possible negotiator. This frequently occurs when an executive is kidnapped. The executive, being accustomed to making decisions, tries to apply his or her customary logic to an illogical situation, with predictably dismal results. An active attempt by a hostage to insert himself or herself into a negotiation is a complication that can only work in favor of the kidnappers.

The patriarch of a family had been kidnapped and the kidnappers refused all requests for direct communication. They would neither accept any questions to pass along nor provide any evidence that the individual was safe and sound and in acceptably good health. After a few weeks, negotiations had bogged down; there was a lack of trust on both sides, exacerbated by the kidnappers' reluctance to facilitate any form of communication with the victim. Finally, the kidnappers called and gave instructions that, under a public phone on a certain corner of a designated intersection, the family would encounter a message from the victim. When we arrived at the designated location, we immediately noticed that there were four telephones installed; one on each corner of the intersection. Of course, at the fourth one checked there was indeed a videocassette firmly taped to the underside of the housing in which the telephone was mounted. "Firmly taped" is an egregious understatement. In order to be sure that the cassette would remain in place, the kidnappers had used a double sticky, black, tar-like tape about one-eighth inch thick, with the holding power of reinforced concrete. I felt around under the housing, located the cassette, grabbed it and pulled firmly. When nothing happened, I grabbed it and pulled very firmly, my hand slipped off again, and I stumbled off the curb and into the street, narrowly missing a passing bus.

After having my sobriety questioned and my heritage loudly insulted from the windows of the bus, I indignantly approached the telephone intending to rip loose and pocket the cassette and casually stroll back to the waiting car with my dignity more or less intact. This was not to be the case. For nearly three minutes I wrestled with the cassette before I was able to twist it loose and slink back to the car, videocassette (tape still firmly attached) in hand, dignity in shreds. To his credit, the family friend who accompanied me simply asked if I had retrieved the item, put the car in gear, and drove away. This process was repeated twice more during the kidnapping, each time with the location being in a more dangerous neighborhood to facilitate the (obvious) surveillance of those sent to recover the cassette. By the third time, I was having dreams about a horrible, viscous, sticky substance.

The tapes were of the victim, blindfolded and holding a current newspaper in his lap with the date clearly visible, appealing to his family to immediately pay the kidnappers' demands and secure his release. Each time we recovered a tape, we knew immediately that he was, up until that point in time, in relatively good condition. When a deal was finally struck with the kidnappers they did permit the hostage to speak briefly with a family member prior to dispatch of the ransom payment.

As a general rule, proof of life should be requested and received at least twice a week. In many situations, once a certain level of credibility has been established, the adversary will end a call by asking for the next series of questions and initiate the following call by providing the answers. This arrangement, acceptable during an ongoing negotiation, does not, however, provide immediate confirmation of the victim's well being.

When a deal is struck and a ransom is to be dispatched, a real-time proof of life is necessary. Trading questions from a day or more in the past does not suffice; the family or organization absolutely must know that the hostage is alive (and well) prior to releasing the ransom for delivery. The best way to accomplish this is by speaking to the victim and kidnappers will frequently allow a momentary chat immediately before the drop. If this is not permitted, the minimum acceptable measure would be some questions submitted and answered within a defined time frame ahead of the delivery. This defined time frame cannot be more than a couple of hours and should be strictly limited to ensure that the victim is in good condition when the ransom goes out the door.

Offer Acceptance

A final agreement between kidnappers and negotiator depends solely on the whim of the kidnappers. No kidnapping is over, nor has an agreement been reached, until the kidnappers agree to an offer of a specific ransom amount. They, and only they, decide how much will be accepted and when this will happen. No matter how reasonable the offer seems to the family or organization or how much effort has gone into accumulating the funds and preparing the ransom, if the kidnappers are not satisfied, there is no deal.

Final agreement on a ransom amount can usually be sensed a few days before the kidnappers actually indicate their acceptance of an offer. As the two sides inch closer together and the difference between the amounts offered and demanded shrinks, the negotiation often takes on a sense of inevitability. Both sides realize that they have made their best effort and that there is little left to say that will change things. Neither is willing or able to give much more ground and so a deal becomes more attractive and more likely.

Kidnappers normally try to force a bump in the ransom offer at the last moment. In cases of smaller ransom payments, this might include forcing friends and family members to rush to the nearest ATM machine and withdraw funds; insisting that jewelry, watches or other such items are included; or simply drawing a line somewhat above the current proposal and offering to settle immediately for that amount. This can be a trick to determine whether or not the family or organization is truly reaching the limits of its possibilities, or whether they have conducted a shrewd negotiation. If the kidnappers feel they are being misled, they may reopen negotiations with much higher expectations.

The kidnappers had originally demanded four million dollars ransom for John's freedom, a sum totally beyond all possibility. They knew this from the beginning; however, they used such a staggeringly high figure both to intimidate and as a prod to push the family to come up with as much money as possible. After weeks of negotiations, the family was offering around seventy-five thousand dollars and the kidnappers were demanding around three hundred thousand. They dropped their demand to two hundred thousand when the family was able to come up with another three thousand dollars. Closure seemed near and the family was hoping that within days a solution could be reached.

Unexpectedly, given their prior lack of participation in the situation, the organization for which John worked suddenly delivered one hundred thousand dollars to the family's attorney for use in the ransom payment. This money, offered with no strings attached, could be added to the ransom offer at any time. This sparked an intense debate among the management team, as some family members wanted to immediately add to the offer and others sided with their advisors in believing that this step would send a dangerous signal that all the foregoing negotiations were based on false pretenses.

When the kidnappers called and asked for one hundred sixty thousand dollars, the negotiator immediately agreed. They hung up on him and waited four long hours before calling back. The adversary negotiator stated that, although the band was sure that a lot more money was available, they were going to accept the offer. The negotiator, properly, protested that no more was available and that a donation had been received that enabled him to raise the offer. The kidnappers finally acceded. The ransom was paid and the victim released on the following day.

In this case, the family was extremely fortunate that the kidnappers chose to take the money, rather than reopen negotiations. The timing of a sudden dramatic increase to a sum more than double that of any previous offers, after weeks of arduous negotiations, was suspicious, and the kidnappers had every right to doubt everything that they had previously been told. Destruction of the negotiator's credibility would have quite likely forced a change in personnel and a new process of relationship building to reestablish credibility and achieve a solution.

When a solution is reached, there is normally a sense of unbridled joy among the participants. The feeling that the nightmare is over and that everything will now be fine must, however, be strictly controlled. The situation is not over until the hostage walks safely through the door! In fact the most difficult and dangerous time of the entire situation is about to begin.

8
RESOLUTION

Suffering isn't ennobling, recovery is.

Christiaan N. Barnard

The basis of optimism is sheer terror.

Oscar Wilde, the Picture of Dorian Gray

Ransom Delivery

Delivering an agreed-upon ransom is the beginning of a period of extreme danger for the victim, as he or she becomes a significant liability to the kidnappers once they have received their money. They no longer want to have the victim on their hands and need to release him or her as soon as possible and under conditions that maximize their chances to successfully escape. The period of time from the moment the ransom is physically delivered until the first appearance of or report from the victim is a time of intense anxiety for the family or organization.

If a victim is to be executed after days, weeks or months of negotiation, this normally occurs after the ransom is collected. Sufficient proof of the victim's well-being has been received by the family or organization, funds have been prepared and delivered, and the victim never returns or is later found dead. The trauma, self-examination and recrimination that such a sequence of events can cause are indescribable. Everyone seeks someone to blame; moral persons have difficulty accepting the fact that there are truly evil people in the world who will commit such crimes without a second thought. Fortunately, this represents a small fraction of all kidnappings worldwide; there would be no business to conduct if too many victims were executed.

Ransom deliveries can be structured in a multitude of ways. Negotiators always ask for a face-to-face exchange of money for hostage; however, this is very rare. Such an exchange is a virtual guarantee that the kidnappers will come immediately to the end of a short but illustrious criminal career as they are arrested leaving the exchange. This actually happened in a case in Acapulco, Mexico. The kidnappers agreed to be on hand for the delivery in a parking lot. The money was duly exchanged for the hostage and the victim and his family member immediately departed. As the kidnappers were attempting to leave the scene, they were rounded up and arrested. Stupid kidnappers generally have very short careers.

The reality is that in almost all cases, the money must be dispatched and delivered according to instructions received from the kidnappers that indicate the victim will be released afterward. The wait is agonizing; however, there is no other mutually agreeable course of action in cases in which a single victim is taken. If there are multiple victims, the delivery can sometimes be arranged around the release of one or more victims in a release–pay–release sequence. This, however, can be risky, as the kidnappers may attempt to reopen negotiations for an additional ransom for the remaining victim(s).

In an overwhelming majority of cases, ransoms are delivered within a few hundred kilometers of the kidnap location. International ransoms are rare; however, they do occur and they carry a different set of variables and problems.

When the delivery is to be made to a locale near where the kidnapping took place and was negotiated, the process is generally similar to the following. Once an agreement has been reached, kidnappers normally are in a tremendous hurry to receive their money and insist on nearly immediate delivery of the ransom. This is why any amount offered must always be on hand or nearby and ready to go at a moment's notice. Kidnappers do not want to hear that the negotiator needs a couple of hours or days to prepare the ransom for delivery. They may break off negotiations or insist on more money if delivery of the ransom cannot be quickly accomplished.

Before leaving to make any ransom delivery, a current proof of life must be obtained and verified. Most kidnappers know this and are prepared to permit a brief, direct communication with the victim or provide immediate answers to proof of life questions to reassure the family or organization that the victim is alive and well and that the money can be released. As good businesspersons, kidnappers will wish to facilitate payment.

In most cases, a local ransom is delivered by a family member or trusted friend. A concerted effort should always be made to insist that two people make the delivery. This, rather than being an opportunity for law enforcement, permits the delivery person to operate much more efficiently and easily follow all instructions from the kidnappers without having to drive, juggle cell phones, look for landmarks, get in and out of the vehicle, etc.

The mere suggestion that more than one person should accompany the delivery will normally elicit a spate of objections because kidnappers will immediately assume that the second person is a police officer either looking to gather information for later investigation and prosecution or present to try and facilitate an arrest. Negotiators need to stand firm on the requirement and insist that, for security reasons, no family member or friend is going to make a delivery alone. In many cases with which I am familiar, kidnappers have acceded to the demand and allowed a second individual to drive while the designated delivery person follows instructions and actually drops the ransom. In others, they have absolutely refused to permit a companion in the vehicle and insisted that only a single person make the delivery.

Kidnappers often ask that the negotiator be the one to deliver the ransom since he or she is the one individual with whom a credible relationship has been built. My perception is that in many cases they just want to get a look at the person who has been involved. In cases in which the negotiator is a female, a much firmer stance can be taken on the need to send two persons and the kidnappers normally more easily accept this. No matter who conducts the negotiations, delivery by two persons should always be sought, although the kidnappers may not agree no matter what justification is provided. For the family or organization, sending an additional person on the delivery is a security issue that makes the event much less stressful on the individual who must conduct the actual drop. Adding a second person to the delivery team also reduces the possibility that a prepared ransom may be diverted.

Joe volunteered to deliver a ransom for a family that had suffered a kidnapping. As a close family friend, he was trusted and there was no one else available who could be made acceptable to the kidnappers. They spoke directly with him, called his residence to verify his identity, and

*agreed that he was not a police officer and could make the delivery. He
left, following their instructions and was gone for four hours, after
which he reported that he had been held up and the money taken from
him at gunpoint. At approximately the same time, the kidnappers called
demanding to know why he would not answer their calls and insisting
that they receive their money.*

*The family had no recourse but to believe him, reopen negotiations
with kidnappers and continue to seek resources for the liberation of their
loved one, a process that lasted a further six weeks. No one was able to
determine with certainty whether Joe had actually been robbed or if
he had pocketed the money. This uncertainty was never fully resolved.
In addition to making an already difficult situation virtually unbear-
able and causing the nightmare to continue another six weeks, a lifelong
friendship was destroyed by suspicion and mistrust.*

Kidnappers sometimes will request that the delivery be made in a vehicle of a specific make, model and/or color. This is seldom a measure to
afford them an opportunity to steal a specific vehicle; most kidnappers
are far too paranoid to have the delivery team leave a vehicle for them
to take. They would probably expect that any vehicle left for them
would have multiple tracking devices installed. They may even insist
that the delivery person or team wear specific clothing or certain col-
ors. They may insist that a certain cellular phone be taken, a marking
be put on the windshield of the delivery vehicle, or impose any number of other conditions. None of these conditions can realistically be
refused, unless they interfere with a safe delivery. As long as the funds
can be safely dispatched and delivered, the members of the delivery
team can shave their heads if that pleases the kidnappers. Remember,
the overriding priority is to achieve the victim's safe return.

The vehicle to be used for the ransom delivery must be in excellent
mechanical condition. If a vehicle has been identified and set aside for
use, the vehicle should receive any necessary maintenance and always
have a full tank of gasoline. Some deliveries last for hours and the
vehicle must be adequately prepared. Vehicles should be equipped
with water, some sort of food items, a medical kit, an empty bottle
or two for necessities, and one or two spare cellular telephones. If a
vehicle tracking system is available, this should be installed, tested

and function properly. A record of all the vehicle's movements can be downloaded afterward for analysis if necessary.

After 26 days of negotiation, an agreement was reached. The kidnappers would allow two persons to deliver the ransom; the woman with whom they had negotiated and a driver. They insisted that the family obtain a white pickup truck with an uncovered bed and that both members of the delivery team wear white overalls. The family obtained a white pickup truck and the bed was loaded with damp sand and two-by-fours to provide extra traction on unimproved road surfaces. Both occupants were dressed head-to-toe in white overalls and they remained so for seven hours while being maneuvered to and fro until the kidnappers were satisfied that no one was tailing them. After the hostage's safe return, the delivery driver was forever dubbed, "the Good Humor man."

In most cases, the vehicle will depart from the office or residence and begin to receive instructions via cellular telephone from the kidnappers. These are driving directions, for example, "Go onto Route 234 and continue west." At some point along that route, an observer will be posted who normally notes the characteristics of the vehicle and any following vehicles. Directions will be called in periodically and the driver will be put through a variety of turns, be told to double back or made to stop and wait in a given location. Almost any observer can be part of the kidnapping team and those individuals will be posted and moved as the kidnappers see fit to observe the delivery vehicle as many times as necessary until they are satisfied that no police units are trailing the ransom.

Once the kidnappers are satisfied that the delivery vehicle does not have a tail, then and only then will they direct the vehicle toward the point where the ransom is to be dropped off. This may be a location that has been passed multiple times already or it may be a remote location. Each kidnapping group decides where its members are most comfortable receiving the ransom, usually in a location that they feel is under their control. When the vehicle arrives at or near the location in which the ransom is to be dropped, the kidnappers call with specific instructions.

Bob and Pete (negotiator) were delivering a ransom. They had taken Pete's brother's car since the vehicle was nearly new and in excellent condition. They left the victim's residence with the ransom at the kidnapper's behest and proceeded to a traffic circle, where they parked as instructed. After a wait of nearly half an hour, the kidnappers called, demanding to know their location. The kidnappers were told where they were and asked about Pete's car (obviously having found out the relevant details from the victim). Pete responded that he had borrowed his brother's car and that he was sitting exactly where they had instructed him to be. They made him wait another ten minutes (checking on the brother's car with the victim and/or notifying surveillance team members?) and then proceeded to give further instructions.

After many twists and turns, including repeated sightings of the same individuals trying not to be noticed as the vehicle passed, the kidnappers finally gave the key instructions. Pete was ordered to stop on an overpass where there was a paint bucket lying next to the guardrail and to throw the bag containing the ransom over the railing. He did so and then leaned over the railing to see what he could observe. Once he returned to the car, the team immediately left the area and returned to the residence. Fortunately, two hours later the victim walked in the front door.

This vignette demonstrates a number of things that could have gone wrong. The delivery team switched cars at the last moment, causing needless delay and confusion. The negotiator could have told the kidnappers precisely which vehicle was being used so as not to delay the delivery any longer than necessary. The kidnappers showed inexperience (always a cause for alarm) by using too few observers in exposed positions, any one of which could have been rolled up had the shadowing authorities been so inclined. Pete had no business looking over the guardrail. His mission was complete as soon as the bag left his hand. His attempt to see what was below could have been misinterpreted with potentially fatal consequences.

The authorities in this case were highly professional; they shadowed the delivery at a safe distance and made no overt moves, in spite of the obvious surveillance, until after the hostage had safely returned home. They then made a full-scale effort to apprehend the criminals. In most places, if the police are aware of the situation (and they should be), they will shadow any delivery and not take any overt action until the victim is safe. Their ability to surreptitiously observe the proceedings, however, does facilitate their investigation and can lead to rapid apprehension of the criminals.

The foregoing also displays the need to thoroughly brief a delivery team prior to its departure on any drop. The members must understand a number of basic points. They are on a mission to deliver the money and then get away from the delivery point as quickly as possible; they are not on an intelligence-gathering operation and certainly are not to interact directly with any outsider unless specifically instructed to by the kidnappers. Their function is to drop off the money and leave!

Delivering a ransom can be one of the most nerve-wracking experiences imaginable. Delivery teams do not always receive precise instructions; sometimes they are told only to drive around and then throw money over a guardrail. This is a favored tactic, particularly using isolated overpasses with no easy access from the upper road to the lower, enabling the kidnappers to leave the zone in relative safety. Although a ransom delivery is typically a safe operation for the drop team, they often will have direct encounters with one or more members of the kidnapping gang and need to remember that their only role is delivery, not interrogation or apprehension.

Ralph and Tim spent seven hours on the highways in a mountainous region outside a major city, following instructions and traveling long distances back and forth on the road network while attempting to deliver a large ransom payment. Intermittent cellular signals required that they drive 30 miles along a stretch of highway before they reached a point at which calls and further instructions could be received. After traveling more than 500 miles in one day, they were told to leave the highway and follow a dry wash into a mountain ravine.

After traveling through the ravine for more than a mile over barely navigable terrain, they were confronted by four men armed with AK-47s. They were ordered out of the vehicle at gunpoint, their cellular telephones confiscated, and they were forced to lie face down in the dirt while the ransom was counted and checked for transmitting devices. To this day, Ralph is thankful that he was able to successfully argue against including a transmitter in the bag. After an hour or so (that seemed like a lifetime) they were returned to the car and ordered to back out of the ravine with lights off and then continue on their way. In pitch blackness, this took over three hours; all the while they didn't know whether they were under surveillance or in someone's rifle sights. They returned after almost six hours incommunicado to find that the victim had been released and arrived shortly before they did.

Both parties to the transaction are very interested in successfully concluding any ransom drop. Any action that interferes with this is not acceptable to either side. There have been instances in which interlopers have assaulted the delivery team and stolen the ransom; cases in which corrupt authorities have intervened and taken the money; and even situations in which the money has been delivered to the wrong location due to a misunderstanding or garbled communications. In most cases, proper planning and good execution could have minimized the risk or avoided the situation. Ransom deliveries in general are very safe operations, kidnappers only want to get paid; however, when you step out the door with a bag full of money, anything can, and occasionally does, happen. No matter the circumstances, a cool head and a complete focus on the mission are required to successfully conduct a ransom delivery.

When the kidnapping occurs in one country or province and the ransom must be paid in another, a number of factors impact the equation. Delivery in a different state or province far from the home area, although in the mother country, can be treated as an international drop in most cases because some of the same dynamics are present.

Although always important, communications takes on an even greater significance when larger distances are involved. Consider that the negotiator must coordinate with the delivery team with absolute precision to ensure that a ransom is dispatched in the agreed-upon amount and only after the final proof of life has been received.

Emilio and Juan Jose were in Argentina, prepared to deliver a ransom after a months-long negotiation to free Emilio's brother from the hands of an international band of kidnappers. They were in constant telephone contact with the negotiating team back home and were also receiving regular calls from the kidnappers with instructions as to how the ransom should be packaged and delivered. Once an accord had been reached, they were prepared to depart and make delivery according to the instructions received. Emilio requested a final proof of life and was told to stand by while the questions were submitted and answered. After a delay of some four hours, the negotiating team was given apparently correct answers to the questions. Shortly thereafter, Emilio received final delivery instructions and set out to deliver the ransom. During the ride he received a call from the negotiating team on the spare cell phone he carried, ordering him to immediately return to the hotel. His brother, taking advantage of an opportunity, had escaped from the location in which he was held. He immediately hailed a taxi and went directly home, arriving just in time to prevent delivery of a ransom for an already-freed victim.

Some might think geographic distances do not change the ransom delivery in a fundamental way. After all, money must be paid before a hostage is released; however, in my experience, the greater the distance from base, the greater the opportunity for mishaps large and small. One critical part of the negotiation is reaching agreement as to where the hostage will be released. If the ransom is delivered in a country other than that in which the kidnapping occurred, determining in which country the hostage will be released is important, if only for the peace of mind of the victimized family or organization.

Negotiators should also try to establish timelines vis-à-vis the payment and release. In complicated cases such as these, agreement can often be reached that the victim will be released within a certain timeframe after the ransom delivery. Kidnappers do not often honor such agreements; however, any additional pressure to conform to an agreement is useful. In kidnappings, the only authority with which a family or organization can speak is moral, and every single opportunity should be exploited.

Personal and vehicle tracking systems should be deployed and used as much as possible in all locations associated with the ransom delivery. These facilitate both real-time monitoring and reconstruction of events after the fact should this be necessary. Coordination with local authorities in both places is also recommended, always via a trusted interlocutor. The very act of negotiating with kidnappers is illegal in some countries and care should always be taken to ensure that all actions are within the parameters of that which is permitted.

Release

The most trying time in any kidnapping is the period between ransom delivery and release of the hostage. The family or organization has done the best it could, negotiated in good faith, complied with onerous and often unusual conditions and kept its word to deliver an agreed-upon sum. Once kidnappers have received the money, there are no guarantees, only the expectation that they will keep their word and release the victim unharmed or with no further damage.

The wait seems endless; nervous chatter and self-examination run rampant until the moment news is received. In these moments, the consultant is often taken aside individually by every member of the team to conduct an instant analysis of his or her performance, in the hope that he or she did nothing that might possibly contribute to a less than successful outcome. This is no time for brutal honesty, rather a time in which constant reassurance is the order of the day.

Under "normal" circumstances, the money will be collected, counted and verified; the delivery case or bag will be checked for transmitting devices; and, if all is satisfactory, orders will be given to release the hostage(s). This can be a complicated process; kidnappers see hostages as a distinct liability once they have collected a ransom and feel the need to be very careful in releasing the victim. They need to ensure that the victim sees nothing that might provide a clue to the authorities and that the victim is transported to a safe distance from the holding location and in a manner that makes retracing the route impossible. Many victims report that they spend hours circling and backtracking in a vehicle before being released.

Victims are normally released within 24 to 48 hours of ransom payment; two to four hours is the more common time period. This depends on many factors, such as the settlement amount, distances involved, professionalism of the kidnappers, their level of paranoia, and the geography of the area in which the operation takes place. No matter the circumstances, in more than 90% of all cases the victim is released unharmed after payment of a negotiated ransom.

Eighteen year-old Marcos had spent 28 days in captivity. The ransom had been dropped off at the indicated location after many tortuous hours of driving about the city following the kidnappers's instructions. The family settled in to wait for news. Every few minutes one or another would buttonhole their advisor and ask questions about the case, seeking reassurance that all was going according to plan. After three and one-half hours the phone rang and his mother raced to answer. "Mama, I'm okay, come and pick me up. Hurry!"

The mother broke down in tears and his father grabbed the phone. After a few minutes he was able to ascertain his son's location and told him to sit tight. Two family friends and his uncle, a doctor, were dispatched to pick up the young man. When they arrived at the location he had described, no one was in sight. Two got out of the car and began shouting for the young man. From the shadows of a nearby store, he answered and the uncle raced over to him. He was quickly bundled into the car and the team departed. After a quick call to the family, the uncle checked him for injuries and pronounced him fit. Twenty minutes later he arrived home to a scene of almost indescribable joy.

In any kidnapping case, no moment is more joyful than when the victim is freed. The release can take many forms. A victim may call from a store or residence at a distance from the home or office pleading to be immediately picked up. He or she may suddenly climb out of a taxi and appear at his or her own front door. He or she may be dropped off on a deserted road miles from nowhere and be forced to travel a significant distance to civilization in order to contact family or friends. Every case is different; however, the intense emotion is always the same.

The sheer exhilaration of a reunion of a kidnapped love one with his or her family has been likened to that of a soldier returning from war. Consider, however, that in the case of the soldier, all parties involved will normally have had time to prepare themselves psychologically for the stress and uncertainty of separation. In a kidnapping, a loved one is suddenly torn from the family and his or her release must be negotiated. Emotions are intense and outsiders are well advised to make their goodbyes and fade away as quickly as possible.

Any hostage must undergo a thorough medical examination as soon as possible after being released. In many cases, the family or organization will have a doctor on hand to conduct a rapid examination of the victim to ensure his or her well-being. In cases where severe mistreatment is known or suspected, an ambulance should be standing by to transport the victim to a hospital if necessary. Most victims who have not suffered much physical trauma will insist that they are fine and need no medical attention. Nonetheless, all victims should be examined as soon as is feasible. The level may range from a simple check of vital signs to a complete physical and psychological examination, depending on the victim's age and condition; however, this is a decision that should be taken by a medical professional.

Law enforcement will need to have immediate access to the victim. The sooner he or she can be debriefed, the more timely the information provided. This, however, is frequently a major bone of contention, particularly in countries where the authorities are not well respected. I know of cases in which the authorities followed recently released victims home, only to be refused the opportunity to interview them and fobbed off with a vague promise of a future visit to the police station.

In virtually every developing country, the civilian populace distrusts the police, assumes they are in league with most criminals and wants little or nothing to do with them. This reputation, unfortunately, has been well-earned in most places and contributes to an environment in which kidnappings flourish. Families and organizations must understand that there are honest police officers everywhere and seek to identify and work with them. Only in this way can the scourge be eliminated.

Aftermath

Once a victim has returned home and the kidnapping is over, family members are normally left to pick up the pieces of their shattered lives as best they can. This is a time when support for both victim and family members is of major importance. Families or organizations should expect and be prepared for strange or unusual reactions to common stimuli when a victim returns home. A barking dog, an automobile exhaust, a particular song or television program; all these seemingly innocuous things can trigger a reaction that sometimes borders on panic. Only the victim knows the exact conditions he or she faced during captivity and everyday actions, noises or activities might bring memories flooding back at inopportune moments. Families or organizations should not expect that someone who has spent a period of time (often prolonged) in captivity and was totally dependent upon the whim of those who saw him or her as merchandise for the most basic elements of existence, to simply pick up where he or she left off.

A recently released victim must be treated with respect; however, no family or organization can walk around on tiptoes trying not to offend. In my experience, one of the most difficult hurdles victims face is getting everyone around them to act normally. Many describe the atmosphere as incredibly tense; family members or coworkers are so concerned with making a misstep that they create more problems for the victim. Victims state that they want those around them to act in a normal manner, giving them the opportunity to fit back into the framework of their previous existence.

Nothing can be the same after a kidnapping; however, there are measures that can help ease the transition to a more natural environment. The most important of these is therapy, both for the victim and for close family members. I have always recommended that both victims and families undergo a course of therapy after such an event. Many times, although acknowledging the need, family members opt not to do so. This is understandable; in many places the view is still held that "only crazy people go to shrinks." Unfortunately, not working through the psychological issues derived from a kidnapping situation can lead to long-term deleterious effects in relationships and a lack of productivity for most individuals and family units. Each family member should undergo a course of therapy designed to help him or her work out the issues and conflicts that the kidnapping has caused. I have never met a family member who was unaffected by the kidnapping of a loved one; I have met many whose refusal to embark on a course of therapy left them suffering severe after-effects for years.

Each individual is different. Some victims become reclusive and others insist on returning to work immediately. Each person deals with extremely stressful situations in a different manner; however, all must deal with effects of the events. Victims often fail to perceive they are not alone in their suffering; family or organization members, too, have undergone deep trauma. By the same token, family members sometimes do not fully respect that, although they have suffered greatly, they did in fact have a support structure around them during the negotiation. Everyone involved must realize that all parties to the kidnapping suffered greatly and that mutual respect and collaboration are crucial factors in regaining a sense of normalcy.

Families and organizations should retain experienced legal counsel when dealing with the aftermath of a kidnapping. Laws differ from place to place and the importance of being accompanied by a qualified legal representative when dealing with the authorities cannot be overstated. In some countries, negotiating with kidnappers is technically illegal and can lead to prosecution. In others, retaining the services of a consultant makes the consultant, and sometimes the family or organization, guilty of the same crime as the kidnappers. In still others, failure to report a kidnapping immediately is considered a crime. In each location, a qualified lawyer should be retained to look after the family or organization's interests.

A lawyer should also be able to accompany the victim during any depositions or statements to the authorities and ensure that the victim's rights are protected. This is always good practice, since many victims tend to be fragile and open to suggestion after having recently undergone such a significant ordeal. Most victims, particularly where little faith is placed in the authorities, find making a declaration to be a traumatic experience and they require and appreciate the support and assistance of a qualified legal representative.

In addition, some countries have unusual laws, such as those that require freezing the assets of the families of kidnap victims as soon as the crime becomes known. These laws have been instituted in some countries in which kidnapping has become a true scourge as a measure to discourage kidnappings by preventing the payment of ransoms. The desired effect has not usually been noted, as families either do not report the crime or seek friends and acquaintances to help raise the ransom. In all cases under this type of regime, however, legal representation is a must.

Families and organizations must also consider the need for designating or contracting a qualified individual or firm to handle the media if the kidnapping becomes public knowledge. Many times, the press is relentless in pursuit of a story and can interfere with negotiation, ransom delivery and the process of recovery. No family or organization wants a recently released victim to be hounded by reporters in search of a hot story; professionals should handle dealing with the media.

9

THE CRIMINAL OR
TERRORIST METHODOLOGY

Fighting terrorism is like being a goalkeeper. You can make a hundred brilliant saves but the only shot that people remember is the one that gets past you.

Paul Wilkinson

An intelligent plan is the first step to success. The man who plans knows where he is going, knows what progress he is making and has a pretty good idea when he will arrive.

Basil S. Walsh

The title of this chapter may dismay or confuse some who will insist that not all kidnappers are terrorists. This is undoubtedly true; however, I learned the methodology as such and understand that all terrorists, with the exception of suicide terrorists in the section about escape and all criminals, must follow this methodology to achieve their goals. Understand that this is real and works in all cases.

Each crime is distinct from all others. No two illegal acts are identical; every single incident has individual characteristics. One can, however, define a methodology that every criminal or terrorist must follow to commit his or her crimes. Criminals or terrorists must follow a defined sequence of inevitable activities.

This sequence of activities is particularly appropriate to a kidnapping; all the actions must be taken and performed properly for the kidnapper to have an opportunity for success. Therefore, any person wishing to prevent a kidnapping should begin by knowing the enemy; that is, understanding the sequence of activities that a potential kidnapper must perform. This knowledge will permit potential victims to take concrete measures that should minimize the risk of being kidnapped.

The methodology consists of five phases, each of which must be fulfilled to carry out a criminal or terrorist act except for suicide terrorists, who neither plan for nor are interested in escaping the scene.

Phase 1—Planning

Just as no building can be constructed without plans, no crime can be committed without adequate prior planning. Criminals and terrorists must consider a series of fundamental questions and planning factors before they take concrete actions. Initial planning requires a number of basic decisions.

What type of crime will be committed? This question is not as simplistic as it might appear. Criminals normally specialize in one particular type of activity; bank robbers are not kidnappers, car thieves are not rapists, and so on. Most criminals dedicate their efforts to those types of crimes for which they are prepared by experience and learning. Some criminals do graduate from one type of crime to another, and many ex-convicts learn new "trades" while in prison; however, criminals normally stay within the bounds of what they know best. Therefore, deciding what type of crime to commit is a fundamental decision.

Define the expected profit. Criminals are as dedicated to their profession as the average worker or executive is to his or hers. They are professionals who constantly seek ways to improve performance, mitigate risks and, most importantly, enhance revenues. The planning process must include an evaluation of what type of profit is expected from the action. For example, in a kidnapping, a budget must be developed to determine what amount of ransom to seek and what will be the lowest acceptable offer.

Identify the geographic area. The location of the victim and kidnapper must be identified. Transnational kidnappings have been committed, as well as crimes only blocks from where both parties reside. The precise scene at which a kidnapping or other crime will be conducted, as well as the location of the safe house and other facilities, will form the basis for numerous decisions that must be taken with respect to the crime. Traditionally, criminals operate in areas close to where they live. Criminals who live within the same city or state as the victim perpetrate a significant majority of kidnappings. While some do go far afield to commit their crimes, the majority chooses to operate in environments in which they are most comfortable.

Identify the victim or victims. Choosing a victim is an integral part of any criminal process; without one there is no crime. A criminal must determine, from the available target pool and based on a realistic assessment of possibilities, which individual family or organization is the most attractive and least risky target. The victim's profile has to correspond to the crime under consideration and expected recompense, and fall within the selected geographic area. For example, an armed robber must consider all those persons moving around within the area in which he or she plans to act and a kidnapper must consider those who live, work or travel through his or her favored zone of operation.

Victims and targets are not necessarily the same; this is easily understood by criminals and terrorists when planning and must be realized by the intended victims or targets themselves. For example, in a case in which an executive from a multinational firm is kidnapped, although he or she may be the direct victim of the action, the target may actually be the financial wherewithal that he or she represents as an employee of a huge conglomerate. This may matter a great deal because the target may be much more willing to sacrifice a victim than one might expect. A coldly calculated decision not to pay an exorbitant ransom to a supposed guerrilla group for a kidnapped executive may sometimes be made based on the target organization's cogently reasoned analysis of the threat to other employees and financial considerations. For the family of the victim abandoned to his or her fate, this would be small consolation.

The preceding example of a kidnapped executive may be an unusual one in ransom kidnapping practice; however, the concept becomes clearer if we consider terrorist-style hostage taking. Consider the situation that attended the capture of two Israeli soldiers by the terrorist group Hezbollah in 2006. Hezbollah offered to return the soldiers in exchange for the release of a number of prisoners. Israel, of course, could not easily accede to the demand (although they finally did) because this would have encouraged this and other terror groups to kidnap more soldiers and civilians in search of a ransom.

Consider law enforcement activities. Any delinquent has to consider the risks associated with perpetration of a crime. Those who do not have short, albeit sometimes illustrious, criminal careers. The presence or absence of police or patrols in a preferred zone of operations can be the deciding factor in whether to act; in any case, law enforcement operations in the favored location must be timed, analyzed and considered as part of the planning process. In many places, the level of corruption fosters law enforcement involvement in a more active role in kidnappings. Failure to consider this could lead to turf wars or serious complications for the perpetrators.

The overall risks, combining all the previous factors, will militate for or against moving ahead. The criminal or terrorist will only do so if he or she determines that the outlook is propitious. Once a decision is made to go forward, the process becomes more focused and even more detailed. A detailed level of planning will be evident in all the following steps; however, the necessary level of detail will vary and each step is a critical part of a successful criminal or terrorist operation.

Phase 2—Logistics

Once a decision has been made to commit a particular crime, the perpetrator must delve into detailed planning of the necessary logistics. Every item necessary to commit that particular crime must be identified, obtained and purchased, borrowed or stolen. In the case of crimes such as kidnapping, this requires planning on a very large scale. For professional criminals, this process can be equally as complicated as that faced by a manager who is tasked with opening a new production facility.

The criminal group or team leader must first decide how many people are necessary to carry out the crime and what skill set each person needs. For example, an individual who is planning to commit armed robbery in the street may only need a single accomplice capable of interfering with pursuit or intimidating a potential victim or victims. On the other hand, the leader of a kidnapping band will need to identify persons responsible for committing the actual kidnapping; a group responsible for transportation of the victim to the point at which he or she will be held; a team to keep the victim alive and under guard; personnel to perform both route surveillance and ransom recovery; and a clean-up team to erase evidence and cover tracks.

Frequently, many of these functions are outsourced; however, all must be considered, individuals identified and hired, and a budget set aside for payment. Small kidnapping groups often use subcontractors who are only paid for specific tasks and know nothing of the overall operation.

If weapons are necessary for the commission of a designated crime, those that are not already on hand must be obtained. This requires both contacts and money. In many countries, ammunition is more difficult to obtain than firearms and this is another point of concern. Arrangements also need to be made for training and practice with those weapons that will be used, as well as additional details such as weapons cleaning equipment and storage considerations.

Communication is another point requiring the criminal's attention. Modern telecommunications equipment such as cellular phones and radios are frequently put to use, particularly "throwaway" cellular telephones; those that can be easily acquired with little or no documentation and used with prepaid phone cards. Also, standard telephones, Internet communications and more archaic methods such as dead drops and hand signals are frequently employed. The mix of communications methods and devices is peculiar to each individual type of crime; however, all crimes require some form of communication between team members.

Each kidnapper must set up multiple redundant communication systems, particularly those who have adopted a cellular structure. The leader must know how to get in touch with every member of the group, including subcontractors; however, they in turn can have no idea who the leader is. Contact with the leader might be limited to emergencies only and all members provided with a single email address or throwaway cellular telephone number. On the other hand, communications protocols and fallback positions for transmitting orders and information must be developed and implemented so that the leader can control the organization. Specific guidelines for communication with the victim's family or organization must be developed and practiced. Communications security is an absolute requirement for criminals just as much as for any other type of organization.

Virtually all criminal activity also involves transportation. Criminals need to get to and from a crime scene, transport large or small objects, move personnel as necessary and have a flexible, immediate and versatile capability to move around. Transportation can range from public transport to taxis or hired cars, stolen vehicles or personal automobiles. In some cases, helicopters, airplanes and/or boats are also necessary. Whatever the transportation requirements, criminals and terrorists must plan for them and determine how to obtain, store, use and dispose of all transportation assets used in any given scenario. Planning must also consider fuel, documentation, insurance, licensing and many other details that permit use of each individual item of transport.

The criminal must also identify one or more locations that will be used as a base of operations. In the case of most common street criminals, this would ordinarily be their residence; they leave home in the morning, dedicate their efforts to perpetrating their daily number of crimes and return home at night. For a kidnapping, however, there is normally a need to identify and prepare multiple locations. These may include a safe house for the team; one or more locations at which to hold the victim; and, occasionally, a specialized emergency bolt-hole in which to hide if the pressure from law enforcement becomes too intense. Most criminal gangs also frequently work from a sort of "clubhouse" in which gang members gather to plan, celebrate and use as a place of rest.

Consumable supplies can be of critical importance. Criminals and terrorists generally cannot limit their concerns to what is on the day's lunch menu; rather, there are a multitude of details requiring attention. For example, if flashlights are to be used, they must be obtained along with a sufficient supply of additional batteries and spare bulbs. Criminals need gasoline for vehicles, batteries and cards for cellular phones and radios, and food, water, pencils, paper and any other items necessary to commit their crime. As the proposed crime becomes more complex and involves additional persons, requirements become correspondingly greater. The adage "for want of a nail" is as appropriate to criminal activity as to bona-fide business endeavors.

Documentation, particularly false identification, can also be an important consideration for the criminal. When the average mugger goes out on the street to attack and rob a passerby, he or she ordinarily does not carry any identification or carries a false ID. Fake documentation is universally available everywhere; in the United States one need only go to the local day laborer pick-up spot to easily detect a nearby location from which false identifications are being sold. In other countries, the mechanics are slightly different; however, where there is corruption (almost everywhere), false identification is readily available. For a kidnapper, depending on the complexity of the case, this might involve fake drivers' licenses, fraudulent documentation of properties or vehicles, or even false passports.

When I was kidnapped, the guy who guarded me used to tell me about how he had been doing this for five years. He said that he owned a house on the coast and that he was hoping to retire within a few years. I asked him how he expected to be able to live a normal life after having participated in so many kidnappings. He told me that his home was listed under his real name and that he had never been arrested or fingerprinted; he also said that he had changed his identity five times in the last four years, complete with new birth certificates, driver's licenses and passports. I did not believe him until he showed me three different passports with his picture, all with different names. He covered enough of the information so I could not see the full name, but the first name was different on every one. He told me that changing his identity was easy, he just went to see a "contact" in the government and paid the man a set fee; I got the impression that this is a common practice.

The financial part of any crime is the most important single issue for any criminal or terrorist. Money is the lubricant that enables the wheels of crime to turn; without money any crime is difficult if not impossible to commit. The common street criminal, once having obtained the basic requirements (e.g., gun, knife, running shoes, subway ticket, etc.), is not confronted with a high cost for committing repeat offenses and these costs can normally be subsumed within the daily take. In more sophisticated crimes such as kidnapping, however, there is a significant cost of operations that must be absorbed by the criminal group prior to any payoff. This cost can be significant; all the previously cited aspects of logistics represent cost factors, and the need to organize logistical requirements and pay for goods and services is unavoidable.

Like any businessperson, the criminal needs to define costs and profit margins. In most cases, the more complicated or riskier crimes lead to an expectation of a higher profit. Inasmuch as a book costs twenty dollars and a car twenty thousand, a street thug may get one hundred dollars from a mugging victim while a kidnapper could possibly make millions. This is, in a kidnapping, the principal factor that affects how much of a ransom payment will satisfy the kidnapper's minimum requirements. All kidnappers will ask for substantially more than they expect to receive; however, they all have also established a minimum below which they cannot afford to go. This varies between scenarios, but must be considered in calculating any payment offers. Ransom kidnapping is, after all, a business.

Phase 3—Surveillance

No criminal can act without first conducting surveillance on his or her potential victim. This process may last only a few seconds in the case of a mugger or many months or even years in the case of a high profile international kidnapping or terrorist attack. No matter how long or detailed the surveillance, the goal is similar: identify the easiest victim to exploit. The most vulnerable or attractive target will virtually always be the one chosen.

In most criminal activities, the surveillance process begins with a series of observations of a pool of likely targets. This initial phase is designed to determine which of the potential targets merits further exploitation. Once a few of the most apparently attractive targets are selected, they will be the subjects of a much more extensive surveillance. These targets are chosen for further exploitation based on an analysis of habits, movements, appearance and resources. In a kidnapping case, vulnerability to attack and an apparent ability to pay are conjoined in the kidnapper's mind as the twin factors that make an individual an attractive target.

For example, a criminal looking to rob motorists would ordinarily shun those who drive with their doors and windows locked and no valuable items visible in the passenger compartment; while choosing to assault a driver with the windows down, an arm with an expensive wristwatch sticking out, or packages on the front or back seat in plain view. The criminal looks for the most attractive (easiest and most exploitable) target against which to act.

In more complicated cases, target surveillance can take on many different forms. Criminals will conduct research in publicly accessible forums (libraries, Internet, etc.), look through home or office trash deposits, follow potential targets in their daily routines and purchase information from those in the potential victim's surroundings, among many other techniques. The amount of personal information available in the trashcans of most residences is truly astonishing. This often includes bank statements, credit card receipts, investment information, data on schools and places of employment and a wealth of other details that are quite useful to the potential kidnapper.

For example, in a residential area, a criminal needs to blend in to be able to acquire information without rousing suspicions. To this end, criminals will adopt disguises that make their presence unremarkable. This might be as a salesperson or religious propagandist, worker, repairman or city official. The aim is to be accepted by the populace so that the criminal may ask questions, glean information and conduct observations.

In one European case, two of the kidnappers took their baby to a park outside the victim's home every day for months. Over time, both the family and the security detail became accustomed to their presence and began to treat them almost as part of the scenery. At one point, the couple even feigned a flat tire and gained access to the victim's home on the pretext of using the telephone. Obviously, no better evaluation of residential security systems could have been obtained, unless blueprints were delivered. The target was subsequently kidnapped in front of his home and held for nearly three months.

Kidnappers are also adept at conducting what is known as "false-flag" recruitment of information sources. They approach individuals who may have information they need, posing as private investigators, police or pollsters in order to put the potential source at ease and gain the necessary information. In many cases, criminals try to obtain information from those close to the victim, either by relationship or by geography. If a street vendor operates a stand near a potential victim's home or office, kidnappers will frequently befriend the vendor in an effort to get information on the victim's habits or timelines of his or her movements.

Neighborhood children are often an excellent source of information. They are normally quite suspicious of strangers who ask questions; however, if they can be put at ease, they are enormous potential sources of information. For example, in one case, one of the surveillance team members dressed as a priest and frequented the neighborhood playground where the children gathered to play soccer. Over time, he was able to gain the trust of the neighborhood children and obtain information that facilitated the kidnapping of the nine-year old scion of a wealthy family.

In the developing world, where there are normally few programs to assist the handicapped, persons with serious disabilities are often reduced to begging on street corners. Kidnappers have used these people as sources of information since their physical inability to flee from trouble forces them to develop superior powers of observation. They can often cite from memory the hours at which a specific vehicle passes a certain point and provide particulars about the occupants. This information is of inestimable value to kidnappers in planning their attack.

Surveillance on a kidnapping victim will be conducted for as long as necessary. Depending on the type of kidnapping, this may last from minutes to months or years. The salient point is that the surveillance will be conducted until kidnappers are sure that the intended victim is a viable target and that they have sufficient information upon which to act.

The surveillance phase is the only time during which a potential victim has an opportunity to truly influence the outcome of a criminal act. The most viable way to accomplish this is by demonstrating to the surveillance that one is not an attractive target. This is relatively easy to do and involves varying one's routine, observing basic security precautions, and avoiding ostentatious behaviors that attract criminals' attention.

Most kidnappers use the least experienced and most expendable team members or contractors to conduct surveillance. This makes their activities more identifiable due to a series of common mistakes, which include:

- frequently checking the time as people or cars travel past
- staring at particular individuals or vehicles
- clothing that does not conform to the scene
- footwear or headgear that is out of place
- making notes for no apparent reason
- taking photographs without justification

In most cases, if surveillance is detected, simply letting the observer know that he or she has been detected is sufficient to discourage further interest. In any case, such activities should always be reported, as other information may be available that might indicate a more imminent threat. In a notorious case from Mexico in the early 1990s, an executive chauffeur noted that his vehicle was being followed on the day before his principal was kidnapped. He did not report the incident because, "I lost them and didn't think it was significant." When the principal was kidnapped near the same location on the following day, the family was forced to pay a multimillion-dollar ransom. One can only speculate as to whether appropriate preventive measures might have been taken had the tail been reported.

The goal of any surveillance operation is to identify where and when the criminal will find the victim in conditions that are favorable for action. When these conditions can be precisely identified, the criminal can prepare for the next phase of his or her action.

Phase 4—Action

Most crime victims comment in one form or another, "If I had only..." In this comment we see the tremendous advantage that the well-prepared criminal has over typical victims. One should understand that, if a situation develops through the action phase, there is a 99% percent chance that the attacker will succeed in perpetrating the crime. There are a number of factors that virtually guarantee a criminal's success at the actual moment of commission.

The first factor is surprise. No one leaves home in the morning expecting to be victimized. The criminal chooses the time, the place and the conditions under which to act and no person can be completely alert at all times. The average person has no idea how to react when suddenly confronted by one or more armed individuals, nor does he have any way of responding successfully once assailants gain control of the scene.

The second factor in a criminal's favor is violence. Criminals normally have weapons and are willing to use them. The average citizen typically is not armed and even if he or she does carry a weapon, a professional assailant will not afford the victim an opportunity to draw the weapon. The criminal will use whatever level of force is necessary to complete his or her attack, irrespective of the consequences. This is why a number of kidnap victims have been murdered for resisting during the takedown.

Another factor is the speed with which a criminal strikes. One or more armed assailants suddenly confront an individual and he or she has virtually no opportunity to react. A criminal will normally have practiced his or her action under similar conditions or have committed the same type of crime, affording him another enormous advantage.

What follows is a description of the action that resulted in a kidnapping. The operation was fully planned; the point of attack carefully selected; necessary logistics on hand and utilized; the attack performed in such a way as to leave minimal opportunity for the victim to escape; and, the kidnappers' escape very well orchestrated.

I was on my way to play tennis on a quiet street called Belgrano. Between Herodes and Concepción it narrows and there is parking on both sides. A car pulled in front of me and I had to brake. He backed up, so I did too, but there was a VW bus behind me. He backed into me and the driver's side guy got out and said, "Hey, you hit me." My reaction is to get out of the car so I did and responded, "Wait, you ran into me." Then suddenly two other guys appeared with submachine guns and I said, "Take the car, there it is." It was an 1987 Cougar, a year old, and I thought they wanted the car. "No," the one guy said, "get in face down in the back seat of the car." I got in face down and a nurse got in, she had on a nurse's shoes and stockings, and she told me to take off my jacket. I was wearing like a sweat suit for exercise and she gave me a shot and I became unconscious and woke up in the place I was to stay for the next three months.

The presence of a guard, driver or protection team is only an impediment to a determined attacker. They simply represent another, normally not insurmountable, obstacle and their neutralization or elimination will be included in planning the attack. From the attack phase, the criminal moves forward to, for him or her, absolutely the most important part of the operation.

Phase 5—Escape

No one commits any crime without having previously scouted and planned an escape route from the point of attack to a safe place. If this route is not available, any planned attack will be cancelled or rescheduled. Obviously, in the case of a suicide terrorist, escape is not an issue;

however, in all other crimes the perpetrator desires to escape and will plan extensively for this. Normally, criminals plan their escape in reverse, beginning with the safe location and working back to the scene of the crime; attempting to ensure that the escape route is secure and available before acting. There is nothing to be gained by committing a crime in a situation from which there is no escape.

For example, most kidnappings occur while the victim is in transit, or arriving or departing from a given location. Potential victims, however, are much safer in traffic jams than on an open road. In a traffic jam, the kidnappers may count on an immobile target; however, their escape route is extraordinarily difficult as well. They are also immobilized and cannot escape. In open road situations, if the target vehicle can be immobilized, escape routes are much easier to plan and execute.

An integral part of the escape for most criminals is to leave behind a clean-up team or element whose function is to impede any pursuit. This can range from a single person on foot to a team of persons in multiple vehicles, depending on the scale of the operation. The mission of the clean-up team is to ensure the safe escape of the strike team with the booty and they will intervene violently if necessary.

Synopsis

The methodology described above works for any crime or terrorist act. Just as there is a method to preparing a tax return or changing the oil in a car, the terrorist methodology must be followed in order to commit a crime. The following example illustrates the way in which this methodology might be used to perform a very common crime:

> A man is seeking to commit robbery at knifepoint in a public park, hoping to obtain whatever valuables the victim may be carrying or wearing (*planning*). He has obtained dark clothing, a six-inch folding knife, a hat that goes low over his eyes, a good pair of running shoes and a partner to watch his back (*logistics*). He carefully observes all who pass by his location, looking for the individual who presents the most attractive target (*surveillance*). Once he chooses the target, he moves into position, springs out and assaults the victim at knifepoint (*action*). He immediately runs to a nearby subway station, trashes the hat, reverses his jacket

and boards the train while his accomplice interferes with any pursuit (*escape*).

There are an infinite number of examples; every criminal must follow this methodology in one form or another. There are no exceptions!

10

Avoidance and Survival

In the land of the blind, the one-eyed man is king.

Desiderius Erasmus, Adagia

There is no such thing as luck. There is only adequate or inadequate preparation to cope with a statistical universe.

Robert Heinlein, Time enough for Love

Personal Security

Anyone who lives in a developing country and owns a business, makes a good salary or is an executive in a major corporation is a potential kidnap victim. So, too, are all direct and most extended family members. If you think you might be a potential victim, you undoubtedly are one. Those who live in more developed countries typically face a significantly lower risk of kidnapping, except for frequent international travelers.

Individuals who consider themselves and the organizations they work for at risk have an obligation to take the necessary measures to reduce their vulnerability to kidnapping. The cost of kidnapping is immense to both families and organizations, so "an ounce of prevention is worth a pound of cure."

Any organization or concerned family's first task is to identify the threat level. The kidnapping threat varies, not only among countries but also among cities and regions within individual countries. In fact, the threat in one neighborhood can be significantly higher or lower than the threat only a few streets away. In many places these are truly dangerous times and a wise individual will study the terrain carefully before acting.

Establishing a preventive security program begins with an understanding of the situation. Perils abound, and the wise man tries to avoid becoming a victim rather than picking up the pieces afterward. This is neither intended to be a paean to security consultants in general nor an implied or implicit recommendation of any particular service. Families and organizations can do much of the necessary work on their own; however, a knowledgeable security professional can be worth his or her weight in gold in determining the set of measures best suited to each individual and group situation for preventing a kidnapping. That said, the necessary components of a functional kidnap prevention plan form part of an overall executive or personal security effort.

A proper threat analysis directed toward kidnap prevention will also lead to a much higher level of personal security and protection against more common crimes such as home invasion, armed robbery, car jacking and burglary. This analysis will focus, however, on preventing a kidnapping with the understanding that numerous corollary benefits accrue. A proper threat analysis is composed of a number of activities, all of which are necessary to draw conclusions as to how an individual or family must be protected.

An initial step is to identify the frequency and type of kidnappings that have occurred in the area where the family lives and works. This requires an analysis of the frequency and location of incidents in the surrounding area, home, schools, workplaces and centers of diversion that the family commonly frequents. As much detailed information as possible should be developed about each incident. Significant similarities and differences between the profiles of the victims and that of the family must be identified and analyzed to determine the potential susceptibility of the family to targeting by kidnappers. Also, analyzing the frequency, level and types of kidnapping in the environment around the family aids in later decisions with respect to resource allocation.

Obviously, the data needed to make sound decisions about the protection of one's family are not easily available; no one can simply look up the required information on the Internet or go to the local bookstore and read about the situation. Obtaining the information is only possible by asking questions of the right people. Neighbors can be a excellent source of general information and in many countries a network of friends will have more up-to-date information than the local authorities since so few kidnappings are reported. One must, however, consider that the rumor mill will tend to wildly exaggerate any story and that all gossip should be viewed with skepticism.

Contact should also be made with those responsible for security in the organizations for which family members work; security managers maintain networks and have an absolute interest in helping to prevent incidents against fellow members of the organization. Consultants will, for a nominal fee in most cases, provide briefings on the current situation from their perspective. The local authorities should also be contacted, through intermediaries in many cases, for information on the threat level. One should understand that in many countries inviting the authorities to participate in an assessment of a family or an organization's vulnerability is perceived as being akin to "inviting the fox into the henhouse." The level of confidence in the authorities in many places is abysmal; corruption is endemic and the lack of trust has been well earned.

Information development is not limited to security and law enforcement professionals and the neighbors. Store and restaurant owners, service personnel, delivery drivers, priests, rabbis, imams, teachers, the list is endless. The more creative and inquisitive an individual or family proves to be, the more accurate their perceptions with respect to the threat in their environment. All the information collected should be analyzed and a determination made as to how severe the threat may be.

If kidnapping is in fact a threat in the area, the family needs to plan carefully how to avoid being victimized. An important point often overlooked is that any plan is better than no plan. Most people do not make an effort to protect themselves in an organized manner and this contributes greatly to the protection of those who do. Potential kidnap victims in a high-threat environment should clearly understand their position. Those who take no thought for their own protection actually enhance the security of those who are actively taking measures. The effect of preventive security practices is magnified when others leave themselves vulnerable. "In the land of the blind, the one-eyed man is king," describes this situation perfectly. Make your own decisions, but understand and accept the consequences.

The regular routines of each family member must be analyzed to identify repetitive behaviors that could be utilized by anyone targeting them. For example, school-age children are very vulnerable since they are required to be in fixed locations at predictable times. Work schedules also can be points of vulnerability, particularly if family members are creatures of habit and always arrive and leave at the same time. Outside activities such as sports, church attendance, meetings and other social events can be predictable as well. All routine activities of each family member must be identified and catalogued.

Once a sequence of activities has been identified for each family member and routine movements are understood, planning can begin to reduce the vulnerabilities inherent in each family member's routine. Kidnappers look to identify a set of circumstances in which they can successfully perpetrate an attack. Repetitious, predictable movements make the job easy, so a family must look to reduce as much as possible the level of predictability in each individual's daily movements. While many movements are virtually set and unchanging, simple steps can have a significant impact on reducing vulnerability.

For example, although school starts and ends at a specific time, there is no reason why children cannot be dropped off within an approximate window of thirty or so minutes prior to the school day. If school starts at 8:00 a.m., children can be dropped off anytime after 7:30 a.m. (although anyone who has had school-age children will understand how difficult just getting them there on time can be). However, this varies the departure time from the home and arrival time at the school, making the kidnappers' task much more difficult.

The same practice can be applied for travel to and from the workplace. Arriving or leaving the workplace a few minutes earlier or later every day can greatly reduce vulnerability to an attack. For outside activities such as the weekly poker game, a number of strategies may be applied. The location of the game can be varied; however, rotating on a fixed schedule, although harder to detect, is still a vulnerable practice. The weeknight for the event can be varied or starting and ending times can be changed slightly as well. For fixed events such as church services, the family may want to consider attending an earlier or later service on a random basis.

The key factor in varying routines is to inject an element of uncertainty into the kidnappers' planning cycle. In order to strike successfully, kidnappers need to identify a time and a place where they can dominate; they are much less likely to plan an attack if the window of opportunity is constantly sliding. They must set up an operation and have personnel standing by to carry out the attack at the indicated location. Maintaining an attack force poised, ready and undetected for fifteen or so minutes in any major urban or suburban area is difficult and dangerous for them. Varying departure and arrival times can greatly reduce vulnerability by eliminating predictable and repetitious movements.

The majority of kidnappings occur while the victim is in transit, either in a vehicle or on foot. Obviously, not every executive and family member can afford to travel everywhere in an armored vehicle and/or with an escort team. Therefore, all the routes that family members commonly take when traveling from one known location to another require analysis. This is also the case if an escort is provided, but assume for the sake of argument this is not the case. Most people take the same route between two known points all the time; very few will arbitrarily choose an alternate route, particularly if they perceive that the secondary route takes longer.

On regularly traveled routes, vulnerable points must be identified. These are locations that afford potential advantages to the attacker, such as bottlenecks where traffic must slow down or intersections where a vehicle has to stop. They provide both good nearby cover and easy escape for an attacker. While street crime is common in areas of heavy traffic congestion, kidnappings are less so; kidnappers need to ensure a clear escape route before striking. Analysis of likely vulnerable points must include this fact. For example, a construction zone in which traffic piles up may not appear at first glance to be a good location to perpetrate a kidnapping; however, if the victim can be moved on foot for a short distance and placed into another vehicle on a road with little or no traffic, the site is perilous indeed.

Every vulnerable location on each route needs to be evaluated and measures implemented to reduce that vulnerability. Similar to risk management principles, vulnerabilities must be eliminated, reduced, transferred or accepted, depending on each specific case. Eliminating vulnerability while in transit may require a change of route to avoid the potential trouble spot. Reducing the vulnerability could consist in changing transit times to pass through the chokepoint at an hour of less traffic or making a rolling stop and wide turn at a residential corner where heavy shrubbery provides good cover for armed men. Cutting back the vegetation dramatically would also help if the possibility exists. Transferring risk is more difficult. Principally, this is done by being more careful than other drivers and presenting a less attractive target. Some readers might suggest that reducing the risk for themselves enhances the threat to others. I would posit, however, that commiserating with the family of a kidnapped neighbor or colleague is eminently preferable to having to console one's own family. Some identified risks may be acceptable; if there is no other viable way to get from one point to another, a certain measure of risk may be necessary.

For every route that is commonly taken, a number of alternate routes should be identified. As important as varying routines, changing routes on a seemingly haphazard basis also throws any surveillance into confusion and makes mounting an operation more difficult for the kidnapper. Each alternate route should be examined as carefully as the principal route for potential vulnerable points and measures taken to counter potential pitfalls. Methods of transitioning from one route to another in case of unexpected delays or interference should also be identified; oftentimes backtracking a distance and changing routes is more secure and faster than waiting for a major traffic jam to clear.

Safe havens should be identified along every route. These are locations where one can go when a potentially threatening situation appears. They include police stations, hospitals, fire stations, military bases, some government facilities and other locales where large numbers of people tend to be present. Each possible safe haven should be precisely located and identified; means of access to each should also be determined. There is little to be gained from outracing a pursuer through the gate of a military installation only to be shot down as a suspected terrorist.

Route planning can be very rudimentary or extremely sophisticated, depending on the level of knowledge of those involved and the amount of time and energy devoted to the effort. This activity is a critical part of any kidnap prevention program. No matter how much or how little route planning is performed, the results will be beneficial.

Since so many kidnappings are carried out against drivers or passengers of vehicles in transit, a few comments about vehicle security apply (see Appendix A for a more detailed list of measures). Any executive or family member who lives in or is deployed to an area in which kidnappings are prevalent should take the time to attend a professionally delivered driver-training course. These courses are available all over the world and, while most are adequate, many do not cover all the necessary aspects. Potential students should strive to ensure that the course is not simply an opportunity to make fancy maneuvers; they should be taught basic skills behind the wheel, but also be trained to understand how to take measures for their own protection. The ability to avoid a dangerous situation is many times more valuable than knowing how to perform a bootlegger's turn.

In many countries, obtaining a driver's license is as easy as slipping a few bills into the hand of the person in charge of issuance; in others, extensive written and practical tests are required. Although the skill level of drivers varies greatly between individuals everywhere; one can safely say that if your license was obtained via the former method, you are most likely even more in need of a training course than someone who has passed through a rigorous licensing process in which a number of transferable skills were learned. Nonetheless, security training for all drivers is an important defense measure against kidnapping.

Any training must be combined with an appropriate level of driver awareness to reduce vulnerabilities. Knowing how to perform evasive or defensive maneuvers is fine; never having to employ them because a kidnapper perceives one as too difficult a target and moves on is much better. Kidnappers will not strike without first conducting surveillance on the target. For example, to an observer, a driver who appears alert, observant, maintains proper vehicle spacing, keeps car securely locked up and constantly checks his or her blind spots is much less attractive a target than one who brakes on the bumper of other cars, has his or her arm hanging out the window and drives carelessly, oblivious to the surroundings.

Even in planning a crime as sophisticated as a kidnapping, the observer will focus on the target that appears easiest. Anyone can reduce his or her profile as a target by practicing secure driving or insisting that his or her driver do so.

Another significant number of kidnappings is committed at the moment when an individual arrives or departs a residence, place of work or other location, particularly involving vehicle travel. When entering or leaving a garage or parking lot, or getting in or out of a vehicle, individuals are very vulnerable. An attack can be launched by anyone close enough to block the victim's path, enter the garage while the door is open or reach the victim physically during the movement.

Captured kidnappers have specifically cited electronic garage door openers as an area of opportunity. They simply hide nearby and enter while the door is opening or closing and the victim is either in the vehicle or in the process of leaving the vehicle. Since most garage doors take around thirty seconds to close, there is ample opportunity for a nearby assailant to act. Another frequent tactic encountered is that of blocking the access of the vehicle between the garage door and the attacking vehicle so that the target is immobilized and an attack can be mounted. This type of attack is frequently noted in residential areas, especially in the evening hours. People tend to relax when they arrive home after a long day; kidnappers take full advantage of this reduced awareness. Another favored tactic is to strike in the parking lot of a commercial center, particularly when a victim is alone and approaches his or her car with an armload of packages. A vehicle suddenly pulls up or armed men spring out from nearby and the surprised victim is taken down while concentrating on loading his or her packages and preparing to depart.

No matter the circumstances, the moment of arrival or departure from anywhere must be a time of heightened alertness. In public places, the area around the vehicle should be scanned and, if any anomalies are noted, one should immediately retreat to a safe place. When arriving home, the area around the garage or parking area should be carefully looked over. If anything unusual is noted, the driver should go around the block one or more times until the potential threat clears. If this does not happen, the authorities should be called immediately to dispatch a patrol car. Many readers might believe that, in their country or city, calling the police is not helpful and possibly even counterproductive. If one feels this way or if no uniformed response is forthcoming, one should consider going elsewhere for a short period of time. What is not acceptable is to go willingly into a potential kidnapping situation. There is always time to drive around the block, particularly if one compares that to a few weeks or months in captivity.

If no clear view of the exterior is available from the vehicle when leaving any given location, every effort should be made to ensure that the area around the exit is clear of danger prior to boarding the vehicle and opening the gate or driving out. This sometimes requires the assistance of a parking lot attendant, valet, maid, assistant or other family member. The point is simple: a few moments of extra precaution or minor inconvenience can prevent a disaster.

I was kidnapped in front of my house. I pulled out from the garage and a car that was parked in front of my neighbor's house pulled up behind me and blocked me in just as the garage door closed. Three guys with guns jumped out and ran up to the door of my car. I couldn't go anywhere, I was trapped. They forced me into the backseat and told me to get down on the floor. They drove away and I didn't see my family for three weeks afterward.

The risks associated with arriving or departing one's residence can just as easily be ignored if the residence itself is not properly protected. Kidnappers who can simply hop a fence or a wall and stroll up to the house have no need to wait for a garage door to open. In places such as the United States where there are few walls, the residence must be hardened as well and care taken when arriving and departing. In other countries, particularly underdeveloped ones, those who are potential kidnapping victims routinely live behind high walls and their security system must start outside the perimeter.

The street outside a residence or in areas where there are no adjacent structures must be properly illuminated. Typically, municipal lighting systems are grossly inadequate and the residents must install additional security lighting (controlled from within, sensor-activated or both) on the exterior of any property. Vegetation around the outside of the residence must be trimmed to eliminate any potential hiding places next or in close proximity to entry points. That decorative shrubbery of which you are so proud may be just what a potential kidnapper needs to confirm you as a viable target.

Perimeter walls and fencing must be solid, or solidly anchored and at least nine feet (2.7 meters) high on the attack side with some sort of anti-climbing measure on top, such as razor wire, iron spikes or an electric fence (non-lethal voltage is mandated by law in most countries). Interior garden and patio areas must be equipped with motion-activated lighting of sufficient wattage and coverage to fully illuminate every nook and cranny of the yard and parking area. These lights must also be controllable from the master bedroom or other safe haven (see below) or sanctuary area established within the residence.

Doors and windows should be as solid as possible. Doors should be equipped with deadbolt locks and securely anchored frames. All door and window hinges and hardware should be installed on the inner side; nothing should be removable on the outside. Many metal window frames have screws holding the frames together on the outside for easy replacement; these should be changed or the screw heads spot welded, although this makes replacement of broken glass a much more difficult proposition. First floor and easily accessible second floor windows and doors should be fitted with security grills (burglar bars). These must be firmly anchored to the structure and sufficiently dense and solidly constructed so that they cannot be easily pulled off or separated by a crowbar or hydraulic jack. Every joint or crossing point in every grill must be independently welded. Grills that are simply screwed to the structure can easily be removed with a screwdriver, thus defeating their purpose. Security grills are often a bone of contention; they limit the view and make some people feel imprisoned in their own home. Anyone who wishes to argue too strenuously for aesthetics over function in an environment in which kidnappings flourish should consider the alternative.

An intrusion alarm system should be installed that includes contacts on every door and window and a series of motion, breaking glass and other sensors. The specific requirements for each residence will vary; however, all possible entries should be covered. A multitude of different types of alarm systems are available and a system suitable to each family's needs (including "pet-friendly" systems) can be found and installed in virtually every country in the world. A very important consideration is response; an alarm is of dubious utility if no response is forthcoming. Obviously, an armed response by qualified personnel is the most positive outcome but, in many places, private security guards are not allowed to carry weapons. In other countries, there are few or no options for patrol services. In still others, the only response is by local police, whose performance generally coincides with the overall level of quality of service they provide.

Within the residence, a safe haven or sanctuary should be designated and outfitted. This is normally a room, often the master bedroom or bathroom, that can be secured against outside penetration for a period of twenty minutes or so under difficult circumstances. The family can retreat to this area during an emergency and summon help. The room should not be accessible from outside the residence;

however, in practice many have grilled windows or windows with no feasible access from the exterior. A safe haven should be fitted with a solid wood or reinforced door and multiple locking bolts. The room should be equipped with a means of communication, water, canned food, flashlights, batteries and other supplies needed for a prolonged stay, should that become necessary.

The use of residential guards is an issue that often arises. In many places, using guards is virtually automatic, the thinking is that without them, everything will be stolen as soon as the residents go out. In other places, guards are seen as a status symbol and no potential victim would be so gauche as to be without them. In others, guards are seldom encountered. To this, one must add the practice of hiring watchmen or doormen, prevalent in many places and normally significantly less expensive than uniformed guards. Users must understand the service they are purchasing and what to expect.

A report was received from an individual deployed in a South American country that persons unknown had entered his property and stolen some items from his yard. Security requested additional information in order to properly follow up with the local authorities. The staff member reported that various gardening tools and one of his two hammocks from the front porch had been taken. When asked by the security manager why only one of the two hammocks had been taken, he responded that the security guard on duty had been asleep in the other hammock.

The preceding anecdote speaks volumes about the quality of private security guard performance, particularly in developing countries. Guards often work multiple jobs to make ends meet, work twelve or twenty four-hour shifts and are too tired or too disinterested to provide effective security. Many families also use the guards to run errands, walk dogs, sweep patios and perform other household chores. This contributes to a lack of professionalism and subverts whatever training and effort the parent company invested in attempting to make the guard perform his or her duties in a professional manner. A residential guard may come in contact with his or her supervisor once or twice per tour; he or she is in constant contact with the family. They are the ones who effectively establish performance standards, not the guard company.

Individuals who work as security guards in developing countries typically come from the same sectors of the population as kidnappers. That is, they are members of the normally underpaid, undereducated and underemployed group of citizens who will work at almost any job that pays. Moreover, work as a security guard is viewed by most sectors of the population as for those incapable of doing anything else. This is not to say that security guards are kidnappers-in-waiting, far from it. They are, however, a potential liability in many cases. Guards get to know the most intimate secrets of a family's daily routine. They know how and when each family member comes and goes and can easily identify weaknesses in any security system. They frequently know which family member drinks too much, if there are marital problems and a host of other potentially exploitable vulnerabilities. If a guard can be suborned or is inclined to work with kidnappers, the kidnappers' job is easy; the guard can provide information, access or both that facilitate a kidnapping. In addition, to expect poorly paid individuals to place their lives on the line when faced with the choice of turning a blind eye or risk being killed is unreasonable. That said, not all security guards are either incompetent or corrupt.

Many security guards work hard and strive to protect their charges to the utmost of their ability. The difficulty lies with the significant percentage of those who do not adhere to higher standards of conduct or morality. Anyone who wishes to contract a security guard or watchman should clearly understand the potential pitfalls inherent in the process. Guards and guard companies must be thoroughly vetted to minimize risks; many companies operate illegally and will basically hire, outfit and deploy anyone who can walk.

Typically, users are as much at fault in the breakdown of a security system as the guards. Many families use guards or guard services as a substitute for sound security practices. Alarm systems are not activated, grills are not installed or doors and windows are not secured because "We have a guard." The practice of relying on an under-qualified and virtually unknown individual instead of employing sound security measures leads all too frequently to tragic consequences. Security guards are but a single tool in a comprehensive security system. Over-reliance on any single facet of a security system is dangerous, and guards are no exception.

Another area in which few of the many necessary security precautions at any residence are undertaken is domestic staff. Maids, gardeners, drivers and other service personnel must be thoroughly investigated on a regular basis to ensure that they remain loyal to the family and pose no unnecessary risks. Service staff must receive training; if they are to answer the telephone they need to know exactly what to say and what information can be given out to callers. Confirming that the head of household is on vacation may be just what potential kidnappers need to move ahead with their plans. As well, anyone who might answer the door must understand that no strangers are ever to be granted access to the residence without express authorization. Front door entry has been a preferred method for kidnappers in many countries. They dress as telephone or cable repairmen, ring the doorbell, announce that they are responding to a maintenance call and are soon inside the residence and in control.

Providing the maid, live-in or otherwise, with a complete set of keys to the residence and alarm deactivation codes is a dangerous practice. Many families have mentioned that they need to have their alarms set up so that the maid can deactivate certain zones in order to be able to bring them coffee in the morning without activating the alarm system. This is the height of folly for any potential kidnap victim, yet many families, even after repeated warnings, continue the practice. Security and quality of life issues may sometimes conflict and each individual must make his or her choices. I prefer to make my own coffee rather than face the possibility, however infinitesimal, of becoming a kidnap victim.

Security in the workplace is similar in many respects to residential security. The physical installation must be protected as well as possible to deny, deter or delay the intrusion of kidnappers. This is obviously a much simpler proposition in a manufacturing facility with a full-time guard force, physical barriers and a properly functioning access control system than in a corner store. Nonetheless, every location in which a potential kidnap victim works should be protected as far as possible. The optimum combination of physical, electronic, human and psychological barriers for each workplace is different and a detailed discussion of all the potential combinations is beyond the scope of this work. Trade-offs between security and the uninterrupted function of any business or organization are always necessary; an impermeable security system by nature would preclude any effective conduct of business. A properly designed security system will both permit an organization to function and minimize the opportunities for kidnappers. Extreme situations, however, can and do occur.

> *Alejandro was in his office at the successful car dealership that he had built from scratch through twenty years of intense labor. Suddenly, three armed men burst into his office, subdued him, put a hood over his head and hustled him downstairs to a waiting vehicle. He was held for many days before being rescued by police. Investigation revealed that a group of eight armed men had taken over the auto dealership and gone into his office to effect the kidnapping, then quickly disappeared. Alejandro later commented that the kidnappers told him that his normal security practices made attacking his workplace the only option for them to strike.*

In any workplace open to the public, operational procedures and access practices inimical to security will exist, some in larger numbers than others. The automobile dealership cited above is an example of a type of business that depends on customer access and cannot easily be defended against a determined band of kidnappers. Potential victims can harden their offices, put filters in place between themselves and outsiders and be very security conscious; however, a car dealer pretty much has to go to the showroom to sell cars. The best approach is to make oneself as difficult a target as possible. Remember that kidnappers, like all criminals, are interested in the easiest targets possible and will normally select someone else when their primary target is too well protected or perceived as too risky an operation.

A friend who has reason to know once told me that if a kidnapper is willing to invest the necessary time, effort and resources, no one is truly immune to kidnapping. When we discussed a number of specific cases, one factor became readily apparent. Although they target a specific individual, kidnappers will often change their focus to a less well-protected target if they perceive that the reward sought is more easily available from the second target. Very rarely do they focus exclusively on a single individual in a ransom kidnapping situation; this is after all a business and everything invested and more must be recouped.

Survival

Many times I have been asked by attendees at a personal security seminar to evaluate their comportment during a recent situation in which they were victimized. The typical interlocutor will provide a detailed retelling of the incident and then ask what they might have done better. Unless the story contains some egregious error that made their survival truly miraculous, my answer is virtually the same every time. "You are here now sharing the experience with us; you survived. Everything else is unimportant. Survival is the key factor in any criminal incident; money, jewelry, possessions and almost anything else can be replaced, your life cannot."

Many questioners are somewhat taken aback by this reply and will press onward, seeking to determine if they really, truly did the right thing. Frequently, the questions go into a level of detail that can be almost comical. "If the assailant had been carrying a three-inch knife instead of a five-inch knife and if he had come at me from the side instead of behind…." Explaining that once an assailant with a knife closes in on you, irrespective of the size of the blade, you are in a difficult situation and need to think primarily about survival may not be the most ego-gratifying response; however, surviving a kidnapping, mugging or other assault is the most important and sole acceptable outcome.

As a Crime Victim

During an actual attack or crime situation, one must focus on those actions or attitudes necessary to maximize the chance of survival. This, particularly during a kidnapping, is one of the most dangerous times. The attacker has established immediate dominance of the situation and is very sensitive to any implied or perceived threat to that dominance. He or she will normally react with extreme violence if control over the situation is threatened. Victims therefore must adopt attitudes that, while avoiding abject submissiveness, permit the captor or attacker to feel as though he or she is in complete control and not threatened in any way.

The first tactic to employ in any crime situation is calm cooperation. If the attacker feels that you are not resisting, chances are greatly improved that the potential for violence will be reduced. If an attacker demands your watch, give him the watch. Even if the watch is an heirloom inherited from your great-grandfather, a possession is not worth your life. If a kidnapper insists you lie on the car floor and cover your head, do so and do not overtly try and sneak peeks around the vehicle.

I was assaulted in a taxi. We had been working late and I made the mistake of jumping in the first taxi I saw. The distance to my home was quite a ways and I was half asleep. I sort of noticed that the driver had turned down a very dark street that was a shortcut between two major roads when suddenly, he pulled over and a guy with a knife jumped in. He made me lie down on the floor and warned me not to raise my head or make a sound. They went through my wallet and my briefcase and got my ATM card and made me tell them the PIN number. He put his knee across the back of my legs and kept poking me in the rear with his knife, saying "Te parcho o te mato?" (Should I rape you or kill you?) I was terrified and kept telling him they could do anything they wanted to do, just let me live. This happened at about 10:30 at night and they drove me around for hours. First they went to an ATM and took out as much money as they could, then we drove around for a while until after midnight so they could make another withdrawal. They kept asking me about how much money my family had and lots of questions about money; I told them that all I had was what was in my bank account and that I wouldn't get paid again for two weeks. They said that they had my address and my house keys and would come for my family if I reported the incident to the police.

Finally they let me go. At about 0230; they had me crawl out of the car and lie face down in the street. They told me not to move for ten minutes or they would kill me. They started to pull away, then stopped and backed up. I thought I was dead for sure. After a minute or so they fired a shot into the street right next to my head and drove away laughing. Believe me, I didn't move for at least ten minutes after that! I finally got up and saw that I was in an industrial area. I walked a few blocks until I came out on a road with some traffic. I stopped another taxi and convinced the driver to take me home.

If you must move, reach into a pocket or take any action that could conceivably be misinterpreted, make sure to announce the action and request permission to do so. Reaching into your jacket for a wallet can easily be misconstrued as an attempt to pull out a weapon and may cause a violent reaction. Explain what you are about to do before doing so and use a calm and matter-of-fact tone. If you are ordered out of your vehicle, let the abductors know that you have to reach down and release your seatbelt in order to do so; do not suddenly move your hand out of sight and expect them to remain calm. Do not get into an argument with your assailants over whether you can bring along your briefcase, a picture of your wife or your cellular phone.

Maintain your composure and try to be as cool as possible under the circumstances. Panicked screaming and thrashing about violently will only exacerbate the tension and make the situation worse. Breathe deeply and do your utmost to control yourself. Try to absorb as much information as possible without overtly observing your kidnappers or the environment. If you are being transported in a vehicle, try to remember the route traveled. This can include the number and direction of turns, road surfaces, outside noises such as construction, sirens or loudspeakers and duration of the trip. This will keep your mind occupied, help you to remain calm and may possibly assist in a later reconstruction of the crime.

Speak only when you are spoken to. Kidnappers are not interested in holding lengthy conversations with the victim; they want a pliable and submissive victim who gives no trouble. Any other type of conduct is very likely to result in physical violence, so do not make threatening statements or adopt menacing poses. Never look directly at any of the kidnappers. If you can discreetly observe the features and characteristics of the kidnappers, this may be of use at a later time; however, your first priority is to stay alive and diminish as much as possible the potential for violence.

The best opportunity for escape may occur in the first moments of a kidnapping. Sometimes, kidnappers will let down their guard momentarily or do something that affords the victim an opportunity to escape. They may not have considered that a victim may react by fleeing or taking a chance and, if circumstances permit, try to get away. Few victims escape successfully and some are seriously hurt or even killed in the attempt. The decision to try to escape is a matter of personal choice when faced with an opportunity, no matter how large or small.

I was kidnapped when I pulled up in front of our plant, located on a small street just off a main thoroughfare. I was a little late, so I had to park about thirty meters away from the door along the curb in front of a high hedge. As soon as I turned off the engine, a guy with a gun appeared at my car door and made me move over to the passenger seat. He told me that they had been watching my sister and me and that my dad would pay big money for me. He told me to shut up and not to move, put the gun under his left leg and drove off. We turned right onto the main road and about one hundred meters down was a major intersection. As we got to the intersection I could see that there was a street market going on and so as he turned left through the intersection I opened the door to try and roll out of the car. He grabbed for me and scored my neck with his fingernails and tore my blouse, but I was able to roll out of the car onto the street. Hitting the asphalt took a lot of skin, but I was so high on adrenaline that I didn't even think about it much at the time. As soon as I hit the ground I started screaming "Socorro, secuestro!" (Help, Kidnapping!) at the top of my lungs. Some people, including a policeman, came running over from the market and the guy took off with my car.

I knew that if I didn't take the chance to get away, I was going to be held for God knows how long and I had to try and do something. A couple of my friends had been kidnapped and the stories they told me were horrible. Fortunately, I got away, but I was terrified the whole time and it only lasted a couple of minutes. I can only imagine what it must be like for someone who is kidnapped for weeks or months. After that, my family called in a consultant who helped us put together a security program.

The young lady in the preceding anecdote is one of the bravest individuals I have ever met. In a perilous situation, she acted upon the opportunity that she saw and successfully escaped. Most victims, however, are not given such an opportunity. The kidnapper in her case, working alone, had too many responsibilities between driving the car and controlling the hostage to be able to completely dominate the situation.

As a Hostage

In any hostage situation, survival is the absolute priority. Anyone who has ever been taken hostage understands that no matter what the hostage taker says or does, the only successful conclusion from a hostage's perspective is survival. The location to which a kidnap victim is taken, which normally will be his or her home for the duration of any negotiation, varies dramatically between kidnapping groups. Most kidnappers plan for the need to maintain a hostage and in urban settings will have obtained or rented a place in which to "store the merchandise." In more rural settings, the hostage may be taken into the jungle or placed in a cave on the side of a mountain. No matter where the hostage is taken, the earliest stages of the process are normally the harshest; kidnappers are still very nervous and no routine has been established. Even if the band of kidnappers have taken many hostages and placed them in the same location, the process will differ slightly depending on the individual victim and the circumstances.

Psychological reactions to kidnapping vary, but almost all hostages report feelings of terror, rage, impotence, depression (to some degree) and frustration. Understanding these feelings and taking measures to combat them is important; left unattended, any or all can have devastating consequences. Victims must come to grips with the reality and realize that every effort is being made to secure their release. Somehow, they must learn to practice patience and wait for the situation to conclude.

In order to survive a kidnapping or any other hostage situation, victims must adopt fundamental behaviors that enhance their possibilities. None of the following guarantees hostage survival. A hostage who does everything right can still be executed on a whim or by design; however, these behaviors have been shown to maximize the chances of survival.

Victims should understand that they may not be fed regularly nor are they going to receive their customary diet. No matter what is offered, as long as the food is edible, hostages should eat as well as possible. Drink as much liquid as possible, preferably water; however, soft drinks, juice and other non-alcoholic beverages are acceptable. Try to keep the body hydrated and energized. Getting enough exercise is also important to maintain good heath while in captivity. While captors are not likely to permit hostages to go for a run every morning, victims can do sit-ups or pushups and similar exercises; if no such exercise is permitted, isometric exercises can be done, even surreptitiously if necessary. The point is to maintain as high a level of physical fitness as possible. Long-term hostages are often malnourished and sickly upon their release; every effort must be made to avoid this.

Victims should exercise their minds as much as possible. They should make mental notes of every single detail possible about the place in which they are being held and practice remembering the details. One should also avoid too narrow a focus only on the captivity and the circumstances surrounding the situation. Hostages should perform mental exercises every day to keep their minds sharp and help regain and retain perspective. Simple exercises such as multiplication tables, remembering quotations from great literary works (or bad movies), or reconstructing dialogues with loved ones can be of great help in maintaining mental acuity.

Preserving physical, mental and psychological stability is very important; one never knows when an opportunity to escape might arise. Even if such a chance never becomes available, the actions necessary to maintain one's fitness will make the rigors of captivity more bearable and the recovery afterward swifter.

If kidnappers insist on making videos or audiotapes, the victim should participate willingly. The family will most likely see these and this is their only way to know that the victim is alive and in what condition. The tapes may also provide clues to investigators; however, trying to blink out the location in Morse code or some other heroic stunt is much more likely to end in violence than in rescue or release. Cooperation may also lead to increased privileges, better treatment or more opportunities for communication.

Believing in a higher being is very helpful. Faith is a tool that helps those affected endure much suffering and can be a key factor in survival. Placing all of one's psychic energy into hating those who committed the kidnapping and focusing exclusively on revenge normally only ends in tragedy. As corny as this may sound, love for family and others will make the unthinkable that much easier to bear. Anger can eat a person up from the inside and send him raving mad; love can make almost anything bearable.

11
CONCLUSION

Philosophy triumphs easily over past evils and future evils; but present evils triumph over it.

Francois, duc de la Rochefoucauld, Maxim 22

Every society gets the kind of criminal it deserves. What is equally true is that every community gets the kind of law enforcement it insists on.

Robert F. Kennedy, Eradicating Free Enterprise in Organized Crime

In 2008, kidnapping is a global phenomenon. All over the world, individuals and groups are committing kidnappings to raise funds for their causes, to make political statements, to intimidate and terrify, or simply to make easy money. Virtual, express and traditional ransom kidnappings are endemic in Latin America, the Philippines, Haiti and parts of Africa. In Iraq, Afghanistan, Pakistan, Somalia, Yemen and other countries, political or terrorist kidnappings are common; making a statement by taking and holding hostages is a favored tactic. In Chechnya and the other former Soviet Republics, kidnapping is rife as well.

Those are some of the particularly troublesome hot spots in which kidnappings have been occurring at a tremendously increased rate in recent years. In Mexico, the government's war on drug traffickers has had an impact on the customary cash flow for narcotics traffickers. The effect of multiple large seizures has been to force the traffickers to seek other means of access to the large amounts of cash they are accustomed to and many of them have taken up kidnapping. This has led to an eighty-plus percent increase in reported kidnappings in the first half of 2008 in some areas of the country, particularly the states along the northern border and in the northwestern part of the country. Criminals take note of the scope of the problem and add to the difficulty by committing more kidnappings that get lost in the fog of blame on the drug traffickers.

In Haiti, kidnapping has rapidly become endemic to the point where the country may now have the highest per capita kidnapping rate in the world. Ineffective law enforcement, high unemployment, increasing food prices and a sense of hopelessness have contributed to an environment in which the crime is flourishing. Kidnappings are occurring at all levels of society on the island and victims are frequently executed for non-payment of a ransom demand. The United Nations Stabilization Mission and the Haitian National Police have been unable to stem the rising tide of incidents.

In Nigeria, although Western oil workers seem to feel they are the focus of all kidnappings, the local populace is increasingly being victimized. From government functionaries to schoolteachers to children of middle and upper class parents, no one is immune. Added to this is the incessant kidnapping of Christian girls to be raised as Muslims. The Nigerian authorities arrest kidnappers every day; however, corruption continues and the citizenry is reluctant to file reports for fear of worse consequences.

In India, the plethora of insurgent groups, religious conflicts and criminal gangs make the country a constant leader in kidnapping, with no sign that kidnappers are slowing down. Argentina, Brazil, Indonesia and Venezuela also are reporting very high numbers of incidents. One can almost say that kidnapping in one form or another is a growing problem in "insert name of country" and have a very good chance of being correct no matter what name is used.

Kidnappings are also becoming more violent. Reports from virtually every country on the globe indicate an increased death rate among kidnap victims. While kidnapping is still primarily viewed as a business, sources everywhere indicate that the death toll as a percentage is rising. Mutilation or sexual abuse of the victim or victims as a tool for leverage is also becoming more commonplace; kidnappers are willing to do whatever is necessary to force the issue and obtain the maximum amount of ransom money in the shortest possible time.

The phenomenon of virtual kidnapping is becoming particularly problematic. This is easy money for kidnappers in an environment in which the populace is loath to report incidents for fear that law enforcement may be involved.

The threat of kidnapping opens an entirely new area of exploitation for criminals: extortion. Where the population fears or distrusts the authorities, and this is the case in most countries in the developing world, the mere threat of kidnapping can result in a handsome payment to the extortionist. A few years ago, I received a call from a client with whom I was working to put together an executive protection program. He was in a panic and showed me a fax he had received at his office earlier that morning. The document threatened to kidnap his son if he did not pay a ransom of thirty thousand dollars. We discussed the situation and took a number of additional security measures; he ignored the threat and responded to a follow-up call with a threat to notify the police. Nothing happened and after that neither he nor any family member has ever been kidnapped. When we discussed the case some months later, he mentioned that nearly one hundred businessmen in his professional association had received similar faxes and that by his estimate about ten percent of them had acquiesced and paid the money without taking time to analyze the feasibility of the threat.

This is good business for the criminals. Send one hundred faxes, make some threatening phone calls, pick up the agreed-upon ransom and count your money. Kidnappers and extortionists rely on a lack of knowledge and fear of consequences and operate with virtual impunity, certain in the knowledge that potential victims are unlikely to report such attempts. In many countries, sending such a threat is not illegal, only actually receiving a payoff for doing so. Imagine if you will, a potential victim reports receiving a threatening communication; the local authorities indicate that they cannot act unless an actual payment is made or an act of aggression committed; and the victim is left to his or her own devices. Readers in the United States may correlate this concept with the dubious utility of restraining orders issued against abusive spouses or lovers.

An activity such as kidnapping or extortion via the threat of kidnapping can only flourish in an environment of fear and uncertainty. Unfortunately, such an environment exists today in nearly every developing nation in the world. In most countries, law enforcement is weak and confronted with multiple other issues such as drug use and trafficking, street gangs, murder, rape and robbery. Police are generally underpaid, poorly trained and equipped, and come from the poorest and least educated sections of the population. The middle and upper classes of societies do not respect the individuals or the institutions, seeing the authorities as a threat or a hindrance rather than as a public service that supports good government and a safe society. Many wealthier citizens of developing countries will openly state that inviting a policeman into their home to take a report is tantamount to scheduling another robbery. Citizens complain loudly about the poor quality of policing; however, they do not take kindly to increased taxes to pay for better law enforcement.

The issue of corruption is also a major contributing factor to the rise of kidnapping. Imagine an officer in a specialized anti-kidnapping unit in a developing nation. He goes through a door equipped only with a pistol (and maybe a bulletproof vest that has been shown to be ineffective because it was purchased from a vendor who paid off the contracting officer and used inferior materials to make a higher profit) and maybe a handheld radio, to assault a band of kidnappers armed with automatic weapons. If the assault is successful, he encounters a room containing bags filled with hundreds of thousands of dollars or the equivalent in local currency. The captured kidnappers suggest a trade; he will report that they escaped through a window and he can keep the money and the hostage(s). The team leader agrees, the criminals flee and the money is divvied up, with a few stacks held over for turn-in. The official report states that the hostage was rescued and that some money was recovered; payoffs are shared up the chain of command and everyone is happy. Unfortunately, the kidnappers immediately go after another victim to replace the funds they lost in the last operation and they are probably going to be in a hurry to get paid and less willing to negotiate amicably.

This is a classic case with which most law enforcement personnel worldwide are familiar. The vast amounts of money are so tempting that men or women who may be dedicated to their craft are pushed to the limit when confronted with an opportunity. Add to this the fact that most are underpaid, under-funded and feel absolutely unappreciated and such denouements are not at all surprising. The unfortunate result of this type of situation is a creeping corruption that slowly overtakes a huge percentage of the police force. Easy money is hard to refuse once an individual has overcome his or her initial moral resistance to taking a bribe or payoff. Like a drug, more and more is needed to feed the monster and more crimes will be overlooked or set aside as the need for money to support an improved lifestyle increases. Under such conditions it is amazing that any criminals at all are apprehended.

Corruption is not limited to the police officer on the beat. A number of situations have been reported in which highly placed politicians, senior members of law enforcement or wealthy denizens of society have been found to be behind kidnapping bands. Those who have sworn to protect and improve society and those of economic power and privilege are often the brains behind the band. The arrogance of such actions is almost incomprehensible. Every time a powerful figure is caught in a web of kidnapping, the entire society suffers a blow in that overall trust in government institutions is diminished.

I once conversed with the senior law enforcement advisor to the governor of a key state in a developing nation. This state is a hub through which a majority of highway and rail traffic passes and is considered one of the keys to detaining drug shipments and controlling criminal groups of all sorts, including kidnappers. In response to a question about police corruption, he stated, "I have never stolen anything...in the last eight years" (since he retired from a senior police position and went to work for the governor). "But before that... whoa." Everyone in the room laughed, some more sardonically than others, and he went on to state, "I have what I need, I don't need to steal anymore." This sad commentary on the reality of corruption in developing nations is an example of one of the factors that foments the growth of the kidnapping problem.

For the poor people of a developing country, a corrupt authority can hardly be considered a reliable resource for the administration of justice. Poor people perceive that justice is only for the rich; they must pay protection in order to sell their wares on the street or operate a market stall. They understand that when they are victimized, their case will be shuffled to the back of the stack of priorities at the police station because they cannot "grease the wheels of justice." The poor do not have the resources to pay stiff fines or bribes and therefore are at the whim of the police officer or bureaucrat. Their lives are endlessly complicated in a corrupt society.

For example, a poor man wishing to renew his driver's license may have to travel more than an hour to the nearest location, wait in line for four to six hours, and then return home. For this he must ask for a day off from his (normally) blue-collar job, run the risk of the supervisor's wrath and probably lose his pay for the day. Furthermore, the boss is angry and may fire him because he knows that renewing a driver's license only takes him an hour or two in total. He (the boss) drives over, pays someone to watch his car, sidles up to the back door, arranges a quick turnaround for a nominal cash service charge, receives his new license and is on his way in an hour. His scheming employee is obviously trying to weasel out of coming to work all day just to run an errand for a couple of hours. This may seem almost comical to the casual observer; however, some version of this is repeated in hundreds of locations throughout the developing world every day.

The wealthier classes also, albeit from a different viewpoint, perceive that justice or the administration of essential services is only for those who can pay and the result is a self-perpetuating system of corruption in which nothing gets done without someone receiving a payoff. A police investigation costs money, as does getting a problem solved with the electric company or installing a new telephone line. The wealthy can and do pay for these services as a matter of course in most developing countries.

Many times I have been exposed to campaigns started via the Internet or among friends in which everyone agrees to no longer pay any type of bribe. These campaigns usually last until someone is pulled over for speeding or running a red light or needs to get something accomplished through the governing bureaucracy. One encounters a distinct lack of enthusiasm for being the first to actually have his or her driver's license confiscated and to have to go down to the local station to pay a fine and pick up the document. It is, after all, much easier to just "pay the fine on the spot" or treat the officer to a soda or a meal.

Other societal factors contribute to the problem. Poor people in most countries have little hope of improvement and perceive few avenues to success. Make no mistake, the majority of citizens everywhere are honest and hard-working; however, an increasing element of the populations sees crime as the easiest way to achieve a consumer goods-laden lifestyle. History is full of examples of people who have been willing to do almost anything to make what they see as an upward move in society and this is almost always reflected in economic or purchasing power. When a hungry young person who must work a menial job at a young age to help his or her family scratch out a meager existence notices that one of their friends is wearing new clothes, eating at restaurants and always has money, questions will naturally follow.

The attraction of "good things" is irresistible to many, particularly in societies where television is king. People are constantly bombarded with advertisements for the good things, little or none of which they can ever hope to afford. Programming such as soap operas glorifies corruption, lying and cheating as ways to succeed and then one wonders why people act in criminal ways. Some may perceive this as a superficial rationalization; however, the impact is undeniable. Many detained kidnappers have cited the desire to have all they saw on television or the feeling that making a lot of money in a hurry by kidnapping was the only way they could get ahead in life as justifications for their actions.

Jobs are also an issue. Most developing nations do not create a sufficient number of jobs for those entering the workforce, particularly in countries in which the majority of the population is young. A lack of opportunity often is used as a justification for entering a life of crime. One may find it easy to pontificate about how there is no excuse for becoming a kidnapper and that jobs are there for those who wish to work; however, that is an unreal perspective. Jobs are not universally available and a small percentage of any population will choose crime as an alternative. The problem grows larger as jobs become scarcer.

The upper levels of society must bear significant responsibility for the tenuous employment situations in many countries. Tax evasion is not only an art form but also a way of life for many of the wealthy worldwide. For example, although conditions are improving as more efforts are made to collect taxes, as recently as five years ago only an estimated eleven percent of Mexicans paid their taxes, forcing the government to operate on a severely restricted budget. This situation is not unique to Mexico; while the percentages may vary, the practice is not dissimilar in other countries around the world. Those unpaid taxes lower a government's ability to finance and train law enforcement, create employment opportunities, support social programs and foster economic development. The resulting lack of opportunities augments the cycle of poverty and contributes to crime and corruption at all levels.

Another issue is the "Robin Hood" effect. In many places, the local populace sees individuals or groups that commit kidnappings as heroic figures who are defying the authorities and helping the poor and weak. In Colombia, drug baron Pablo Escobar built schools and playgrounds in poor communities with the fruits of drug trafficking and kidnapping. In India, the *dacoits* were long viewed by the local population as heroic bandits although they made their living by kidnapping and robbery. In Mexico, *narcocorridas* (ballads portraying drug traffickers and kidnappers as heroic anti-establishment figures) receive considerable radio airtime and can be heard at sidewalk cafes and on the streets throughout the northwestern part of the nation.

When ideology, race or religion come into play, support from certain sectors of the population is much easier to obtain. Chinese Communist leader Mao Zedong is quoted as saying that the guerrilla needs to swim like a fish among the population. To this end, kidnappers who consider themselves revolutionaries have long tried to establish a base of operations among some segments of the population. This is an area or locale in which their activities, if not viewed entirely favorably, at least receive tacit approval from a majority of the locals. Investigators make little headway in resolving kidnappings committed by Shiites in Sadr City, the FARC in Colombia or the NPA in Compostela Valley province in the Philippines. Ideologically or politically motivated kidnappings, particularly those for ransom, tend to be extremely difficult to resolve.

In countries where drug trafficking is a serious problem, kidnapping flourishes as well. Drug traffickers encourage kidnapping as a means of diverting law enforcement attention and resources from their principal activities, as well as using the crime as a fundraising tool when times get tough or law enforcement pressure begins to affect cash flow. They also use kidnapping and abduction as a measure to intimidate and terrorize rival traffickers, law enforcement and the local population. This has contributed to an increase in the violence associated with kidnapping, as drug traffickers are notoriously quick to use violence and short of patience in negotiations. The relationship between drug trafficking and kidnapping can be noted when one considers that many of the countries most often cited as world leaders in kidnappings (Colombia, Haiti, Mexico, Pakistan, Venezuela, etc.) are also routinely considered among the most problematic points for production and/or shipping of drugs.

Many countries previously considered supplier countries or transshipment points for drugs are encountering an ever-larger problem of drug consumption. Governments and law enforcement turned a blind eye to or profited from drug smuggling in prior years and the chickens are now coming home to roost. A situation that was viewed as purely an American or European problem is becoming a serious social issue as entrenched smuggling networks have turned to selling their wares to local populations, creating an entirely new class of users as a source of ready cash and a way to expand their markets. Weak and often corrupt law enforcement agencies are not prepared to take on well-organized and extremely wealthy drug cartels. Kidnapping is viewed as easy money and more drug users are turning to a ready source of large amounts of cash to finance their consumption.

Kidnappers and drug traffickers typically are better armed and equipped than law enforcement authorities in developing nations; they normally have automatic weapons, personal protection gear, first-rate communications equipment and late-model vehicles. They also have more ammunition, get more practice with their weapons and are much more willing to use them. Police in many countries are hamstrung to a degree by laws that ensure that the officer who uses his or her weapon against a criminal will go to jail until the case is fully resolved or they face restrictions that make using a weapon virtually a crime. Most police officers in developing countries get very little opportunity to use their weapons at a practice range. They typically are afforded one or two opportunities yearly and can only fire a dozen or so rounds each time. In many cases, officers must pay for their practice ammunition and also for the ammunition they carry on duty. This limits proficiency and leads to cases of police officers carrying antiquated rounds that are in no condition to be fired safely.

Another factor impacting the growth of kidnapping is impunity. Most criminals in the developing world are not incarcerated for their crimes. Justice systems all over work inefficiently and limited resources are focused on kidnapping as a specific crime.

In most countries there are multiple legal loopholes through which a kidnapper can pass, not least of which are judges for sale to the highest bidder. If a kidnapper knows there is a less than ten percent chance he or she will be arrested and successfully prosecuted, he has little or no incentive to refrain from kidnapping at will. Ten percent is a wildly optimistic estimate in the case of most developing nations; the actual percentages appear to be far lower.

Assume that fifteen percent of all kidnappings are reported to the authorities in country X (this percentage can be disputed; however, all sources with whom I have talked agree that it is no more than a quarter and probably much closer to an eighth of all kidnappings for ransom are reported). From the start, a kidnapper has an eighty-five percent chance of avoiding prosecution simply because law enforcement knows nothing of the case. Of those reported, maybe fifty percent result in a lead or leads that can potentially be followed up by investigators after the victim has been released (kidnapping is an extremely difficult crime to investigate successfully, particularly if the kidnappers are professionals). Of the remaining seven and a half percent, assume that half of the investigations lead to an arrest. Of those arrested, one must consider the possibility of a poorly prepared case, a bribed judge or juror, improperly collected or processed evidence or a wealth of other possibilities that would prevent incarceration. Finally, assume that one in three arrested kidnappers is actually tried, convicted and jailed. The result is that 98.75% of all kidnappers are free to continue operating with no fear of ever going to jail.

This also does not take into account the fact that rarely are all the members of a kidnapping band arrested; those who survive recruit new members and continue or form their own groups to continue the work. One can substitute numbers in this equation at will; however, no numbers outside of full reporting and complete investigation lead to any percentage that notably increases the risk for the average kidnapper. Any criminal permitted to operate with virtual impunity will continue to commit the same crime over and over.

One might wonder how any kidnapping is ever solved, considering the multiple advantages that accrue to kidnappers. Many solutions to the problem have been proposed; however, most have proven unworkable. I have provided executive protection training to many wealthy

individuals and families over the last fifteen years. During the training, some member of the family or group, obviously designated by
the leadership, has almost always taken me aside and inquired as to
the feasibility of putting together a team to "take care of the kidnappers." The question is always asked delicately and in such a way that a
denial is possible if the issue was to ever come up again. My response
is always that the concept of death squads is not one that can be controlled and that proper security procedures are much better than trying to put together a team of contract killers. The person always nods
understandingly and goes away to report that I am not interested.
Rumors of this practice abound; however, I have yet to see any evidence of such an activity making a positive impact. One only has to
look at El Salvador and the Colombian paramilitary experience to see
that, once unleashed, death squads are impossible to control.

Another solution that is intuitively obvious but totally useless in
practice is often proposed by people who have never experienced a
kidnapping first-hand. They suggest "If every one refused to pay ransom, no one would be kidnapped because there would be no market."
This is undoubtedly true; however, I know of no one who wishes to
be the first to sacrifice a loved one for the good of all. Making such a
statement while comfortably ensconced in one's living room, at a local
bar or in a conference room is easy; acting upon such a premise when
one's husband, wife or child is being held by kidnappers is virtually
impossible. The reality of a kidnapping is that the victim's family or
organization will negotiate some form of payment, despite all claims
to the contrary. One only need remember President Ronald Reagan's
claims that the United States does not negotiate with terrorists, made
while trading missiles for the release of hostages.

What can be done to reduce the scope of kidnapping worldwide?
From a law enforcement perspective, there are a number of steps that
would help alleviate the problem. The principal factor is the need to
create respect for the job of police officer. Respect must be earned;
however, there are a number of measures that might contribute to
developing more respect among the populace. Law enforcement personnel need to be compensated in a manner that attracts better candidates. If salaries are so low that the average police officer must augment
his or her income in some way to provide for his family, opportunities
for corruption are widespread and payoffs are inevitable. In the more

developed countries, all candidates are vetted carefully, in most cases more carefully than candidates for military service. In the developing world, efforts are being made to vet candidates more effectively but results are spotty and this must improve if a better quality of recruit is to be identified and brought on board.

Education and training is another area of emphasis; all officers must receive training that enables them to function effectively. This is inextricably linked to the educational level of candidates recruited for service. A police officer who reads and writes at an elementary school level is not likely to be able to absorb and use sophisticated training as well as one who has a high school diploma or some college. In the United States and Europe, a significant percentage of all law enforcement officers are college graduates and receive training in multiple disciplines. They are expected to use that knowledge on the street every day, as well as operate computers in patrol cars, write reports that can be used in court and perform a multitude of other tasks. Police officers in developing countries are often expected to comply with a similar level of responsibility; however, they are not given the proper training or are not educationally prepared to make effective use of the training received.

Equipment and other tools of the trade are also critical factors. In developing countries, members of law enforcement are operating at a gross disadvantage in armament, communications and equipment against criminals. Limited resources provide insufficient quantities and often shoddy quality equipment with which the thin blue line is expected to make a stand. Political decisions must be made to equip police with the necessary tools if they are to be expected to make any headway against kidnappers, drug traffickers and other criminals.

A blanket condemnation of the honor and quality of law enforcement in developing countries worldwide would be completely unjust to the thousands of dedicated professionals who do a great deal with, in many cases, very little support. Overall, however, the quality of police work is lacking and more and better training, selection, education and equipment are necessary to facilitate their work. Law enforcement needs to be equipped with the most up-to-date technologies; people tracking systems, remote surveillance and electronic intercept capabilities formerly only in the hands of governments are needed to detect, deter and detain kidnappers.

Political will to make the necessary changes is also important. As an initial step toward common understanding, kidnapping needs to be defined on an international basis. Governments and legislatures need to agree on what constitutes a kidnapping and how the crime will be penalized. Obviously, complete agreement on all aspects is a dream; however, much more can be done to standardize definitions and penalties. Even more important are the changes in socioeconomic conditions that would reduce the fertile field in which kidnappers now operate. More and better jobs and education for the masses in most countries will spawn development that strengthens societies and reduces the inequalities that are frequently cited by kidnappers as an underlying cause for their activity. I am not suggesting that the world become some sort of utopia in which everyone lives in peace and harmony; this is apparently against human nature. I do, however, posit that, if the enormous gulf that exists in much of the world between the haves and the have-nots begins to lessen, people will perceive more opportunities for success via traditional paths and the rationale for kidnapping might well diminish.

Civil society also has a role to play. Grassroots organizations in Spain and Colombia were able to mobilize the populace and increase public awareness of the kidnappings committed by the ETA and FARC, respectively. These campaigns obliged the governments to act and also applied pressure on the guerrilla organizations to reduce the scope of kidnapping activities. This did not, in either case, eliminate the problem; however, both counties were able to slow the growth of kidnapping incidents. Citizens can have an impact. In Mexico City in June 2004, nearly one million people marched in the streets against the scourge of kidnapping. Despite the local mayor's dismissive remarks about the elitist nature of the marchers, a strong statement was made, enormous pressure placed on the federal and local authorities, and kidnappings in the area were reduced somewhat for a time.

These recommendations are not new and, for the most part, are unlikely to be implemented on any broad scale. Poor quality law enforcement, economic inequalities, corruption and the diversion of public resources for private benefit are going to continue around the world. There is also too much money, opportunity and easily available victims for kidnappers to voluntarily give up their profession. They will continue to become more professional and more sophisticated, keeping pace with improvements in law enforcement. As long as kidnapping is still "the best business around," the plague will continue. Kidnapping has existed since the dawn of human history and there is no reason to expect that to change in the modern world. Our interconnected world affords virtually any kidnapper with an agenda the opportunity to be noticed and, in certain ways, foments the commission of more kidnappings. However, since we cannot go back to the Stone Age, these issues must be addressed head on.

Most of us probably share the perception that governments are unlikely to take the sweeping measures necessary to reduce kidnappings worldwide, thus leaving the prevention and resolution of kidnappings in the hands of individuals and organizations. We the people are those who must take appropriate actions to avoid becoming victims. If you believe yourself to be a potential kidnap victim, do not hesitate to take measures to reduce your vulnerability and that of your family and/or organization. Develop a personal security plan for all potential victims and implement that plan; get professional help, if necessary. The worst thing you can do is stand idly by trusting that kidnapping will happen to someone else. Security measures need not necessarily be prohibitively expensive; judiciously apply a suitable set of measures to your particular situation and incorporate prevention into your daily routines. Simply becoming a more difficult target will lower your risk significantly.

If you or a member of your family or organization become a kidnap victim, understand that there is a solution in most cases. The process described herein may vary slightly among venues; however, a methodical approach that covers all the necessary elements is the best opportunity for a successful resolution. Discuss the process with your family and implement a plan within your organization; preparation is the key to success. A properly managed response to a kidnapping will result in the victim's safe return in more than ninety percent of cases. Endeavor to avoid becoming a victim; however, if a kidnapping occurs, take the necessary measures to ensure that you are in the ninety percent of those having joyful reunions with loved ones and colleagues.

Appendix: Personal Security and Avoidance Tips

Any individual or institution wishing to reduce the risk of kidnapping in today's world must learn to adjust his or her lifestyle and methods of conducting business. The security recommendations in this appendix should be carefully reviewed and discussed with family members and those staff considered at risk. Personal habits and business and professional activities form the basis of an individual diagnosis of specific security requirements. The physical and procedural security characteristics of residences, offices, recreational locations and commonly used methods of transport must also be considered.

While a complete and detailed security analysis of any at-risk individual is always the safest course of action, anyone can apply basic concepts that will enhance security and reduce the possibility of falling victim to a kidnapping or other crime. A fundamental precept of any security plan is that changes necessary to implement the plan should never be so complex that they interfere with a normal private life. Plans should be adjusted to suit each individual. Adopting a simple and realistic plan is much easier than trying to implement a series of complicated and wildly exaggerated security measures.

The security measures contained in this appendix are not new; rather they are a compendium of sound, common sense measures derived from the efforts of countless security professionals over many years. No matter how extensive or complete a list one encounters, the best possible security measure is the individual's common sense and good judgment. The information herein is presented in an easily accessible manner to facilitate its use by both professionals and laymen.

Residential Security Measures

- Get professional advice.
- Understand that security is an essential part of your life and act accordingly.
- Motivate your family members to exercise sound security practices.
- Install and use deadbolt locks on all doors and windows.
- Install adequate perimeter and exterior lighting that can be controlled from within the residence.
- Keep a list of emergency numbers next to each telephone and preprogram those numbers into cellular phones.
- Have a list of telephone numbers of friends and locations that each family member frequents.
- Keep family members informed if delays in returning home are encountered or expected.
- Always change lock combinations when occupying a residence or when any domestic staff member with possible access to keys has been terminated; change combinations any time keys are lost or stolen.
- Use peephole viewers in all solid exterior doors.
- Keep vehicles locked even when on the property or in a garage.
- Install burglar bars or security grills on all accessible windows and doors.
- Install security film on larger windows.
- Ensure that nearby street areas are adequately lighted and install additional security lighting on the exterior of the property as necessary.
- Use motion-activated security lights in inner garden or yard areas.
- Maintain curtains and blinds closed to deter observation, especially at night.

- Trim shrubbery and trees to reduce potential hiding places and make access to the residence more difficult from the exterior.
- Never put names on the outside of the house or on the mailbox.
- Install and use an intercom or video intercom system for granting street access. Do not allow remote opening of exterior property gates or doors without a visual check of the exterior.
- Ensure that any workers or service personnel arriving at the residence are authorized and duly identified prior to granting access.
- Establish and practice a family emergency plan.
- Prepare and keep available a "bug-out" kit with passports, cash and other essential documents that can be easily grabbed and carried in an emergency.
- Ensure that perimeter walls and fences are of sufficient height (9 feet on the attack side) and have anti-climbing protection (barbed wire, etc.) on the top.
- Check the serviceability of fire and alarms and fire extinguishers on a regular basis.
- Install, use and regularly test an intrusion alarm system.
- Purchase insurance against robberies and fires.
- Verify the identity of any strangers noted in the area with neighbors or authorities.
- If strange vehicles are noticed near the residence, note the license plate and characteristics of the vehicle and report to the local authorities or security company.
- Carefully evaluate security service vendors and choose only those of good repute.
- Avoid leaving exterior doors open, even momentarily, while sweeping sidewalks or other such activities.
- Ensure that family members and domestic employees are aware that personal information should never be given to strangers, telemarketers or anyone who calls or comes to the residence.
- Do not allow friends or family members of domestic staff to enter the property.
- Investigate domestic staff personnel or have a background investigation conducted; simply calling a couple of references is not sufficient. Keep current photographs and locator information on hand.

- Make an effort to maintain good relations with neighbors and the local authorities.
- Refrain from accepting packages or gifts sent by persons or organizations unknown.
- If a stranger asks to use your telephone, offer to make the call for him or her and relay a message without permitting that person entry to the premises.
- When traveling away from home, suspend services such as newspapers and do not post notices announcing your absence.
- Leave lights on or set timers to turn them on and off when you are not at home.
- Never leave an extra key outside your home under a rock, in a planter, etc.
- Try to vary your arrival and departure times from home as much as is feasible. Purchase a portable document shredder and destroy all bank and credit card statements, as well as any other document containing personal or financial information.
- Prepare a personal file, including medical information, on each family member that contains information necessary to support a response to a kidnapping.
- Do not leave ladders lying about in the yard, chain them to a fence or store them inside.
- Establish a safe haven within the residence to which you can retreat in case of emergency.
- If you notice that someone is trying to enter your residence, go to your safe haven and call for help.
- Immediately investigate any alarm signal to determine the cause; call or respond to the alarm company's call by asking for a patrol if there is any doubt at all.
- Consider purchasing a fire- and water-resistant safe for storing important papers, credit cards and valuables. Ensure that the safe is bolted to the floor.

Outside the Home

- Do not carry a lot of cash, take only what you expect to need and carry only a single credit or debit card.
- Dress in a low-key fashion.

- Do not wear flashy jewelry or watches.
- Avoid walking alone. If possible, travel with a friend.
- Plan your route and travel well-lit, busy streets.
- Carry a personal alarm device.
- Carry a solid or sharp object with you.
- If you will be gone a long time, let someone know your schedule.
- Be constantly aware of your surroundings.
- Exude confidence, walk quickly and strongly, keep your eyes open and look around.
- Walk at a distance from alley entrances, shrubs, and other potential hiding places.
- Watch areas with shadows.
- Walk near the curb and be very attentive to vehicular traffic.
- Avoid public parks and other locations with few people and many hiding places.
- Carry your purse close to your body like an American football or under a jacket and keep your wallet in a front pants pocket.
- Try to avoid walking encumbered by purses, bags, books, etc.
- Walk facing vehicular traffic.
- Watch for strangers and suspicious behavior.
- Do not hesitate to seek assistance or safe haven if you feel threatened by suspicious persons or behavior.
- Know the areas in which you walk. Locate in advance police stations and other locations where you could get assistance.
- Be watchful of people asking for directions or other assistance from a vehicle.
- Do not approach unknown persons in vehicles.
- If threatened by someone in a vehicle, run in the opposite direction.
- Never accept rides from strangers.
- Schedule your walking, to and from work, around the block, etc., in such a way as to be unpredictable.
- Avoid using public restrooms alone if possible.
- Do not become involved in fights or violent disturbances that do not directly concern you.
- Keep an eye on your purse, briefcase, shopping bags and other items at all times.

- If you fell that someone is stalking you, discreetly seek help. If in a public place, remain there until the situation is resolved.
- When entering any public place for the first time, always identify the nearest emergency exit. For example, in most restaurants an emergency exit will be located near the rest room or through the kitchen.
- In restaurants or cafes, always sit away from the door and as close as possible to an emergency exit.
- If you are traveling with a group, stay with the group.

Leaving and Returning Home

- Look over the yard and points of entry into the home to check for forced entry or anything out of the ordinary.
- Look outside doors and windows to ensure that no one is lurking about.
- Check the street before opening garage doors.
- Never enter the home or compound alone if there appears to have been forced entry during your absence. Go to a neighbor's house and call the authorities.
- Avoid entering dark yards, porches, stairwells, etc., when alone.
- Trim shrubbery around residence to eliminate hiding places for attackers.
- Install lights along dark walkways, driveways, and in yard.
- Leave entrance and garage lights on.
- Use a flashlight at night.
- Do not stop to retrieve mail at night if you live in a high crime area.
- Do not get out of a vehicle if the area appears for any reason to be unsafe.
- If you notice a strange person or vehicle loitering near your residence, circle the block. If that person is still there, go somewhere safe and request assistance.

Security Measures for Children

- Teach your children basic self-defense measures.
- Teach your children to enter and exit vehicles quickly.

- Check the route your child takes to and from school.
- Pay attention to danger spots along the route and at school bus stops.
- Review the school's security, check-in and check out procedures.
- Tell your children to report any unusual incidents or suspicious people.
- Warn your children against accepting rides or gifts from strangers.
- Know the names and phone numbers of your child's playmates, their parents, and where they live.
- Make sure each child knows his or her phone number, address, and the phone number of another trusted adult.
- Know the playgrounds your children frequent. Avoid letting them go alone.
- Teach your children traffic laws.
- Establish the practice of having older children report when they reach a destination.
- Teach small children the difference between "good" touching and "bad" touching.

Weapons in the Home

The issue of weapons in the home is contentious and there are always two sides to the argument. If an individual decides to keep a weapon at his or her residence, a number of very strict rules should apply:

- Ensure that the weapon is of a type and caliber that is authorized under local law.
- Be sure to register the weapon with the local authorities.
- Learn to safely handle the weapon, and teach family members to do likewise.
- Store the weapon and any ammunition in separate, locked containers.
- Never leave a loaded weapon in a night table, under a mattress or under a pillow.
- Before cleaning, remove the magazine and check the chamber to make sure the weapon is clear. If a revolver, unload the cylinder.

- Do not carry the weapon outside of your residence unless you have legal permission to do so.
- If an incident occurs, do not try and use the weapon unless you have been trained to do so.
- If the weapon is used in defense of your home, immediately obtain legal advice.

Workplace Security Measures

No matter which organization an individual works for, there are likely to be a number of security measures in place. Part of any individual security plan is the responsibility for knowing and understanding security measures in the workplace. Whether you own your own business or work for a large organization, security is still an absolute requirement. Consider the following measures as the minimum necessary.

- Know the organization's internal security procedures.
- Understand and abide by all access control procedures.
- Establish or recommend the implementation of such procedures where none exist.
- Identify all emergency exits and principal and alternate evacuation routes.
- When attending meetings outside the principal workplace, ensure that the location is a public place with adequate security.
- Let someone know your schedule, when you will depart and when you expect to arrive, call to report any unexpected delays or changes.
- Establish a duress signal with your secretary, co-worker or supervisor to communicate an emergency situation.
- In locations where explosions of any type are possible, do not place your desk in front of a large window.
- Do not go near a window if you hear an explosion; take cover behind or beneath something solid.
- Report suspicious packages or other objects to security; do not touch or open any suspicious package.
- Parking spaces should not be marked with the name or position of any executive or member of the organization.
- Keep personal information under lock and key in the workplace.

Travel Security

Crime against travelers is increasing worldwide. Assaults on you or your family, and theft of money and belongings, can be avoided. Helpless and unaware persons are the easiest prey and frequently become targets and victims. Most individuals who were crime victims while traveling report that they were vulnerable for one of the following reasons:

- Inattention to personal belongings while in public places (restaurants, hotel lobbies, shops, etc.).
- Leaving personal belongings in easily accessible positions or places.
- Not reacting when a threat was detected or first materialized.
- Assuming that "It can't happen to me."
- Using unauthorized or unreliable transport services.

Potential Threat Situations

- Movements on foot in major cities.
- Vehicular movements in taxis or private vehicles.
- Hotel lobbies, restaurants and shopping centers.
- Airports, particularly baggage claim and taxi stands.
- Credit card scams such as skimming or double billing.
- ATM machines.
- Marches, demonstrations and other street protests.
- Electoral periods (violence between opposing groups).
- Unpopular government decisions or policies.

General Travel Security

- Always plan your travel.
- Be aware of risks, threats, and scams.
- Be constantly aware of your surroundings.
- Watch for suspicious persons or behavior.
- Protect yourself and children.
- Protect your luggage.
- Be ready to react to any situation.

- Do not keep all identification cards, cash, and important papers in one place.
- Hide money in different pockets.

Know before You Go:

- At least a few phrases in the local language.
- Culture and people.
- Political and economic situation.
- Upcoming major events, such as elections or holidays.
- Severe weather concerns or potential seismic zones.
- Potential health concerns.
- Potential threats and trends in crime.
- Terrorist or guerrilla activity.
- Status of any civil unrest or protest activity.
- Emergency numbers (not all countries use 911).

Avoid:

- Flaunting your wealth or position.
- "Red light" districts and high crime areas.
- Slums and shantytowns.
- Antagonizing local officials.
- Offending the local populace.
- Dressing immodestly.
- Wearing jewelry and openly carrying other valuable items.
- Being ostentatious.
- Carrying large amounts of cash.
- Drinking to excess or drug use.

Hotel Security:

- Stay in hotels near where your meetings are to be held or as near to your tourist destination(s) as possible.
- Identify and locate emergency exits and evacuation routes.
- Read the security instructions on the back of your hotel room door.
- Locate the nearest fire control equipment.

- Do not allow any unauthorized individuals (other than cleaners, room service, etc.) access to your hotel room.
- Make sure that interconnecting doors between hotels rooms are securely locked.
- Always use the room or hotel safe for valuables.
- Refrain from leaving laptop computers, cameras and other high-value items unsecured in your hotel room.
- Do not allow hotel maintenance personnel into your room while you are present.
- Consult with the individual in charge of hotel security on potential trouble spots in the area of the hotel.

Security at Airports, Seaports, Train and Bus Stations:

- Take note of strangers who appear and disappear frequently.
- Check in early.
- Never leave your luggage unattended.
- Do not let strangers carry or help you with your luggage.
- Never agree to carry packages or mail for anyone you don't know and trust.
- Avoid crowds, overly congested areas, and completely isolated areas.
- Request identification from anyone claiming to be an authority or official.
- Locate emergency exits and emergency assistance stations.
- Dress modestly, casually, and comfortably.
- Avoid ostentatious behavior, activity and conversation.
- Avoid exhibiting large amounts of money, traveler's checks, or credit cards.
- Do not purchase anything from freelance vendors.
- Know where you are going or need to go, and avoid becoming lost.
- Use only authorized taxi services or hotel shuttle buses.

Safety on Board a Plane, Train, or Boat:

- Check your seat area for potential hazards or illicit materials.
- Never agree to watch a stranger's luggage, even for a minute.

- Window seats are most secure for you and your carry-on luggage.
- Listen to emergency instructions and locate emergency exits.
- Mentally prepare for how you might react in any given situation.
- Assess fellow passengers—be alert for suspicious persons and behavior.
- Limit your intake of alcoholic beverages and caffeine.
- Never accept beverages, food, or cigarettes from strangers.
- Rest as much as possible.

Safeguarding Your Luggage:

- Lock your luggage and carry-on bags. (Use TSA-approved locks or straps)
- Keep unattended luggage locked, even while you sleep.
- Use distinctly colored nylon straps to further secure and easily identify luggage.
- Use fold-over ID tags to protect your identity and nationality.
- Do not use distinctive luggage tags that show you are a platinum or gold card or club member.
- Do not use luggage or tags with your organization or company logo on the side.
- Secure additional identification tags inside luggage.
- Never place travel documents, sensitive papers, currency, or other valuables in checked luggage.
- Maintain an inventory of luggage contents in the event of loss, damage, or theft.

Basic Precautions:

- Leave an itinerary with a trusted friend.
- Make sure your personal affairs are in order. Consider bills and obligations.
- Take extra medicine and eyeglasses.
- Reconfirm flights and itinerary upon arrival and just before departure.
- Allow extra time to make connections.

- Keep the address and phone number of your embassy or consulate.
- Safeguard passport or visitor's card.
- Carry small change for tips and sundries.
- Place high-value items in your carry-on luggage.
- Photocopy your airline tickets, passport and other important documents.

Vehicle Security:

The single most vulnerable location for most persons is in their vehicles. More than eighty percent of kidnappings occur while in transit, as well as armed robberies, car jackings, smash and grabs and numerous other crimes. The following list of recommendations is provided to reduce your chances of becoming a victim:

- Use vehicles that are not unique or attention-getting.
- Always carry a cellular phone and emergency numbers.
- Identify residences of known persons and safe havens (hospitals, police stations, etc.) along regular routes.
- Vary routes to and from frequent destinations; and be aware of multiple options.
- Use seatbelts and keep doors and windows locked.
- Never leave children in a vehicle without an adult.
- Check the backseat for intruders before getting in a vehicle.
- Do not leave identification documents in a vehicle.
- Lock valuables in the trunk.
- Know the vehicle's capabilities—take a test drive.
- Sound the horn if someone tries to enter the vehicle.
- Travel on main roads and position the vehicle in center lanes as much as possible.
- Keep flashlights, flares, a blanket, non-perishable snacks, and bottled water in the trunk. Once a month, check the pressure of the vehicle's spare tire.
- Drive to a safe haven if harassed.
- If required to exit the vehicle due to an accident or breakdown, take the keys and lock the doors.

- Leave space in front of your vehicle so you have room to maneuver if necessary.
- Keep the vehicle in gear at brief stops.
- Avoid troublesome areas and traffic jams.
- If someone tries to stop your vehicle saying that you have a flat tire or other malfunction, go to a safe, well-lit area to check.
- Maintain the gas tank at least half full at all times.
- Approach your vehicle with keys in hand, get in and go.
- Whenever arriving home or at a frequent destination, take care to observe potential risks such as strangers or impediments to movement.
- When departing, take note of any strangers loitering in the area.
- Never park in isolated areas that lack a security presence.
- Do not drive in uninhabited areas or construction zones unless absolutely necessary; never let someone stop you in an isolated area.
- Never leave the vehicle to converse with a stranger.
- If your vehicle breaks down, do not accept help from strangers; call for assistance.
- Do not offer rides to unknown persons or stop to look at accidents.
- If the police stop you, do not leave your vehicle. Make a note of the characteristics of the officer and vehicle. Try to proceed to a well-lighted and well-traveled area before stopping.
- Maintain a safe distance from the vehicle in front of yours at all traffic stops (make sure you can see the rear tires of the vehicle in front of you in contact with the road surface). This will provide enough room to escape in the event of an emergency.
- Be cautious when motorcycles appear to be matching your pace.
- If trapped in an exchange of gunfire, get down on the floor of the vehicle.
- If chased by another vehicle, seek a safe haven; stop next to a police car or in a very crowded area.
- Never leave an automobile running when you exit the vehicle. Get out with keys in hand in case a rapid return to the vehicle is necessary.

- Do not travel with valuables (purses, briefcases, packages, etc.) on passenger seats and in view.
- Protect vehicles with alarms, interrupter switches, immobilizing devices and the like.
- Consider the possibility of hiring a driver with security training.
- When using valet parking, always leave only the valet or ignition key.
- Get a receipt from parking lot attendants or valets for any valuable items left in the vehicle.
- Inspect vehicle to check for damages, strangers or missing items before accepting control from parking attendants.

If You Become a Victim:

- Stay calm and reassure the attacker.
- Do not try to flee unless the situation permits.
- Obey all instructions; don't argue about a ring, a watch or a wallet.
- If you know the aggressor, do not call him or her by name or give any sign that you can identify him or her.
- Let the assailant feel as though he or she is in control.
- Avoid responding in kind to aggressive behavior.
- Make sure your movements are not abrupt or threatening.
- Everyone has a limit, be sure you know yours.
- The goal in any situation is survival; if you survive the incident you have done the right thing.
- Make an effort to discreetly memorize any unique characteristics that could later be used to identify the attacker.
- Never try to follow or chase an assailant.
- Immediately make sure that you and all members of your party, if accompanied, are unhurt and provide first aid to anyone in need.
- Conserve and protect any evidence left at the scene.
- Report immediately to the local authorities and your embassy.
- When making a criminal complaint, particularly in a foreign country, be sure to retain a qualified lawyer as your representative.

- Report any loss of credit cards or personal documents to the appropriate bank, financial institution or organization.
- Any damage to physical security barriers (door locks, windows, etc.) should be immediately repaired and strengthened as necessary.

Response to a Telephone Threat:

- If you receive a call threatening you or your family or claiming to have kidnapped a member of the family, remain calm.
- Quickly evaluate the truth of any statements made by the caller such as school names, vehicle descriptions, family member names or other information.
- Decide whether the information provided is in the public domain or could be easily obtained by an outsider.
- Rapidly contact or attempt to contact affected family member(s).
- Do not enter into an argument; simply ask why your family was chosen.
- If the threat or action is believable and money is demanded, insist that you do not have the requested sum and need time to gather resources.
- Do not peremptorily negate the possibility of payment; rather, assure the caller that you will do your utmost to meet their expectations.
- If the caller insists on a payment, get precise delivery instructions and try to fix a location for the delivery.
- Ask questions about the delivery; this will help you gain some control in the situation.
- Keep the interlocutor on the telephone as long as possible to lower the tension level and make the dialogue more civil.
- Write down everything you can about the caller and the conversation; notes are always better than memories.
- Never summarily offer to deliver a ransom yourself.
- Immediately seek professional assistance and determine jointly whether the authorities should become involved.

Hostage Behavior:

- If you are kidnapped, do not resist in the initial, most dangerous stage.
- The first half hour is the most critical period; stay calm and follow all instructions.
- Speak only in answer to direct questions and offer no information that is not requested.
- Acts as normally as you can, do not argue with your captors; showing your fear is natural and normal.
- Once the initial tension has passed, seek to establish rapport with your captors. Do not, however, try to tell them their business.
- Try to memorize the route taken from the crime scene to your eventual destination and recall any unusual noises or characteristics.
- Let the kidnappers know if you have any medical requirements or need a particular medicine.
- Memorize the substantive aspects of conversations with the kidnappers.
- Try to avoid providing information about family members, co-workers and friends. If specific information is requested, be as vague and general as possible.
- Escape is a personal choice that, however, often leads to tragedy. The best advice is to sit tight and wait out the situation.
- Prepare yourself mentally, physically and spiritually for a lengthy stretch of captivity.
- Discreetly observe as much as possible; try to remember everything about the people and place for later investigation.
- Stay alert, keep track of time and exercise your mind and body as much as possible.
- Make no promises of payment to the kidnappers and avoid becoming involved in the negotiations. The victim is the worst possible negotiator.
- Kidnappers may try to convince you that no one is willing to negotiate for your freedom or that no one cares. This is simply a pressure tactic to break down your resistance and make you more malleable.

- If forced to write messages with which you do not agree, understand that those on the receiving end will recognize that the messages were prepared under duress.
- Have faith that many people are working very hard to obtain your release.
- Exercise your faith in whatever religion or creed you believe.
- If violence breaks out during a rescue attempt, take cover and wait for the rescuers.
- If you are released, make a careful note of the circumstances, location and method of your release.
- Once you have returned home, get immediate medical and therapeutic help.

Bibliography

Alix, Ernest K. 1978. *Ransom Kidnapping in America, 1874-1974/ The Creation of a Capital Crime.* Carbondale, IL: Southern Illinois University Press.

Bies, Mark and Robert Low. 1987. *The Kidnap Business.* London: Pelham Books.

Birmingham, Frederic. 1976. Kidnapping Victims: Tragic Aftermaths. *Saturday Evening Post.* April 1976 62-65, 106-107, 113, 116.

Blinkhorn, Martin. 2007. Avoiding the Ultimate Act of Violence: Mediterranean Bandits and Kidnapping for Ransom 1815-1914. *Cultures of Violence: Interpersonal Violence in Historical Perspective.* Stuart Carroll, ed. 2007 192-211. New York: Palgrave Macmillan.

Blinkhorn, Martin. 2000. Liability, Responsibility and Blame: British Ransom Victims in the Mediterranean Periphery, 1860-81. *Australian Journal of Politics and History,* 46, no. 3 336-356.

Blythe, Bruce T. 2002. *Blindsided: A Manager's Guide to Catastrophic Incidents in the Workplace.* New York: Penguin Group.

Briggs, Rachel. 2001. *The Kidnapping Business.* London: Foreign Policy Centre.

Brodman, James William. 2006. Community, Identity and the Redemption of Captives: Comparative Perspectives across the Mediterranean. *Anuario de Estudios Medievales (AEM)* 36, no. 1. (January): http://estudiosme-dievales.revistas.csic.es/index.php/estudiosmedievales/article/viewPD-FInterstitial/5/5 (accessed December 12, 2007).

Colley, Linda. 2002. *Captives: The Story of Britain's Pursuit of Empire and How Its Soldiers and Civilians Were Held Captive by the Dream of Global Supremacy, 1600-1850.* New York: Pantheon Books.

Council on Foreign Relations. 2007. *Basque Fatherland and Liberty (ETA).* http://www.cfr.org/publication/9271.

Garcia Marquez, Gabriel. 1997. *News of a Kidnapping.* New York: Alfred A. Knopf.

Giersbach, Walter. 2006. Governor Kieft's Personal War, Military History Online.com (August 26, 2006): http://www.militaryhistoryonline.com/indianwars/articles/kieftswar.aspx (accessed March 23, 2008).

Gonzalez Placencia, Luis. 2006. Una Aproximacion Critica del Problema del Secuestro en Mexico. *Insyde en la Sociedad Civil* 11. (July): http://www.insyde.org.mx/images/Secuestro__listo__1_.pdf.

Griffiths, John C. 2003. *Hostage: The History, Facts and Reasoning behind Political Hostage Taking.* London: Andre Deutsch.

Hagedorn, Ann. 1998. *Ransom: The Untold Story of International Kidnapping.* New York: Henry Holt.

Hauge, Arild. 2002. *Viking Traveling Routs.* Denmark: Arhus. http://www.arild-hauge.com/eraids.htm (accessed March 12, 2008).

Jenkins, Brian and Janera Johnson. 1975. *International Terrorism: A Chronology, 1968-74.* Santa Monica CA: Rand Corporation.

Jessup, John E. An *Encyclopedic Dictionary of Conflict Resolution 1945-1996.* Westport CT: Greenwood.

Jimenez Ornelas, Rene. 2002. *El Secuestro Problemas Sociales y Juridicos.* Mexico: Editorial UNAM.

Keller, David Neal. 1995. Shanghaied, *American Heritage Magazine* 46, no. 5 (September): http://www.americanheritage.com/articles/magazine/ah/1995/5/1995_5_66.shtml.

Kertzer, David I. 1998. *The Kidnapping of Edgardo Mortara.* New York: Random House.

Kramer, Samuel N. 1950. Inanna's Descent to the Nether World, *Journal of Cunieform Studies* 4, 4, 199-214: http://www.jstor.org/stable/3515910?seq=2.

Lofkrantz, Jennifer. 2005. *Ransoming in 19th Century West Africa.* Working Paper, Harriet Tubman Seminar York University. http:// www.yorku.ca/seminars/2005_6/Lofkrantz-RANSOMING_IN_19TH_CENTURY_WEST_AFRICA.pdf.

Madrid-Nassif, Guillermo A. 2006. *El Primer Secuestro en Colombia.* Bogota: Editorial Oveja Negra.

Martin, Paula. 1998. *Spanish Armada Prisoners: The Story of the Nuestra Señora del Rosario and Her Crew, and of the Other Prisoners in England, 1587–97.* Exeter: Exeter University Publications.

Messick, Hank and Burt Goldblatt. 1974. *Kidnapping: The Illustrated History.* New York: Dial Press.

Moorehead, Caroline. 1980. *Hostages to Fortune: A Study of Kidnapping in the World Today.* New York: Atheneum.

Newton, Michael. 2002. *The Encyclopedia of Kidnappings.* New York: Checkmark Books.

Patterson, Orlando. 1982. *Slavery and Social Death: A Comparative Study.* Cambridge, MA: Harvard University Press.

Philippine Center for Investigative Journalism. 2006. 20 Filipinos 20 Years after People Power. *The Investigative Reporting Quarterly* (Jan-Feb 2006) http://www.pcij.org/i-report/edsa20/teresita-ang-see.html. (accessed Jan 14, 2008).

Pickard, Kate E.R. 1856. *The Kidnapped and The Ransomed, Being the Personal Recollections of Peter Still and his Wife "Vina" after Forty Years of Slavery.* Syracuse: William T. Hamilton. Electronic Edition retrieved from Documenting the American South Collection, University of North Carolina at Chapel Hill. http://docsouth.unc.edu/neh/pickard/menu.html.

Plutarch. 75. *Caesar, Lives Vol. VII.* http://classics.mit.edu/Plutarch/caesar.html. (accessed Nov 24, 2007).

Prescott, William H. 1843. *The History of the Conquest of Mexico.* New York: Random House Modern Library, Inc.

Prescott, William H. 1847. *The History of the Conquest of Peru.* New York: Random House Modern Library, Inc.

Rubio, Mauricio. 2003. *Del Rapto a la Pesca Milagrosa Breve Historia del Secuestro en Colombia.* Bogota: Universidad de los Andes http://www.economia.uniandes.edu.co/es/ content/download/2081/12310/file/d2003-36.pdf.

Seton-Watson, R.W. 1966. *The Rise of Nationality in the Balkans.* New York: H. Fertig.

Smith, Arthur L. 2002. *Kidnap City: Cold War Berlin.* Westport, CT: Greenwood Press.

Steinhoff, Patricia G. 2004. Kidnapped Japanese in North Korea: The New Left Connection. *Journal of Japanese Studies* 30, no. 1: 123-142. http://muse.uq.edu.au/demo/journal_of_japanese_studies/v030/30.1steinhoff.pdf.

Turbiville, Jr., Graham H. 2004. ETA Terrorism, the Americas, and International Linkages. *Crime & Justice International* 20, no. 81 (July/August): http://www.cjcenter.org/documents/pdf/cji/Cji0407-08.pdf.

Turner, Mark. 1995. The Kidnapping Crisis in the Philippines 1991-1993: Context and Management. *Journal of Contingencies and Crisis Management* 3 (1), 1–11 (March): http://www.blackwell-synergy.com/doi/abs/10.1111/j.1468-5973.1995.tb00049.x?cookieSet=1&journalCode=jccm.

Whitaker, Brian. 2000. *The Kidnapper's Toll.* Middle East International website http://www.al-bab.com/yemen/artic/mei61.htm . (accessed May 31, 2008).

Zimbardo, Philip. 2007. *The Lucifer Effect: Understanding How Good People Turn Evil.* New York: Random House.

Index

A

Abu Ghraib, 42
Abuse of victims, 42–43, 186
Acquaintances, 90
Action phase, 161–162
Adversary negotiator, 95–96, 128
Afghanistan, 21, 27
Africa, 27
Airline hijackings, 20
Airports, 209–210
Alarm systems, 174, 177
Alexander III, 13
Alexander the Great, 4
Americas, 8
Anti-kidnapping units
    corruption in, 82
    description of, 78
    family's monetary support of,
        82–83
    "operating expenses" for, 82
Antiquity, 1–6
Arizmendi, Daniel, 44
Arrivals to residence, 170–173, 202,
    204

Asia, 8
Assistant, 69
Atahualpa, 8
"ATM abduction," 34
Attila the Hun, 5
Attorney, 86, 149–150
Audiotapes, 101–102, 184
Authorities. *See also* Law
        enforcement; Police
    competence level of, 78
    corruption of, 82–83, 188–189
    importance of involvement by, 81
    political influences on, 78
    reporting to, 77, 81, 86, 149
Aztecs, 8

B

Baader-Meinhof, 20
Baldwin II, 6
Barcenas, Jose, 14–15
Base of operations, 156
Beatings, 43
Beheadings, 28

Bela IV, 7
Biehl, Eugenio, 21–22
Bielazki, Bruce, 14–15
Black Hand, 15
Brazil, 26
Bribes, 190, 194
Brutalities, 56
Buddhism, 3
Bus stations, 209
Business contacts, 70

C

Caesar, Julius, 4–5
Call forwarding, 101
Caller ID system, 90, 100
Calls. *See* Telephone calls
Caretakers, 43
Cellular structure of kidnapping
        bands, 40–42
Cellular telephone calls, 67, 69, 155
Central America, 25
Cervantes. *See* Saavedra, Miguel
        Cervantes de
Charles V, 8
Children
    information gathering from,
        159–160
    security measures for, 204–205
    varying the routines of, 167–168
Circassians, 5
Civil War, 13
Code of Hammurabi, 3
Colombia, 15, 20, 23–26, 28, 54, 87,
        124, 192, 197
Communication(s)
    ceasing of, 123
    equipment necessary for, 99–100
    goal setting for, 126
    handling of, 102
    with kidnappers, 79, 125–128
    with media representatives, 84,
        150

methods of, 125–126, 155
    telephone calls as. *See* Telephone
        calls
Composure, 181
Consultants
    family involvement with, 75–76
    functions of, 74–75
    honesty by, 76–77
    laws regarding, 87, 149
    legal requirement to report
        kidnapping, 77–78
    meeting with decision makers,
        76
    as negotiator, 74–75, 96–97
    payment of, 93
    word-of-mouth referrals, 74–75
Consumable supplies, 156
Consumerism, 190–191
Contingency plans, 59
Cooperation, 179–180
Coors, Adolph III, 16
Coroners, 71
Corruption, 82–83, 188
Costa Rica, 25
Crime
    action phase of, 161–162
    escape phase of, 162–163
    logistics phase of, 154–158
    planning phase of, 152–154
    surveillance phase of, 158–161
Criminal penalties, 85
Crisis control center
    in family homes, 98–99
    in organizations, 99–101
Crisis management program, 66
Crusades, 6–7
Cudahy, Edward Jr., 14

D

Dacoits, 15, 192
Darius of Persia, 4

Death, 111–112
Death squads, 195
Delivery of ransom. *See* Ransom delivery
Departures from residence, 170–172, 202, 204
Descent of Ishtar, 3
Diplomats, 21
Discretion, during verification process, 71
Documentation, 156–157
Domestic staff, 177, 201
Doors, of residence, 174, 200
Dozier, James, 25
Drake, Francis, 9
Driver training, 171
Drug trafficking, 20, 185, 192–193
Duvalier, Jean Claude "Baby Doc," 16

E

Ear cuttings, 44, 56
Eastern Europe, 13, 27, 41
Eder, Elisa, 15
Eichmann, Adolf, 16–17
Eilenburg, 9
El Salvador, 25
"El Tempranillo," 11
Electronics equipment, 99–100
Emotions, 52–55, 97, 184
Empathy, 95
Epaminondas, 4
Escape
    by kidnappers, 162–163
    by victim, 181–182
Escobar, Pablo, 192
ETA, 20–22, 24–25
Exercise, 183
Exodus, 1, 3
Express kidnappings, 25, 34–35, 45
Extortion, 35, 187

F

Faith, 184
Fake documentation, 156–157
False kidnappings
    description of, 68
    payments for, 67, 71
    verification methods to prevent, 68–71
"False-flag" recruitment of information, 159
Family
    acquaintances of, 90
    anguish feelings by, 56–58
    behaviors after kidnapping, 90
    consultant's involvement with, 75–76
    crisis control center in home of, 98–99
    discretion by, 103
    "do's and don'ts" for, 65–66
    freezing the assets of, 150
    isolation of, 90
    life support for, 103–105
    negotiations by, 92–93
    organization's support of, 59, 93
    physical violence against victim used to pressure, 44
    preparations by, 66–67
    psychological pressure on, 50–51, 64–65, 121–125
    ransom delivery by, 139
    reporting avoidance by, 86
    rescue operations performed without consultation of, 80
    shock reactions by, 104
    sleeplessness by, 104–105
    speaking with kidnappers, 95
    support for, 104, 148
    telephone calls to, 65–66
    therapy for, 149
    uncertainty for, 57
Fangio, Juan Manuel, 16

FARC, 23, 124
Finances of victim, 110–111
First Opium War, 12
Food, 183
Frustration, 54–55

G

Genghis Khan, 7
Getty, Paul, 22
Gold, 8–9
Grassroots organizations, 197
Greece, 4
Grey Automobile Gang, 14
Guards, 175–176
Guatemala, 25
Guerrillas, 21

H

Haiti, 16, 186
Hauptmann, Bruno, 15
Heads of household, 48–49, 91
Hearst, Patty, 22, 53–54
Hebrews, 1
Helen of Troy, 3–4
Helplessness, 54–55
Hezbollah, 153
Hiding location, 182–183
Higuita, Rene, 87
Honduras, 25
Hostage. *See also* Victim
    death of, after ransom delivery,
        112
    recommendations, 215–216
    survival as, 182–184, 215–216
Hostage taking
    in antiquity, 3–4
    of cities, 9, 12
    in Industrial Age, 10–17
    in Middle Ages, 6–10
Hotel security, 208–209

Huarte, Felipe, 22
Huerta, Victoriano, 15
Hundred Years War, 7

I

Impunity, 193
Incas, 8
Incident
    authorities. *See* Authorities
    consultant's control of, 81
    example of, 63
    kidnap-ransom insurance effects
        on, 72–74
    professional consultant's effect on,
        74–77
    responses to, 64–66
    verification of, 67–72
India, 15, 27, 186
Indonesia, 26
Industrial Age, 10–17
Information gathering, 44–45,
        158–159
Insurance, 72–74, 97
Inventory rotation, 77
Iraq, 28
Israel, 153
Italy, 20, 22–23

J

Jackson, Geoffrey, 21
James I, 8
Japan, 16
Jobs, 191, 197
Joseph, 3
Journal notes, 89

K

Kampusch, Natascha, 54

Kazakhstan, 27
Kelly, Ned, 12
Kidnapped, 13
Kidnappers
    apprehension of, 38
    base of operations for, 156
    as caretakers, 43
    characteristics of, 24–25, 35–36,
        40
    communications with, 79,
        125–128
    contact with, 114–116
    conviction of, 40
    cooperation with, 179–180
    crimes committed by, 37
    decision to become, 37
    demands by, 64
    identification protocols for, 115
    information gathering about
        victims by, 44–45
    interrogation of victims by, 117
    looking at, 181
    media portrayal of, 85
    negotiation with
        denial of police or law
            enforcement involvement,
            116
        identification protocols, 115
        initial contact, 114–116
    negotiator and
        bonding between, 118
        communications between, 79
        rapport building, 94, 117
    punishments for, 85–86
    ransom delivery requests, 140
    rapport with, 94, 117
    religious affiliations, 36–37,
        117–118
    sexual abuse by, 42–43
    socioeconomic influences, 37
    tactics used by, 28–29
    telephone calls from, 65–66, 90
    threats of violence by, 122, 124

    traits of, 42
Kidnapping
    action phase of, 161–162
    analysis of, 166–167
    as business, 123, 126
    consumerism and, 190–191
    cyclical nature of, 40
    definition of, 32–33, 85
    duration of, 108, 123
    escape phase of, 162–163
    false. See False kidnappings
    financial costs of, 108
    geographic area for, 153–154
    global prevalence of, 185–186
    high-risk areas for, 185
    incentive for, 190–191
    length of, 108
    logistics phase of, 154–158
    media awareness of, 83–85, 150
    money obtained through, 31–32
    planning phase of, 152–154
    psychological effects of, 52, 183
    recommendations for reducing,
        195–198
    risks associated with, 153–154
    surveillance phase of, 158–161
    types of, 33
    uncertainty associated with, 57
    verification of, 67–72
    virtual, 35, 67, 186–187
Kidnapping bands
    cellular structure of, 40–42
    description of, 37–38
    leader of, 43
    logistics planning by, 154
    negotiator in, 95–96
    reforming of, after arrests, 194
    subcontractors used by, 40–41,
        155
Kidnap-ransom insurance, 72–74,
    97
Koran, 3, 32
Korea, 16

L

Latin America, 86
Law(s)
    asset freezing for victim's family,
        150
    country-specific variations in, 85,
        149
    improvements in, 197
    knowledge of, 77–78
    negotiation-prohibitive, 149
    reporting of kidnapping, 77–78,
        149
Law enforcement. *See also* Police
    briefing of, after victim release,
        147
    corruption of, 80, 82, 188–189
    denial of involvement by, 116
    equipment improvements for, 196
    mission of, 81
    weakness of, 187–188
Lawyer, 86, 149–150
Legal system, 193–194
Leopold V, 7
Life, proof of. *See* Proof of life
Life support, 103–105
Lindbergh, Charles Jr., 15
Location
    for hiding of victim, 182–183
    for ransom delivery, 141–142
Logistics
    in kidnapping planning, 154–158
    of response, 101–103
Loss of control, 49
Luggage security, 210

M

M19, 20, 23
Macedonia, 12
Malaysia, 26
Mao Zedong, 192
Mara Salvatrucha, 25

Mazzotti, Cristina, 22
Media, 83–85, 150
Medical conditions, 92, 111
Medical facilities, 69
Mental exercise, 183–184
Merchant Seaman's Act, 11
Mexico, 15–16, 24, 28, 44, 47, 87,
    185–186, 191
Middle Ages, 6–10
Middle East, 27
Ming Dynasty, 8
Mitrione, Dan, 21
Moctezuma, 8
Money
    extortion for, 35
    as kidnapping purpose, 31–32
    planning considerations, 157–158
    as ransom, 128–130
Mongols, 7–8
Montoneros, 22
Moro, Aldo, 22
Mortara, Edgardo, 32
Mortuaries, 71
Movimiento Revolucionario Tupac
    Amaru, 25
Mujaheddin, 21
Murder, 111–112
Muslims, 5, 28, 32

N

Narcotics trafficking, 20, 185,
    192–193
Native Americans, 8–9
Nazis, 16
Negotiation
    arguments presented during,
        127–128
    composure during, 66
    congruent strategy for, 109–110
    decision making in, 93–94
    false expectations about, 55

with kidnappers
  denial of police or law
    enforcement involvement,
    116
  identification protocols, 115
  initial contact, 114–116
laws regarding, 149
offer development, 118–121, 128
outcomes of, 111–114
priorities in, 107
psychological pressure, 121–125
responsibility for, 92–94
schematic diagram of process,
  119–120
strategy for, 107–111
techniques of, 116–118
threats of violence effects on, 122,
  124–125
"vaccination" strategy for,
  108–109
Negotiator
  actions congruent with promises
    of, 109–110
  adversary, 95–96, 128
  changing of, 95
  consultant as, 74–75, 96–97
  credibility of, 116–117
  decision-making power of, 93–94
  emotions of, 97
  in family kidnappings, 94
  friends as, 94–95
  function of, 94
  kidnappers and
    bonding between, 118
    communications between, 79
    rapport building, 94, 117
  language skills of, 96
  ransom delivery by, 139
  recommended practices for,
    97–98
  selection of, 94
  telephone calls to, 114

threats of violence handled by,
  123–124
victim as, 132–133
Nicaragua, 24–25
Nigeria, 27, 32, 186
No-negotiation policy, 123
Nutrition, 183

O

Offer
  acceptance of, 134–135
  development of, 118–121, 128
  proof of life before acceptance of,
    133
Olympic Village kidnappings, 21, 80
Organizations
  crisis control center, 99–101
  crisis management program, 66,
    84
  kidnap-ransom insurance, 72–74
  offer development, 118–119
  psychological pressure on,
    121–125
  reactions and responses by,
    59–60, 91, 118–119
  remaining employees affected by
    kidnapping, 60
  security enhancements by, 59
  support from, 92–93

P

Pakistan, 27
Paramilitary groups, 23
Parking lots, 172–173
Penalties, 85
Personal security
  arrivals and departures from
    residence, 170–173, 202,
    204
  information gathering, 167

need to develop, 198
residence. *See* Residence
routine variations, 167–169
street lighting systems, 173
threat analysis. *See* Threat
   analysis
tips for, 199–216
transportation routes, 169–170
Peru, 25
Peugeot, Eric, 16
Philip of Macedonia, 4
Philippines, 12, 26
Photographs, 131–132
Physical violence, 43–44
Pizarro, Francisco, 8
Police. *See also* Authorities
   calling of, 64
   communications between
      kidnappers and negotiators
      given to, 79
   compensation for, 188, 195
   control of situation by, 81
   corruption by, 80, 82, 188–189
   denial of involvement by, 116
   derogatory comments about, 116
   distrust of, 148
   education of, 196
   firearms practice, 193
   importance of involvement by, 81
   ransom access by, 80–81
   ransom delivery shadowing by,
      142
   reporting of incident to, 79
   respect for, 195–196
   tactical operation planning by, 79
   training of, 193, 196
   underpayment of, 188, 195
   vetting of, 196
Police blotters, 70
Political kidnapping
   difficulty of resolving, 192
   duration of, 123–124
   high-risk areas for, 185

   kidnappers involved in, 36
Political purposes, 32
Polybius, 5
Poor people, 190
Popular Front for the Liberation of
   Palestine, 21
Post-traumatic stress disorder, 61
Preexisting medical conditions, 92
Press-ganging, 11
Pressure
   psychological, 50–51, 64–65,
      121–125
   time as method of applying, 124
   violence used for, 121–124
Prince Friedrich of Austria, 7
Prisoners of war, 2
Private security guards, 175–176
Proof of life
   after acceptance of offer, 133
   audiotapes, 101–102, 184
   frequency of, 133
   importance of, 130–131
   photographs, 131–132
   questions used to establish,
      91–92, 114, 131
   before ransom delivery, 138
   speaking with victim, 131, 133
   videotapes, 131–132, 184
Psychological kidnapping, 35
Psychological pressure, 50–51,
   64–65, 121–125
Psychologist, 103
Public security, 202–204
Publicity, 60
Punishments, 85–86

Q

Quemuenchatocha, 9
Quesada, Gonzalo Jimenez de, 9
Questions, proof of life, 91–92, 114,
   131

R

Rage, 57
Ransom
    agreement to, during initial
        contact, 115
    amount of, 108
    insufficiency of, 112
    last-minute increases in, 134–135
    media's role in conveyance of, 85
    money used for, 128–130
    non-cash items, 130, 134
    offer of
        acceptance of, 134–135
        development of, 118–121, 128
    police access to, 80–81
    reduction of, 119–121
    refusal to pay, 195
    verification of, 129–130
Ransom delivery
    death of hostage after, 112
    in different state or province,
        144–145
    drops, 143
    geographic distance effects on,
        144–145
    instructions for, 138, 141–142
    interference with, 143–144
    kidnapper requests for, 140
    location for, 141–142
    logistical considerations for, 103
    by multiple individuals, 139
    negotiation continuance after,
        112
    by negotiator, 139
    persons involved in, 139, 142–143
    police shadowing of, 142
    proof of life before, 138
    release of victim after, 145
    repeat kidnapping after, 108, 113
    structuring of, 137–145
    timing of, 129
    vehicle used for, 140–141

Ransom kidnapping
    in antiquity, 1–6, 3–4
    as business, 44
    of cities, 9, 12
    definition of, 34
    duration of, 34
    high-risk areas for, 185
    in Industrial Age, 10–17
    in Middle Ages, 6–10
    survival rates after, 34, 44
Red Brigades, 20, 22, 25
Release of victim, 145–148
Religion, 36–37, 117
Religious laws, 32–33
Repeat kidnappings, 108, 113
Reporting
    to authorities, 77, 81, 86
    avoidance of, 86
    legal requirement, 77–78, 149
Rescue operations
    description of, 113–114
    examples of, 79–80
    family consent for, 80, 113
Residence
    arrivals and departures, 170–173,
        202, 204
    description of, 69–70
    kidnappings at, 171–172
    security guards for, 175–176
    security measures at
        alarm system, 174, 177
        domestic staff, 177, 201
        doors, 174, 200
        perimeter, 173–174
        recommendations, 200–206
        safe havens, 174–175
        vegetation, 173, 201
        weapons, 205–206
        windows, 174
Resolution
    goals for, 107–108
    ransom delivery. *See* Ransom
        delivery

Response
    crisis control center, 98–101
    initial steps in, 89–92
    journal notes about, 89
    logistics, 101–103
    responsibility for negotiation,
        92–94
Revolutionaries, 192
Revolutionary organizations, 15–16,
    20
Richard the Lionhearted, 7
Risks, 153–154
Rivers, 27
"Robin Hood" effect, 192
Rojas, Clara, 54
Romans, 5
Ross, Charley, 13
Routes, 69
Routine variations, 167–169
Russia, 27

S

Saavedra, Miguel Cervantes de, 9
Safe havens
    in residence, 174–175
    on transportation route, 170
Schools, 71
Scott, Walter, 13
Seaports, 209
Secretary, 69
Security
    at airports, 209–210
    at bus stations, 209
    for children, 204–205
    hotel, 208–209
    of luggage, 210
    personal. See Personal security
    in public, 202–204
    residential. See Residence,
        security measures at
    at seaports, 209
    on trains, 209–210
    travel, 207–211
    vehicle, 170–171, 211–213
    workplace, 177–178, 206
Security grills, 174
Security guards, 175–176
Sembat I, 6
Sexual abuse, 42–43, 186
Sharia law, 32
Shock, 104
Sinatra, Frank Jr., 17
Slavery
    in Africa, 10–11
    kidnapping and, relationship
        between, 2
    in United States, 12
Sleeplessness, 104–105
Smart, Elizabeth, 54
Social engagements, 70
Sociopaths, 43–44, 123
Soviet Union, 16, 20, 28–29
Spain, 11, 197
Spreti, Karl Maria von, 21
Still, Peter, 12
Stockholm syndrome, 52–54, 56
Street lighting systems, 173
Subcontractors, 40–41, 155
Suffering, 48
Surveillance, 158–161
Survival
    as hostage, 182–184, 215–216
    rates of, 34, 44
    as victim, 179–182, 213–214
Symbionese Liberation Army, 22,
    53–54

T

Tactical operations, 79
Taoism, 3
Target surveillance, 158–161
Technology, 32

Telephone calls
    arguments presented during, 127–128
    briefing of recipients of, 90
    caller ID system, 90, 100
    copying of, 102
    dedicated line for, 90
    to family, 64–65
    from friends or relatives, 105
    from kidnappers, 90
    to negotiator, 114
    practicing of responses between, 127
    reviewing of, after completion, 126
    threat placed using, 214
    to victim, 67, 69
Terrorists, 19–20
Therapy, 149
Thirty Years' War, 9
Threat(s)
    telephone, 214
    of violence, 122, 124
Threat analysis
    arrival and departure from residence, 170–173, 202, 204
    daily routines, 167–169
    overview of, 165–167
    safe havens, 170
    street lighting systems, 173
    transportation routes, 169–170
Time, 123–125
Tobago, 26
Trains, 209–210
Translation services, 89, 102–103
Transportation
    alternate routes for, 170
    in kidnapping planning, 155–156
    schedules for, 68
    threat analysis of routes, 169–170
Travel security, 207–211

Treaty of Aix-la-Chapelle, 10
Trinidad, 26
Trinitarians, 9
Tupamaros, 21

V

"Vaccination," 108–109
Vehicle security, 170–171, 211–213
Venezuela, 25–26
Verification of kidnapping, 67–72
Victim
    abuse of, 42–43, 186
    age ranges for, 48
    avoidance of becoming, 198
    beating of, 43
    brutalities against, 56
    cellular telephone calls to, 67, 69
    characteristics of, 47–48
    composure of, 181
    death of, 111–112
    emotions of, 52–55, 184
    escape by, 181–182
    friends of, 51
    frustration by, 54–55
    gender of, 48
    heads of household as, 48–49
    helplessness of, 54–55
    hiding location for, 182–183
    identifying of, by potential kidnappers, 153–154
    information gathering about, 44–45
    information provided by, 110, 117, 132
    interrogation by kidnappers, 117
    loss of control by, 49
    medical examination of, after release, 103, 147
    murdering of, 111–112
    as negotiator, 132–133

normal interactions with, after
  release, 148–149
physical violence against, 43–44
potential, 51
with preexisting medical
  conditions, 92, 111
proof of life of. *See* Proof of life
psychological pressure on, 50–51,
  148–149
recommendations for, 183–184,
  213–216
release of, 145–148
residence of. *See* Residence
reunion with, 147
selection of, 44–45, 153–154
studying of, before kidnapping,
  44–45
suffering by, 48
surveillance of, 158–161
survival of, 34, 44, 178–184,
  213–216
therapy for, 149
Videotapes, 131–132, 184
Violence
  in action phase of kidnapping,
    161
  increases in, 186
  physical, 43–44

psychological pressure created
  through, 121–122
threat of, 122, 124
Virtual kidnapping, 35, 67, 186–187
Visual aids, 127

W

War of 1812, 11
Wealthy citizens, 188, 190
Weapons
  in home, 205–206
  time as, 123–124
  violence as, 121–123
Weyerhauser, George, 15
Windows, of residence, 174
Witnesses, 70
Workplace security, 177–178, 206

X

Xenophon of Athens, 4
Xia Dynasty, 3
Y
Yemen, 27
Z
Zabala, Lorenzo, 22